This wonderful book speaks to every believer about "the awesome power of the Word within you." I'm so concerned these days that our Christian world focus less on Christianized "principles" and "application" and more on the sacred Scriptures themselves. In Scripture resides the power to change 100 people—and to change us! This book is proof.

Anne Ortlund, author of *Children Are Wet Cement*

Too often it is forgotten that the Bible is timely as well as timeless. This readable and most enjoyable educational book shows just why and how the Scriptures have been so important for so many influential people in Western history. Among the volume's many virtues is its contribution to both historical and biblical understanding.

Mark A. Noll, McManis Professor of Christian Thought, Wheaton College

Whenever I sign my name in a Bible, I always include my life's verse—1 Samuel 12:24. I have often wondered what verses have significantly impacted other Christians. Thanks to the Petersens, I now know. For most Christians there is at least one verse in the Bible that sticks in their heart, a verse that motivates and inspires them. Once you have read the 100 verses that changed the lives of people through the centuries, you will never read these verses the same way again. What a joy to discover that some of these verses have also inspired me in my life. Only God's Word changes lives. Nowhere is that more evident than in *100 Bible Verses That Changed the World*. Read how these verses impacted others and you can't help but be impacted yourself.

Dr. Woodrow Kroll, president and senior Bible teacher, Back to the Bible

A finely crafted journey through history, biography, and theology that will instruct and inspire you. But don't run through the book. Walk slowly, savor each chapter, and make what you read a part of your life. You are in for a treat—and a jolt!

Warren W. Wiersbe, author, conference speaker

This very readable book is particularly valuable in helping Christians appreciate how Scripture is a Living Word and how it has marvelously interrupted and redirected lives and situations in other times and places. Equally important is the valuable gui[...] [Scrip]ture in our own lives. How enriched we [...] [th]rough the Word in other times and cultu[...] [th]at he is trying to show us today.

Dr. Ken[...] [...]y Institute

OTHER BOOKS BY William J. Petersen

The Christian Traveler's Companion: Western Europe with Amy Eckert (Revell, 2001)

The Christian Traveler's Companion: U.S.A. and Canada with Amy Eckert (Revell, 2000)

100 Christian Books That Changed the Century with Randy Petersen (Revell, 2000)

The One Year Book of Psalms with Randy Petersen (Tyndale, 1999)

25 Surprising Marriages (Baker, 1996)

The One Year Book of Hymns with Randy Petersen (Tyndale, 1996)

Jeremiah: The Prophet Who Wouldn't Quit (Victor, 1984)

The Discipling of Timothy (Victor, 1980)

Two Stars for God (Warner Books, 1974)

Those Curious New Cults (Keats, 1973)

Astrology and the Bible (Victor, 1972)

Another Hand on Mine (McGraw-Hill, 1967)

OTHER BOOKS BY Randy Petersen

Angry with God with Michele Novotny (Pinon Press, 2001)

100 Christian Books That Changed the Century with William J. Petersen (Revell, 2000)

The Stress Test with Thomas Whiteman (Pinon, 2000)

The One Year Book of Psalms with William J. Petersen (Tyndale, 1999)

The Christian Book of Lists (Tyndale, 1997)

The One Year Book of Hymns with William J. Petersen (Tyndale, 1996)

Adult ADD with Thomas Whiteman and Michele Novotni (Pinon, 1995)

Men Who Love Too Little with Thomas Whiteman (Nelson, 1995)

Becoming Your Own Best Friend with Thomas Whiteman (Nelson, 1994)

The Family Book of Bible Fun (Tyndale, 1994)

How to Fear God without Being Afraid of Him with David New (Victor, 1994)

The 100 Most Important Dates in Church History with Kenneth A. Curtis and Stephen Lang (Revell, 1991)

Giving to the Giver (Tyndale, 1990)

God
doesn't look at
how much we do,
but with
how much love
we do it.

MOTHER TERESA

100
Bible Verses
That Changed
the World

WILLIAM J. PETERSEN
and RANDY PETERSEN

Fleming H. Revell
A Division of Baker Book House Co
Grand Rapids, Michigan 49516

Published by Fleming H. Revell
a division of Baker Book House Company
P.O. Box 6287, Grand Rapids, MI 49516-6287

Printed in the United States of America

Library of Congress Cataloging-in-Publication Data

Petersen, William J.
    100 Bible verses that changed the world / William J. Petersen and Randy Petersen.
        p.   cm.
    Includes index.
    ISBN 0-8007-5760-2
    1. Bible—Quotations. 2. Christian biography. 3. Bible—Influence. I. Petersen, Randy. II. Title.

BS391.3 .P48 2001
220′.09—dc21   2001041865

For current information about all releases from Baker Book House, visit our web site:
http://www.bakerbooks.com

Contents

Contents

Contents

7

Contents

Contents

Contents

Preface

Can you imagine a book entitled *100 Shakespearean Texts That Changed the World?* Or even *100 Lines from Great Movies That Changed the World?* Probably not.

100 Bible Verses That Changed the World is a different story. For two millennia the Bible has been in the business of changing the lives of people who in turn have changed the world. There is an old hymn that states, "Thy Word is like a garden, Lord," but we have found that God's Word is often more like a stick of dynamite. In some cases a Bible verse caused a dramatic conversion or a life calling; in other instances it was a Bible verse that moved civilization in an entirely new direction.

Perhaps you can give some examples of how a Bible verse dramatically changed your world; we certainly can think of ways that verses have changed ours. Undoubtedly, the Bible is like no other book.

Yet we must provide a warning notice. Not all the subjects in this book are examples to be followed. Several of our world-changers used the point-and-shoot method of biblical guidance, but we have to admit that it worked for them. Some people misinterpreted a Bible verse, as John Quincy Adams did when he formulated the American policy of Manifest Destiny, but like it or not, that's how the West was won. But most of the people you'll meet in this book have experienced changes because they heard God's clear direction in Scripture, and they had a redemptive influence on the world around them.

We hope and pray that this book will inspire you to explore God's Word for yourself and discover how specific Bible passages can change your world. We also trust that this book will give you a new appreciation for the men and women in church history and inspire you by their examples.

The Light of the World

PAUL THE APOSTLE (?-68)

The missionary was brought from his prison cell to meet with the king. The room was filled with government officials, Roman and Jewish, as the king strode in with great pomp and ceremony. The Roman governor Festus opened the proceedings with a few remarks about the history of this case: The prisoner had been arrested for disturbing the peace; he was opposed by Jewish leaders on religious matters; as a Roman citizen, he had made a legal appeal to Caesar. Festus shook his head as he explained that he was ready to send the missionary to Rome for trial, but he didn't know what to write on the report. Maybe King Herod Agrippa would have some ideas.

When King Agrippa nodded his way, Paul, the missionary, began his testimony, telling of his background as a loyal Pharisee, his mission to persecute Christians, and the light from the sky that knocked him from his horse on the road to Damascus. Along with that light came the voice of Jesus, giving him a new mission to the Gentiles. "So then, King Agrippa," Paul continued, "I am saying nothing beyond what the prophets and Moses said would happen—that the Christ would suffer and, as the first to rise from the dead, would proclaim light to his own people and to the Gentiles."

Isaiah 49:6

I will also make you a light for the Gentiles, that you may bring my salvation to the ends of the earth.

Beginning in Isaiah 42, we find several Servant Songs that describe someone on a mission from God. Who is this Servant? At times it seems like a personification of Israel itself (49:3 says, "You are my servant, Israel"), but elsewhere it sounds like a separate person (49:5 says this person's mission is to gather Israel back to God). Christians believe that Jesus was the Servant who would suffer for human sin and enlighten the Gentiles. Fittingly, it was a Servant Song (Isa. 53) that the Ethiopian eunuch was puzzling over as he traveled from Jerusalem back to his particular end of the earth. He asked Philip, whom he met along the road, "Who is the prophet talking about?" And Philip "told him the good news about Jesus" (Acts 8:26–40).

13

A light for the Gentiles. This idea is packed into the Book of Isaiah in the section known as the Servant Song. Early Christians grabbed on to these prophecies and applied them to Jesus. He would be the one "despised and rejected," the "man of sorrows" on whom "the Lord laid the iniquity of us all" (Isa. 53:3, 6). He would be a light for the Gentiles (Isa. 49:6). And a heavenly vision had commanded Paul to carry the torch.

After receiving this commission, Paul went through several years of preparation. Then the cutting-edge church at Antioch sent him out, along with Barnabas, with the Good News.

In one of their first stops, Paul and Barnabas preached at the local synagogue and drew great crowds. While some Jews accepted their message, others forced them out of the synagogue. Paul and Barnabas replied, "We had to speak the word of God to you first. Since you reject it . . . we now turn to the Gentiles. For this is what the Lord has commanded us: 'I have made you a light for' the Gentiles, that you may bring salvation to the ends of the earth'" (Acts 13:46–47). Yes, that's Isaiah 49:6 quoted there, Paul's theme verse.

In town after town, these missionaries followed the same pattern: Preach in the synagogue, using the Hebrew Scriptures to convince people about Jesus; gather a base of believing Jews; then, when opponents turn up the heat, move on to bring a light to the Gentiles. As a result, the local churches that Paul started included both Jews and Gentiles. The wall between these groups was falling down. Christ was their peace.

After three missionary journeys, Paul still wasn't finished. Arrested in Jerusalem, he told Festus and Agrippa about his commission as the torch bearer to "proclaim light to his own people and to the Gentiles" (Acts 26:23). Then he used his Roman citizenship to get a free ticket to the capital city and a few appearances before governors and kings along the way. This light simply would not go out.

The Man of Peace Who Fought for Truth

IRENAEUS (CA. 125-202)

His name meant "peaceful," but Irenaeus declared war on a dangerous heresy. The Gnostics were the New Agers of their time, promising a fuller experience of God through various secret formulas. Since they used Christian language, they led many believers astray. But Irenaeus stepped up and wrote his master work, *Against Heresies*, exposing the Gnostic fraud. He did as much as anyone to keep Christianity on track in the second century.

Born about 125 in Asia Minor, Irenaeus learned from the bishop Polycarp, who had learned from the apostle John. It was a time of scattered persecution for Christians. Regional authorities would turn up the heat from time to time, and occasionally a Roman emperor would declare a major offensive against the church. In 156 Polycarp died in one regional persecution, standing in a packed arena, refusing to deny his faith. "Eighty-six years I have served the Lord," the old bishop had

> ## 2 Timothy 2:2
>
> *And the things you have heard me say in the presence of many witnesses entrust to reliable men who will also be qualified to teach others.*
>
> ---
>
> Timothy was a valuable assistant on Paul's ministry team. In fact, he was like a son to Paul. After accompanying Paul on several journeys, Timothy landed in Ephesus as a leader of the church there. Paul's two letters to Timothy emphasize the importance of personal purity, solid church leadership, and proper doctrine. In these epistles you can sense that Paul is passing the torch to a new generation of leaders. That's why it was so important to establish a chain of reliable teaching: Paul to Timothy, Timothy to his students, these students to theirs, and so on to the present.

declared to the crowd, "and he never did me any wrong. How can I blaspheme my king who has saved me?" Undoubtedly, Polycarp's dogged devotion inspired Irenaeus. In 177 persecution broke out in Lyons, in what is now France, and the local bishop was killed. Irenaeus replaced him.

Irenaeus soon found that the church's worst enemies were not from without but from within. False teachers were saying that Christ was merely the first rung on a ladder of many angelic beings who would usher a soul into God's fullness. They devalued the human body and denied that Christ was a physical being. Many Christians were falling for this heresy. Irenaeus wrote powerfully in defense of the supremacy of Jesus. Many of the basics of our faith were expounded by this bishop of Lyons in the second century.

What backing did Irenaeus have? The Bible? Well, many Gnostics claimed that the Old Testament had no relevance for their lives, and the New Testament wasn't put together yet—it was just a batch of documents. Without a common Scripture, how could Irenaeus support his arguments?

That's where 2 Timothy 2:2 comes in. In this verse Paul tells Timothy to take his teachings and pass them on to others who would faithfully pass them on to others. As Irenaeus saw it, Paul was setting up a chain of apostolic teaching. In fact, Irenaeus himself could claim that, through Polycarp, his teaching came straight from the apostle John. So he drew on the teachings in Paul's letters, the four Gospels, and John's letters to compile a definitive theology for the church.

"Although scattered across the earth," he wrote in *Against Heresies,* "the Church has received from the apostles and their disciples its faith in one God, the Father Almighty, who made heaven and earth, and the seas, and all that is in them; and in Christ Jesus, the Son of God, who became flesh for our salvation; and in the Holy Spirit, who proclaimed God's activities through the prophets—the comings, the virgin birth, the suffering, the resurrection from the dead, and the bodily ascension into heaven of our beloved Lord, Christ Jesus, and his return from heaven in the glory of the Father to restore everything, and to raise up all flesh."

You might see the beginnings of the Apostles' Creed in that statement. And if you listen carefully, you might hear the Gnostics wincing at his emphasis on the physicality of Christ.

Irenaeus never set out to create theology. He was just defining what had been given to him by the apostles and Polycarp—faithful people who in turn taught others.

A Bible Born in Bethlehem

JEROME (CA. 340-420)

As a young man, Jerome received a broad education in Rome, reading the Latin classics—Cicero, Ovid, Virgil. He couldn't get enough of these respected authors. He eagerly studied the best scholars of his day, devoting his life to language and learning.

But there was a culture war going on. A generation earlier, Constantine had made Christianity the official religion of the Roman Empire, overturning centuries of persecution. Suddenly Christians were stepping into positions of power in government and society. But the old pagans of Rome didn't go quietly. They kept pushing the traditional gods of Rome—Jupiter, Mars, Minerva, etc. In fact, in the 360s, while Jerome was going to school in Rome, Emperor Julian briefly turned the tables on the burgeoning Christian movement.

> ### Psalm 1:2
> But his delight is in the law of the LORD, and on his law he meditates day and night.
>
> ---
>
> The first psalm draws a sharp distinction between the righteous and the wicked. The first verse pronounces blessing on the person who avoids being drawn into wicked behavior by wicked companions. Then two verses describe the righteous and two describe the wicked. Not only does the righteous person enjoy meditating on God's law, but he is "like a tree" (v. 3) with a steady water supply. By contrast, the wicked are "like chaff that the wind blows away" (v. 4). Note that the righteous person considers God's Word not an obligation but a "delight."

Roman culture was changing too. The old Roman authors whom Jerome loved had all worshiped the pagan gods. Jerome was baptized as a Christian in 365, shortly after Julian's death, but he continued to struggle with how a good Christian could keep reading pagan authors. He was haunted by one dream in particular, in which he was challenged: "Are you a follower of Cicero or of Christ?"

This dream helped Jerome deepen his commitment. You can imagine how Psalm 1 also helped crystallize his decision. Verse 1 offers blessing to the person who forsakes the company of the ungodly, willful sinners, or mockers of true faith—people like Emperor Julian, or perhaps some of Jerome's favorite writers. Verse 2, which became Jerome's

17

favorite verse, describes this blessed person delighting in the law of the Lord and meditating constantly upon it. No longer would he be devoted to the Latin classics. Now he would have a new devotion—the Bible. He adopted a monastic lifestyle and studied the Scriptures as much as he could. He traveled throughout the Middle East, learning Hebrew and Greek, reading the theology of Origen and others, and sitting under the tutelage of Gregory Nazianzen, a leading Bible scholar of that time.

In 382 Jerome became a personal secretary to Damasus, bishop of Rome, and received a unique assignment. His new boss wanted him to translate the Bible into Latin. Part of the motivation behind this assignment was a political ploy to help make Rome (where Latin was spoken) the center of church power. But it was also a way to make the Bible available to the wide population in the Western Empire that didn't speak Greek. (Jerome's translation became known as the Vulgate, from the Latin word for "common people." Many Western Christians had been saying about the Bible, "It's Greek to me," relying on educated priests to translate. With Jerome's Vulgate they could understand for themselves. (Ironically, a millennium later, when no one but the priests understood Latin anymore, the church upheld the Vulgate as the sacred text.)

This assignment brought everything together for Jerome. In this exciting new project, he could unite his broad scholarship with his desire to serve Christ. He hunkered down in Rome and began translating portions of the New Testament. But in 385 the bishop died. Jerome wasn't getting along with the new leaders (some say he wanted to be the new bishop), and so he moved out to Bethlehem to complete his work. After more than twenty years, in that famous birthplace, a new translation of God's Word was finally completed. Jerome's love of language and of God's Word made it possible for common Christians throughout the Roman Empire to delight in the law of the Lord and meditate on it day and night in the language of their own souls.

Pick Up and Read

AUGUSTINE (354-430)

Professor, politician, playboy—Augustine was a man on the move. He grew up in North Africa, near Carthage, but his brilliance soon propelled him to Rome, where he took a job as a professor of rhetoric. Augustine gained the support of a powerful senator, who saw great potential in him. Some day this bright young man might change the world.

The time was the late 300s. Christianity had become the official religion of the Roman Empire, but the old paganism was still hanging around. All sorts of new and old ideas found a forum in Rome. Though his mother, Monica, was a devout Christian, praying constantly for him, Augustine was living a rather wild life.

The emperor lived not in Rome but north in Milan. So did the notable bishop, Ambrose. While Rome still courted the old paganism, Milan had become the Christian power base. And since Christians were in power, Milan was the place for an ambitious young politician. So Augustine moved there, landing a job on the emperor's staff, teaching and probably speech-writing. Like many other ladder-climbers of his day, Augustine made a preliminary claim to be a Christian because it was the thing to do. He began to listen to Ambrose's sermons, but he wouldn't commit himself to Christ. After all, he had a political future to consider. He had a career. He had a mistress.

He also had a mother who kept praying for him.

Romans 13:13–14

Let us behave decently, as in the daytime, not in orgies and drunkenness, not in sexual immorality and debauchery, not in dissension and jealousy. Rather, clothe yourselves with the Lord Jesus Christ, and don't think about how to gratify the desires of the sinful nature.

The earlier chapters of Romans tell us that we all need a Savior, and that through his death, Jesus has not only brought us the free gift of God's grace but also set us free from the constraints of the law. How then are we to live? Romans 12 begins a discussion about the Christian life. We are to be "living sacrifices," "transformed," and "overcoming evil with good." In chapter 13 Paul offers the revolutionary statement: "Love is the fulfilling of the law." The New Testament's fashion statement is that we are to clothe ourselves with Christ.

19

Augustine began to wrestle with religious thoughts. Once he had followed the dualistic cult of the Manicheans. He ditched that for the teachings of the Neoplatonists, who urged him to purify his soul. But how? He had often felt guilty about his hedonistic lifestyle, even as he continued it. He finally broke up with his mistress, thinking that might help, but his soul was still restless.

One day Augustine was walking in his garden. Tortured by his inability to give up his vices, he threw himself on the ground and wept. Then he heard a child's voice saying, "Pick up and read." Was it just a kid playing next door? But he didn't know any games with that phrase. He heard it again: "Pick up and read." Was this God talking?

Augustine found a Bible and flipped it open at random. His eyes fell on Romans 13:13, which urged the reader to "behave decently," to put aside sexual immorality.

"It seemed as though light broke in upon me," he later wrote. This was his moment of conversion. Here was his answer. As the Scripture instructed him, he decided to clothe himself not with sin but with Jesus.

Augustine delighted his mother with the news. On Easter Sunday, 387, he was baptized by Bishop Ambrose. Ironically, now that he could legitimately rise to power in a Christian government, that wasn't important to him. His rampant ambition was gone. The next year he moved back to North Africa, intending to live quietly in his hometown.

It didn't work out that way. When Augustine visited the North African town of Hippo, the congregation there forced him to be their priest. In 396 he became bishop. And that's when he began to change the world.

As a church leader, Augustine sought to heal a major schism. As a theologian, he spoke out against paganism and heresy. As a writer, he broke new ground with his autobiographical *Confessions* and the twenty-two-volume *City of God*. In short, he was the most important Christian thinker since Paul. And all because of a child's voice and a Bible verse.

The Shepherd at the End of the Earth

ST. PATRICK OF IRELAND (CA. 389-461)

So many legends have entwined themselves around the life of St. Patrick that it's hard to know what's true and what isn't. This much we know. Born in Roman Britain near the end of the fourth century, Patrick was kidnapped as a sixteen-year-old from his father's farm and sold as a slave in County Antrim, Ireland. He spent six years there as a shepherd. As a slave in a foreign land, he had time to think back on his religious training in childhood. He came to place his trust in Jesus Christ.

After six years Patrick escaped from his master, fleeing back to England. Here he received more Bible training and was accepted for the ministry by the British church. However, in a dream, he heard the voice of the Irish calling, "We beseech you to come and walk among us once more." It was like the apostle Paul's Macedonian vision.

He finally heeded that call when he was forty-one years old, returning to Ireland as a bishop sent from the English church. He was now steeped in Scripture, as his writings indicate. While he loved the psalms and the Book of Romans, the verse that impelled his evangelistic work was Matthew 24:14: "This gospel of the kingdom will be preached in the whole world, as a testament to all nations, and then the end will come."

Matthew 24:14

And this gospel of the kingdom will be preached in the whole world as a testimony to all nations, and then the end will come.

Matthew 24 is the beginning of the Olivet Discourse, when Jesus taught his disciples from the Mount of Olives shortly before his death. His disciples asked him, "What will be the sign of your coming and of the end of the age?" Jesus responded with a collection of warnings and prophecies that have tantalized readers for centuries. Some of the prophecies were fulfilled in the Roman defeat of Jerusalem in A.D. 70, but others seem to await the last days. Many missionaries, like Patrick, have claimed verse 14 as a mandate, understanding that Jesus will not return until all people (or people-groups) have heard the gospel.

21

In Patrick's day Ireland was at the end of the world. Nothing was farther from the civilizations of Athens and Rome, nor was anything less civilized than Ireland. So Patrick believed that when he had preached the gospel to all of Ireland, Christ would return. "I always give thanks to God," he wrote, "because . . . he has taken notice of me so that in spite of my ignorance and of our being in the last days, I should venture to . . . declare his gospel as a testimony to all nations before the end of the world . . . and we see as a consequence that it has been fulfilled just so; you can see that we are witnesses that the gospel has been preached as far as the point where there is no one beyond."

As a missionary, Patrick didn't allow any clover to grow under his feet. He planted about 365 churches and won about 120,000 converts to Christ. Several Irish kings were converted. Because of Patrick's love for the Bible and his concern for evangelism, the Irish church became both a center of education (from the sixth to the eighth centuries it was regarded as the most learned country in western Europe) and a center for continued missionary effort. Missionaries were not only sent back to England but also to central Europe. Some of the greatest missionaries of the Middle Ages were sent out by Patrick's successors in the Irish church. One Irish missionary, Brendan, is said to have ventured westward across the Atlantic to see if there were any more lands to reach for Christ before the end came.

Building a Civilization by the Book

CHARLEMAGNE (742-814)

This king of the Franks is often called the father of modern Europe because of his efforts to bring disparate European tribes together in a common civilization. However, Charlemagne thought of himself not as the father of Europe but as an Old Testament king.

Which Old Testament king? Since he was the first king of that particular empire, you might consider him another Saul. Since he was the shrewd developer of a mighty civilization, you could see him as a Solomon. But the king Charlemagne chose as his model was a more obscure one—Josiah, the boy king of Judah, who brought spiritual renewal to the nation.

Josiah had assumed the throne at age eight and was still only twenty-six when a temple housecleaning uncovered an old copy of the Book of the Law. God's commands had been long forgotten, but this dusty volume led the nation into revival. King and commoners alike pledged themselves to a renewed covenant with their neglected Lord.

> ### 2 Kings 23:3
> *The king stood by the pillar and renewed the covenant in the presence of the LORD—to follow the LORD and keep his commands, regulations and decrees with all his heart and all his soul, thus confirming the words of the covenant written in this book. Then all the people pledged themselves to the covenant.*

The king in this case was Josiah, who had become king of Judah in 640 B.C. His great-grandfather, Hezekiah, had led a revival in Judah around 700 B.C., but those spiritual gains were lost under the lengthy reign of Manasseh, who promoted pagan practices and the worship of false gods. After a priest happened to find a copy of the Mosaic Law during a fix-up project at the temple, Josiah led the people in corporate repentance and recommitment.

Charlemagne had become king at age twenty-four. Like Josiah, he lived in a dark age. Sometimes Charlemagne quoted the words of Jesus about the increase of wickedness in the last days when the love of many would grow cold. He wanted to bring some light into the darkness.

Though illiterate and uncultured at the start, he brought in brilliant Christian advisors—Alcuin from England and later Theodolf from Spain. After Charlemagne learned to read and write, he became president of his own royal academy, a patron of scholars, and founder of parish schools throughout his realm. As a religious reformer, he reprimanded clergy who had become lax.

Like Josiah, he loved God's Word. He pictured himself as a king who "stood by the pillar and renewed the covenant in the presence of the LORD" (2 Kings 23:3). "A priest should be learned in Holy Scripture," he said, and he wanted a fresh Bible translation because Jerome's Vulgate was nearly four centuries old. He encouraged preaching in the language of the people and opposed the worship of icons in the churches. His favorite book, apart from the Bible, was Augustine's *City of God*. He loved to argue theology and thought up questions to stump his advisors.

Charlemagne also loved music. He often sat on the church steps and listened to the choirs inside. Sometimes he would even go in and tell them how to sing.

To his own Frankish people, Charlemagne was a genial leader. To his foes he was often vicious, blood-curdlingly vicious. For more than thirty years he was in continual warfare, battling the Lombards in Italy, the Saxons in Germany, the Moors in Spain, and also the Danes, the Bavarians, the Huns, the Bulgarians, and the Slavs. We bristle at his attempts to convert the Saxons. "Believe or die" was his motto, and in one day he executed 4,500 of them. But by the year 800 Charlemagne had united most of Europe under one government. That was the year he decided to stop fighting and devote himself to civilizing his people. He moved his empire from a dominion of force to a dominion of law.

You don't have to love everything about Charlemagne. He had several wives and many mistresses, and undoubtedly he was a very proud man. But it's hard to question his love for the Bible. Like Josiah of old, he used the Scriptures to rebuild a nation. And fittingly, a carving on Charlemagne's tomb depicts him holding a copy of the Gospels on his knee.

The Man behind the Magna Carta

STEPHEN LANGTON (CA. 1160-1228)

The Magna Carta, signed at Runnymede, England in 1215, is hailed as one of the most significant documents in history and the charter of a democratic age. Yet the man responsible for that historic happening has almost been forgotten. His name is Stephen Langton, and Winston Churchill called him "the indomitable, unwearying builder of the rights of Englishmen."

Born in Lincolnshire, England, Langton crossed the channel to study in Paris, where he became a great Bible scholar and teacher. He loved to compare Scripture with Scripture. To make it easier to do this, he divided the Bible into chapters. (Others had tried such divisions, but Langton's arrangement stuck—it's what we use today.)

In his writing and preaching, Langton often focused on forgiveness. One passage in particular impacted his life: "'Lord, how many times shall I forgive my brother . . . ?' Jesus answered, 'I tell you, not seven times, but seventy-seven times'" (Matt. 18:21–22). In theory it was easy to apply, but in the real world, Langton had far more than seventy-seven opportunities to put those Matthew 18 teachings into practice.

In 1207 Pope Innocent III named Langton the archbishop of Canterbury, head of the English church. King John of England had others in mind for the position, but the pope vetoed his suggestions. In response King John vetoed Langton, considering him obnoxious. Back

> **Matthew 18:21–22**
> Then Peter came to Jesus and asked, "Lord, how many times shall I forgive my brother when he sins against me? Up to seven times?" Jesus answered, "I tell you, not seven times, but seventy-seven times."
>
> Matthew 18 has several teachings about forgiveness. In verses 15–20, Jesus gives instructions for reconciliation with a "brother" who "sins against you." Confront him alone. If that doesn't work, bring others with you. Finally, "tell it to the church." Then Peter asks his famous question. What limits should we place on forgiveness? "Seventy-seven" is not a new calculation but a measure of infinity. Jesus follows up with the parable of the unmerciful servant. Forgiven people should forgive others.

and forth it went. The tug-of-war continued, with Langton caught in the middle. When King John confiscated church property, Pope Innocent placed an interdict on England and excommunicated John.

In 1213, after military defeats in France and the loss of support from the barons, King John reluctantly decided to accept Langton as archbishop of Canterbury after all.

When he arrived in England, Langton put forgiveness into action, bargaining with the pope on King John's behalf. Soon this "obnoxious" archbishop became a counselor to the king. In a public ceremony Langton absolved the king from excommunication as Psalm 51:9–10 was sung: "Hide thy face from my sins, and blot out all mine iniquities. Create in me a clean heart, O God" (KJV). Then the king announced amnesty to rebels as well as restitution to the clergy. Forgiveness was occurring on a grand scale.

Next Langton began working with the barons. The barons wanted to overthrow the king, but Langton talked them out of it, saying he would get the king to accept their demands. After long negotiations, King John agreed, and the Magna Carta was written and signed. It spoke of justice, jury trials, the rights of commoners as well as of nobles, and the need for legal cause to hold anyone in prison. More than that, it restricted the king's power, which meant the king was no longer above the law. Stephen Langton's name was first on the list of signatories.

When the pope heard about the Magna Carta, he ordered that the rebellious barons be excommunicated. Langton refused to do it. The Magna Carta was too important to let even the pope spoil it. For his refusal to obey the pope, he was suspended from all official duties and forced to leave England.

With Langton out of the picture, it looked as if the document would be forgotten and the country would fall into anarchy. But King John died suddenly from eating too many green peaches and drinking too much new cider, and his nine-year-old son, Henry III, took over. Everyone knew that young Henry needed a wise mentor, so Langton was invited back to become chief counselor. The Magna Carta was given official status again and soon became established in English law.

Most historians agree that if any one person deserves credit for the Magna Carta, it is Stephen Langton, who was often offended but just as often forgave.

The Slacker Follows the Savior

FRANCIS OF ASSISI (1182-1226)

As a youth, Francis de Bernardone was known as the flower of his hometown of Assisi, Italy. Born to a wealthy textile merchant, he was good-looking, virile, and smart—a ladies' man who longed to be a knight in the Crusades. When war broke out between Assisi and a rival city, Francis enlisted quickly, hoping to establish himself as a war hero.

Instead he was captured, imprisoned, and then released. At the tender age of twenty, Francis was plagued by self-doubt. With his dreams of crusading dashed, he had no idea who he was or what he would become. One day he shuffled into the church of San Damian. The crucifix in that church was different from most; Jesus looked especially calm and gentle. He seemed to be saying to Francis, "Come unto me."

Francis knelt before the cross and prayed, "O Lord Jesus, shed your light upon the darkness of my mind." While on his knees, he had a vision of Christ telling him to rebuild his church. He rose to his feet a new creation in Christ.

> ### Matthew 10:7–10
>
> *As you go, preach this message: "The kingdom of heaven is near." Heal the sick, raise the dead, cleanse those who have leprosy, drive out demons. Freely you have received, freely give. Do not take along any gold or silver or copper in your belts; take no bag for the journey, or extra tunic, or sandals or a staff; for the worker is worth his keep.*
>
> In Matthew 10, when Jesus sends his disciples on a mission throughout Israel, he seems to be speaking not only to the Twelve but to the generations of Christian ministers who would follow. He warns that his disciples will not always get a good reception, and he asks them to work as he worked, with "no place to lay his head" (Matt. 8:20). While the Christian worker "is worth his keep" and should be provided for, one shouldn't go into the ministry for the money.

He wasn't exactly sure how to interpret the vision. Uncertain of God's call, he spent a few years working with lepers. Then while worshiping in the church of Portiuncula, he heard the verses from Matthew 10 in which Christ commissions his disciples and tells them to go out and serve humbly. Francis understood this as Christ's call to him as well.

As a barefoot preacher in the community, he began proclaiming the kingdom of God. Following the scriptural pattern set forth in Matthew 10:7–10, he went without money or knapsack. In a ragged cloak and a rope-belt taken from a scarecrow, he roamed the countryside, begging from the rich, giving to the poor, and preaching the words of Jesus. Gradually a few others joined him.

Two years later, when Francis was twenty-eight, he got approval from the pope for his new order, the Franciscans, dedicated to apostolic poverty and caring for the poor and sick. Soon Francis was doing missionary work abroad, going to Spain in 1215 and then to Egypt in 1219, where he tried to convert the sultan.

As the Franciscan movement grew, Francis passed the leadership on to others, withdrawing to a hermitage to devote his life to solitude and prayer. Here he wrote the *Testament* and the *Canticle to the Sun*. He enjoyed his solitary life; it was here that he preached to the birds and animals.

As Francis lay dying at the age of forty-four, fifty of his followers came to be with him. He asked them to read John 19, which records the crucifixion of Christ. Still remembering his conversion in the church of San Damian, he said, "In living or in dying, 'God forbid that I should glory, save in the cross of our Lord Jesus Christ'" (Gal. 6:14).

The Franciscan order in their gray cloaks soon became a familiar arm of Roman Catholicism around the world. Francis's followers continued his missionary work throughout Europe, North Africa, and the Middle East. Today there are also Franciscan orders in the Anglican and Lutheran churches. Thousands more from all religious traditions have been inspired by Francis's love of God's creatures and his enjoyment of nature.

Perhaps best known to Protestants and Catholics alike is his prayer, "Lord, make me an instrument of thy peace." It is a prayer that shows an attitude he learned from Jesus.

The "Dumb Ox" Plods On

THOMAS AQUINAS (1225-1274)

As a brawny schoolboy, Thomas Aquinas earned the nickname "Dumb Ox." But the Dumb Ox was smarter than people thought. As a Dominican monk and professor, he changed the way Christians thought, and he has been pulling the cart of Christian scholarship for much of the past millennium.

Born in 1225 into a wealthy family, Aquinas showed early signs of pious devotion, so he was sent off to be educated by monks. At age fourteen he went to the University of Naples, where he was greatly impressed by a teacher who was a member of the Dominican order. Aquinas decided to enter that order himself.

Bad idea, according to his family. A young man as brilliant as he was should practice law or run the government, not bury himself in some monastery. The monk business was fine for getting an education, but he shouldn't *become* one. They had to try to dissuade him, so they hired a prostitute to seduce him. When that didn't work, they kidnapped him and attempted some deprogramming. When he still insisted on entering the Lord's work, they offered to buy him the post of archbishop of Naples. Might as well start at the top.

Aquinas escaped his family's influence by moving to Paris to study theology. Despite his serious, plodding manner, the Dumb Ox became a great debater. He used those skills as a professor and as a writer. He

> ### Romans 1:20
>
> *For since the creation of the world God's invisible qualities—his eternal power and divine nature—have been clearly seen, being understood from what has been made, so that men are without excuse.*
>
> This is the first paragraph of Paul's treatise on sin and salvation, which makes up the bulk of Romans. Paul's point is that God has good reason to be mad at everybody, Jew and Gentile alike. He starts with the Gentiles, asserting that they could know God by looking at the created order, but instead they choose to worship idols and follow their base desires. (In chapter 2 the Jews join the act, since they have God's law but don't keep it.) It doesn't seem that Paul is trying to establish the principle of natural law; instead he's using it to prove universal sinfulness.

penned a number of biblical commentaries but also wrote about philosophy, especially Aristotle's work. In 1265 he began his best work, a compendium of Christian thought called *Summa Theologica*.

Christianity makes sense. That was Aquinas's premise, and it was extraordinary for his day. He dared to say that we can use our human reason to understand the revelation of God. After all, the apostle said in Romans 1:20 that the "invisible qualities" of God can be understood through the creation, even by those who haven't read Scripture.

The medieval church wasn't big on reason. Allegorical interpretations of Scripture and fanciful superstitions marked the age. Since human reason was damaged by sin, how could mere mortals understand the mysteries of the eternal? But Aquinas sliced the issues carefully. Human *will* is corrupted by sin, but not human *reason*. That is still the gift of God that separates us from the animals. Otherwise, how could God's "eternal power and divine nature . . . be understood from what has been made" (Rom. 1:20)?

One of Aquinas's greatest contributions is his effort to prove the existence of God through logic. In *Summa Theologica* he sets out five arguments, including the need for a Prime Mover and the teleological need for a being that exhibits to the fullest all the good qualities we seek. Logic also led him to the principle of natural law, which states that the created order should bear a kind of internal law that parallels what God has given us in Scripture. This formed the basis for many of the legal developments over the following centuries.

Some theologians criticize Aquinas for exalting human reason too much. That was certainly the criticism he got during his lifetime. Shortly after his death in 1274, the University of Paris condemned some of his teaching. For three centuries he was merely a footnote, but the Council of Trent (1545–1563) revived his work, using it for many of the council's decrees, and "Thomism" regained popularity. In 1879 the pope pronounced Thomas's theology "eternally valid."

It seems the Dumb Ox was not as dumb as people thought.

The Morning Star of the Reformation

JOHN WYCLIFFE (CA. 1329-1384)

John Wycliffe is called "the Morning Star of the Reformation," and for good reason. What he began in the fourteenth century kept erupting across the continent of Europe for the next two hundred years.

The first eruption came in Lutterworth, England, in 1381, when the fifty-two-year-old Wycliffe was sick in bed, near death. He had already had a full career. Trained at Oxford, where he was recognized as a leading philosopher, he had served as a chaplain in the king's court in London. He was outspoken in his views on the separation of church and state, the primacy of Scripture, the corruption in the Roman Catholic Church, and the idea that the church consisted of God's chosen people, who did not need a priest to mediate with God for them. The main job of the priest is preaching, he taught, and the content of his preaching must be the Bible. Furthermore, the Bible must be available in the language of the people so that anyone can understand it.

Psalm 118:17

I shall not die, but live, and declare the works of the LORD (KJV).

Picture a prisoner of war returning home after a victory is won and a town throwing a parade in his honor. That's the feeling of Psalm 118. It's full of thanksgiving, it's clearly a processional, and it has an underlying sense of deliverance from near disaster. The psalmist was clearly at death's door, but now there's more living to do. This psalm was part of Jesus' triumphal entry into Jerusalem. Verse 22 mentions "the stone the builders rejected," which "has become the capstone"— a metaphor the New Testament often uses for Jesus. You may recognize verse 26 from that first Palm Sunday: "Blessed is he who comes in the name of the LORD." With that in mind, Wycliffe's verse provides a premonition of resurrection.

As you might guess, Wycliffe's revolutionary doctrines got him into trouble. The archbishop of London banned him from preaching. When Wycliffe asked the king for support, he got none, and so he retired to the small town of Lutterworth, an ill and beaten man.

Though most of his friends had deserted him, his opponents came to his bedside and urged him to repent and confess his error. Surprising everyone, this maverick sat up in bed and quoted Psalm 118:17: "I shall not die, but live, and declare the works of the LORD" (KJV).

Wycliffe was right. He had a few more years of life to declare God's works. In his "retirement home" of Lutterworth, he began translating the entire Bible into English, the first time anyone had done this. English commoners would be able to read the Scriptures for themselves without relying on priests to paraphrase from the Latin. A group called the Lollards gathered around Wycliffe, helping him with the translation and then, after training, going out to preach and teach across the countryside of England.

A second eruption came a generation later. A Czech named Jan Hus read Wycliffe's writings and launched a reform movement in Prague. A third eruption came in the next century. Martin Luther changed the religious makeup of Europe, drawing heavily from the ideas of both Hus and Wycliffe. Name any reformer from the 1500s—Zwingli, Calvin, Melanchthon—and chances are they saw themselves as building on Wycliffe's work. Even Henry VIII was affected by Wycliffe. It was after he read Wycliffe that he separated the English church from the Roman Catholic Church.

Wycliffe's translation efforts paved the way for vernacular versions throughout Europe. William Tyndale took the next step of English translation, and Luther worked on a German Bible. Today a missionary organization called Wycliffe Bible Translators has translated the Bible into hundreds of languages and has a goal of translating it into every language on earth, so that people everywhere can understand God's Word in their own tongue.

"I shall not die, but live," said Wycliffe. He was no doubt grateful for the few extra years he had to declare God's works, but did he have any clue how those declarations would live on after him?

Carrying Christ around the World

CHRISTOPHER COLUMBUS (1451-1506)

The Italians call a person's thirty-third year the *Anno de Cristo*, the year of Christ, in memory of Christ's death in his thirty-third year. It is the year for spiritual revelations and reflection.

For Christopher Columbus it was a time to reflect on his name, Christopher, which means "Christ-bearer." While he and his brother Bartolomeo were working as map makers in Lisbon, Portugal, Columbus had time to reflect also on his love of the sea. Then he came upon a Bible verse that fit these reflections—the opening verse of Isaiah 49. It spoke of islands and "distant nations." It spoke of being "called" before birth. Was that why Christopher was given that name before he was born? Was that why he loved the sea so much? Did God direct him to this Scripture verse because he was calling Christopher to bring the message of Christ to the people in "distant nations"?

> ### Isaiah 49:1
>
> *Listen to me, you islands; hear this, you distant nations. Before I was born the LORD called me; from my birth he has made mention of my name.*
>
> The latter half of Isaiah includes several Servant Songs, which describe the work of a Servant empowered and approved by God. In chapter 49 there is a view toward expansion. The Servant will be "a light for the Gentiles" (v. 6), a promise that is applied to Christ and the Christian message in various New Testament passages.

And so in his thirty-third year Christopher Columbus went to the king of Portugal with a proposal. He asked for underwriting to finance a trip to sail west to get to the Far East. The royal commission called the idea far-fetched. Columbus sent his brother to England, but the English court called his brother a fool. Then Columbus turned to King Ferdinand and Queen Isabella of Spain, who rejected his plan because it "rested on poor foundations."

Disheartened, Columbus retreated to a monastery. There a Franciscan friar befriended him. Soon Columbus was ready to try again. "It was the Lord who put into my mind," he wrote later in his *Book of Prophe-*

cies, "to sail from here to the Indies. . . . I have cried out to the Lord for grace and mercy, and they have covered me completely. I have found the sweetest consolation since I made it my whole purpose to enjoy his marvelous presence.

"The signs are that the Lord is hastening the end. The fact that the gospel must still be preached to so many lands in such a short time—this is what convinced me."

The next morning the prior at the monastery sent a messenger to Queen Isabella, asking her to reconsider the decision. The rest is history.

On August 3, 1492, after receiving Holy Communion, Columbus rowed out to his three ships, all meticulously outfitted, to begin the voyage. During the voyage, the crew was on the verge of mutiny, but Columbus thought of himself as Moses leading the murmuring Israelites toward the Promised Land. When he finally arrived in the New World, he christened the island San Salvador (Holy Savior) and prayed, "Praised be Thy Majesty, which hath deigned to use us . . . that Thy holy Name may be proclaimed in this second part of the earth." He gave gifts to the natives of the island, "in order that we might win good friendship, because I knew that they were a people who could better be freed and converted to the Holy Faith by love than by force."

Later he wrote in his *Book of Prophecies,* "It is simply the fulfillment of what Isaiah had prophesied."

Columbus had many failings. He could be vain, domineering, and arrogant. He seemed obsessed with gold. He was a poor manager, and because of his mismanagement, he was removed as governor of Hispaniola. But despite heartbreak, disease, and despair, he still could say, "God has been good to me." Returning from his final voyage, he had a dream in which he heard a voice assuring him, according to Isaiah 49:1, that God had privileged him to open up "islands" and "distant nations" for the gospel. He wrote his will on the pages of a prayer book and signed it as he usually did—"Christ-bearer."

The Flamethrower of Florence

GIROLAMO SAVONAROLA (1452-1498)

Was Savonarola the real igniter of the Reformation flames? Many historians charge this fiery Italian preacher with striking a crucial match. Luther himself said he was greatly influenced by what Savonarola had done a generation before him.

But Savonarola seemed to be a failure until one Bible verse burst upon him. Much to the displeasure of his physician father, Savonarola had entered a Dominican monastery in Bologna, where he had become a student of Scripture. After seven years in Bologna and four years in a convent in Ferrara, he was sent to Florence, where the Renaissance was at its peak.

Savonarola was disgusted by the immorality of Florence. No one in the city seemed to care about spiritual things— even the clergy were disinterested. When Savonarola preached, no one came to hear him. As a preacher he was a resounding failure.

Then one day as he prayed, the heavens seemed to open. He heard a voice commanding him to go out and preach repentance. He was to carry the message of John the Baptist: "Repent, for the kingdom of heaven is near" (Matt. 3:2).

Strangely, God took Savonarola away from Florence, and he was sent instead to a small town in the mountains to preach—another disappointment, because he knew his message was needed in Florence. As he preached in the smaller cities of northern Italy, however, his fame increased. Great throngs were now coming to hear him. He was preach-

> ### Matthew 3:2, 10
>
> *Repent, for the kingdom of heaven is near. . . . The axe is already at the root of the trees, and every tree that does not produce good fruit will be cut down and thrown into the fire.*
>
> ---
>
> This is the first New Testament appearance of John the Baptist, who preached in the desert and baptized in the Jordan, preparing the way for Christ. John was a fitting role model for Savonarola, a thunderous preacher who challenged the religious leaders and gained the support of the common people— and who died because he condemned sinful behavior.

ing against the evils of the clergy and even the corruption of the monks in his own monastery. The people loved his honesty.

Then he was called back to Florence, and he preached of a judgment coming upon the city for its wickedness. St. Mark's Church couldn't hold the crowds that wanted to hear him. Soon Savonarola was preaching in the magnificent Duomo of Florence. When Lorenzo the Magnificent, the most powerful ruler in Italy, lay dying in a nearby villa, he called for Savonarola, seeking his blessing.

Savonarola continued to preach doom to the city unless it repented. Nevertheless, when the king of France invaded Italy, threatening Florence, Savonarola went out to the invading king, warning him not to destroy the city. If he did, the preacher warned, he would incur the vengeance of God. The French army withdrew, and Savonarola was more popular than ever. He preached to even larger crowds. Now the Duomo wasn't large enough to house the people. Savonarola was named city manager, making Florence a republic—or, more accurately, a Christocracy with Jesus as its head. Savonarola initiated tax reforms, aided the poor, reformed the courts, and condemned gambling, sodomy, and immorality. Overnight, the pleasure-mad city became saintly.

Though Florentines lauded him, Savonarola's fearlessness did not win him any friends in Rome. The pope made a political gesture, offering Savonarola a cardinal's hat. He refused to take it.

The pope had enough. Savonarola was suspended from the priesthood and excommunicated. Besides that, the city of Florence was placed under a papal interdict. That's when the people of Florence changed their minds about the reformer. Of course, he always had his share of foes in the city, but now those enemies flexed their muscles. Savonarola was asked to retract his charges against the pope and admit he was a false prophet. He refused, was arrested, stood trial for heresy, and was found guilty.

After a month of torture, he was sent to the gallows. The execution took place on the city square. After the pope's representative pronounced judgment upon him, saying, "I exclude thee from the militant and triumphant church," Savonarola responded, "From the church militant you may, but from the church triumphant, you cannot."

Choosing Truth over Tradition

ULRICH ZWINGLI (1484-1531)

As the new priest strode to the pulpit on the first Sunday of 1519, the congregation wondered what he might say. Ulrich Zwingli had been appointed to this influential Zurich church as the "people's priest," and he brought an impressive resume. Earned a master's degree from the university at Basel. Studied under the great Erasmus and other noted scholars. Knew Greek and Hebrew. Was a small-town pastor for ten years, chaplain of the Swiss mercenary force for two years. Served two more years as priest in the popular pilgrimage center of Einsiedeln. Whatever the assigned Scripture was for the day, surely this new man would find something interesting in it.

Zwingli surprised them all by tossing out the lectionary. He would be preaching through the New Testament week by week, starting in Matthew. They all had some important things to learn about the gospel.

> ### Psalm 119:30
>
> *I have chosen the way of truth; I have set my heart on your laws.*
>
> Psalm 119 is the longest chapter in the Bible, with 176 verses. It has twenty-four stanzas of eight verses each, one stanza for each letter of the Hebrew alphabet. Each verse begins with the Hebrew letter of its stanza. Scholars think this psalm was used as a primer for children learning to read. And what better subject matter than the Word of God itself? Psalm 119 is all about God's law—knowing it, obeying it, hiding it in your heart. Verse 30, in the "D" stanza, echoes the sentiment of the other 175 verses—the necessity of a personal commitment to follow God's Word.

This might seem harmless, but it was the first step that Zwingli and his people would take over the next few years—steps away from the control of the Roman Catholic Church. Zwingli led a back-to-the-Bible movement, preaching what he found in Scripture even when it went against church positions. His knowledge of the original languages helped him cut through some of the convoluted interpretations of church tradition. Based on biblical teaching about Christian freedom, his followers began to eat meat during Lent in defiance of church rules. Zwingli urged Rome to allow priests to marry, and he got married himself. Images of saints were removed from church buildings. He brought the Eucharist down from its distant, ornate altar and served the people bread and wine from a simple table. Preaching became a more important part of the mass. All of this was Zwingli's way of *choosing truth,* as the psalmist wrote, "I have chosen the way of truth; I have set my heart on your laws" (Ps. 119:30).

It was a time of upheaval in the European church. Luther had nailed his ninety-five complaints to a church door in 1517 and was condemned by the pope in 1520, but he found political protection among the German nobles. Zwingli's reforms continued throughout the 1520s within the protective embrace of the canton of Zurich. When he pronounced his own set of sixty-seven theses in 1523, setting forth his basic theology and complaints against the Catholic Church, the city council backed him up, resolving "that Mr. Ulrich Zwingli continue . . . to proclaim . . . the pure holy scripture."

Zwingli's sixty-seven theses were more basic than Luther's ninety-five. Note number 3: "Christ is the only way to salvation for all who ever were, are, or shall be." Or number 4: "He who seeks or shows another way errs, and indeed he is a murderer of souls and a thief." Strong language but based on the supremacy of Scripture. Number 5: "Hence all who consider other teachings equal to or higher than the gospel err, and do not know what the gospel is."

Zwingli set out a design for living, a "way of truth." Always the pastor, Zwingli wasn't just interested in reforming the church, but also in reforming people. Christians, he said, must obey Christ but shouldn't "burden themselves with foolish laws." Secular government should be obeyed "in so far as they do not order that which is contrary to God." And Christians should make sure their governments "protect the oppressed."

Several Swiss cantons that remained Catholic went to war against Zurich in 1531, and Zwingli accompanied his troops into battle, where he was killed, an early casualty in religious wars that would ravage Europe over the next century.

Yet motivated by a simple desire to follow God's Word, Zwingli had transformed a city. He had set his heart on God's law.

The Book of Love

WILLIAM TYNDALE (1494-1536)

The king banned the book, but still it found its way into the country. In bundles and barrels it was smuggled in. Soldiers seized what they could find, but there were always more. Church leaders kept pushing the king to do something about this offensive volume.

Finally someone hatched an ingenious plan: Send the king's agents to buy up the books and then burn them! Sure, it would cost something, but the elimination of these perilous pages would be well worth the price. The plan was swiftly carried out.

That dangerous book was the Bible. The time was the 1520s. The land was England. A scholar named William Tyndale had dared to translate the New Testament into English so people could read it for themselves. At first Tyndale thought church leaders might support his new project, but instead they vehemently opposed it. Tyndale was forced into exile on the European continent, where he finished translating the New Testament and started work on the Old. Tyndale had to keep moving to avoid English agents, but this was his life's calling. In an argument with a priest, Tyndale had once articulated his vocation in this way: "If God spare my life, ere many years, I will cause a boy that driveth the plough to know more of the Scripture than thou dost."

And the ploughboys and common workers were snatching up the New Testament portions as soon as they were smuggled into England. Of course, the common folk didn't have a lot of money, so Tyndale's publishing project was undercapitalized—until the king started buying up copies to burn. The grand plan backfired mightily as the king's gold

> ## 1 John 4:19
>
> *We love him because he first loved us* (KJV).
>
> Love is a major theme in John's Gospel and his letters, which makes sense because he refers to himself in his Gospel as "the disciple whom Jesus loved" (John 13:23). In this first epistle he makes it clear that "God is love" (1 John 4:16) and the source of love. In response to this love, we love God and others.

served to finance a second edition. Tyndale was able to make revisions and do a better printing.

You might expect such an embattled soul to develop a bitter spirit, but Tyndale seemed to hang on to love. One contemporary noted that the translator was especially fond of the writings of the apostle John— perhaps because of the strong love theme found in the fourth Gospel and John's epistles. When Thomas More wrote a treatise criticizing his translation, Tyndale penned a response that included a reference to 1 John 4:19: "We love him because he first loved us" (KJV).

"Our love and good works make not God first love us, nor change him from hate to love." Tyndale wrote. "No, His love and deeds make us love, and change us from hate to love. For He loved us when we were evil . . . and chose to make us good and to shew us love, and to draw us to Him, that we should love again. . . . If ye could see what is written in the first epistle of John, though all the other Scriptures were laid apart, ye should see all this."

"If I work for a worldly purpose, I get no reward in heaven," Tyndale also wrote in 1531 in his answer to Thomas More. "Even also if I work for heaven, or a higher place in heaven, I get there no reward. But I must do my work for the love of my neighbor, because he is my brother, and the price of Christ's blood, and because Christ hath deserved it, and desireth it for me; and then my reward is great in heaven."

When captured by English agents in Belgium in 1536, Tyndale was condemned as a heretic and executed. His dying words: "Lord, open the king of England's eyes."

His plea, apparently, was granted. Within a year, King Henry VIII changed his tune on Bible translations, supporting a new version by Miles Coverdale, a Tyndale associate. Soon the ban on Tyndale's work was lifted and the king actually encouraged the publication of new Bibles in English. A later monarch, King James, authorized the 1611 translation that remained the standard for centuries. About 90 percent of the wording in the King James Version comes from William Tyndale.

Steps of Faith

MARTIN LUTHER (1483-1546)

The monk gathered his robes and crawled up to the next step. There he prostrated himself again and started a new prayer. Like other pilgrims, he was praying his way up Pilate's Steps, a staircase on which Jesus had stepped. According to legend, these steps had been miraculously transported from Jerusalem to Rome, and now faithful Christians could atone for their sins by climbing these stairs on their knees. The monk, Martin Luther, knew he had many sins to atone for. He was tortured by them daily.

But there was something else on his mind on this fateful day, a Bible verse that rang clear and true. This monk was also a Bible professor at the University of Wittenberg. In his studies, he kept coming back to the writings of Paul, especially the Epistle to the Romans. And there in the first chapter was a pithy quotation from an Old Testament prophet: "The just shall live by faith" (v. 17). This simple truth was dancing through his mind even as he knelt on those steps. "Those who are truly righteous will live through their faith. . . . The righteous will find life in their faith. . . . Those who are righteous through faith will truly live." These words matched everything else Paul had written in Romans. All of us are sinners, but we are justified—made righteous—by Christ's sacrifice, which is ours through faith. Atonement was claimed by faith, not accomplished through pious acts.

As the story goes, this Bible verse finally broke through Luther's defenses, and he stood up and walked down Pilate's Steps. In the following years, he stepped into a whirlwind of activity, questioning the church's actions, starting a revolution, and launching a religious reform

> ### Romans 1:17
>
> The just shall live by faith (KJV).
>
> The quote originates in Habakkuk. The prophet has been complaining about the success of evil enemies, but God assures him that the righteous people who trust him will live. Paul picks up this verse to conclude his prologue to Romans. You might even consider this as Paul's theme sentence. Throughout Romans, Paul maintains that we are justified by faith (see 5:1), and not by keeping the law.

41

that changed the world forever. All because he held true to the simple message of that Bible verse: "The just shall live by faith" (v. 17).

He might have kept the whole thing to himself, except there was this huckster of a priest, Johann Tetzel, who came through the area selling indulgences. The church was raising money for a new cathedral in Rome, so why not offer forgiveness for a price? You could reduce a loved one's stay in purgatory or perhaps get some divine indulgence of your own. Luther was horrified by this, and he said so in ninety-five hotly written complaints that he tacked to the church door at Wittenberg on October 31, 1517. Now the battle was joined.

In 1520 he was ordered to recant his views, and in 1521 he stood before an imperial council that had examined his writings. "Will you recant?" the council demanded, and Luther's final answer came back: "Here I stand; I can do no other." That seemed to be the point of no return. Luther's work was condemned. But a political and religious revolution was underway, redrawing the map of Europe as it spread through Switzerland and England. And for twenty-five more years, Martin Luther was in the middle of the fray as a Bible teacher, songwriter, and translator.

A year before his death, in the introduction to a collection of his writings, Luther recalled earlier moments. "Though I lived as a monk without reproach, as a sinner before God I had an extremely disturbed conscience. . . . I hated the righteous God who punishes sinners. . . . As I thought about this day and night, I finally noted the context of the words, '. . . He who through faith is righteous shall live.' There I began to understand that the righteousness of God is what justifies us, by God's grace, through faith. . . . I felt that I was totally reborn again and had entered paradise itself through open gates. All of Scripture took on new meaning for me. . . . This passage of Paul was truly my gateway to heaven."

No Other Foundation

MENNO SIMONS (1496-1559)

For much of his life, Menno Simons remained on the fringes—thinking but not acting, respecting others who did brave things but not getting involved himself. But when this man finally took a stand, he became the center of a movement that lasts to this day.

Menno Simons was born into a swirling time. He was barely in his twenties when Luther pounded the first beats of the Reformation on the church door at Wittenberg. Ordained at age twenty-eight, Menno served twelve years as a Roman Catholic priest. As Luther was spearheading the German Reformation and Zwingli was changing the religious landscape of Switzerland, Menno was quietly doing his clerical duties in Friesland (near the Netherlands). He admitted later that he seldom opened the Bible during that time. He was afraid of it. He had been educated in Greek and philosophy, but not the Scriptures. He said mass and conducted rituals of birth, marriage, and death as a routine. It was his job. His life was not yet built on the foundation of Christ.

But some intellectual problems began to gnaw at Menno. For one thing, he wasn't buying the Catholic teaching about Communion—that the bread and wine became Christ's physical body and blood. When he dared to consult Scripture on the subject, he found no support for the official view. That scared him even more. Was he ready to challenge the church? He read some forbidden works by Luther and got a new sense of the importance of Scripture.

> ## 1 Corinthians 3:11
>
> *For no one can lay any foundation other than the one already laid, which is Jesus Christ.*
>
> The Corinthians were a cantankerous lot, with scandals, tiffs, and divisions. In the early chapters of this first epistle, Paul deals with factions based on personalities. Some claimed to follow the brilliant teacher Apollos, while others remained loyal to Paul. Apparently another group followed "Cephas" (Peter's Hebrew name). Rather than pushing his own party, Paul asserts that all ministers have their roles, but it's ultimately God's church. There might be various builders, but the foundation must be Jesus Christ.

43

During this time a new religious group was emerging. Their critics called them "Anabaptists," because they rebaptized adults. But the Anabaptists had a broader agenda. It was a kind of "back to the Bible" movement they were pushing; they felt Luther and Zwingli weren't going far enough. If you really stripped the church of all its extrabiblical traditions, they asked, what would you have?

Menno admired the Anabaptists. He acknowledged that Anabaptists, with their lack of organization and loose definitions, could sometimes go to extremes, but he also watched as they stalwartly faced persecution from Catholics and Protestants alike. He was moved by their devotion to the Scriptures.

In 1534 an apocalyptic group of Anabaptists took the city of Münster by force. When authorities besieged and recaptured the city, they massacred the Anabaptists. This event shook Menno. While he preached against the errors of this fringe group, he was also challenged by their dedication. If they could fight to the death for their errant ideas, why couldn't he stand up for the truth of Scripture? After an intense year of soul-searching, Menno resigned his priesthood and underwent baptism into an Anabaptist congregation.

He had stayed on the fringes as he wrestled with his conscience, but now his scholarship and wisdom provided a much-needed center for this scattered group. In his preaching and writing he defined the movement, calling radical groups back into conformity with biblical teaching but also challenging the Catholic and Protestant persecutors to come back to God's truth as well. On virtually everything he wrote, Menno used 1 Corinthians 3:11 as his motto: "For no one can lay any foundation other than the one already laid, which is Jesus Christ."

And Menno paid the price for his commitment. When Charles V put a bounty on his head, he had to wander the continent as a wanted man. Some of his loved ones were killed. Some who helped him elude authorities were executed. But Menno kept preaching and writing. Among his teachings was a belief in pacifism. He felt that Christ commanded his followers to turn the other cheek, and so Menno's Anabaptists would not fight back. The authorities never did track Menno down. He died peacefully in 1561 after a quarter century as an Anabaptist.

Menno's influence was quiet but decisive. His followers became known as Mennonites. The Mennonites in turn influenced other groups like the Baptists, and their simple teaching has remained a challenge for Christians of all persuasions. When you strip down everything else, is Christ your sure foundation?

Picking Up the Pieces

PHILIPP MELANCHTHON (1497-1560)

Superheroes have sidekicks. Sheriffs have deputies. Reformers have . . . people like Philipp Melanchthon. At the turn of the twentieth century, Martin Luther made everybody's list of the most important people of the millennium. But Luther might not have made so much of a splash without the support of Melanchthon. Together they changed the world—but always with the awareness that God was calling the shots.

Luther and Melanchthon met at the University of Wittenberg, where Melanchthon was already teaching Greek at the tender age of twenty-one. He quickly developed an admiration for Luther, fourteen years his senior, a Bible professor who had already tacked his Ninety-five Theses on the church door. As Luther's reform work grew, Melanchthon offered his help. They

> **Romans 8:31**
>
> If God be for us, who can be against us? (KJV).
>
> In the previous chapter Paul describes the frustration of wanting to do right but still doing wrong (Rom. 7:14–24). But then, as the eighth chapter opens, he announces that there is "no condemnation" for Christians. He continues by pointing out the Spirit's work of guiding, empowering, interceding, and encouraging. We face suffering and weakness, but we know that God is working all things out for good. Ultimately we have confidence in the amazing love of God, who gave his Son for us. If God loves us, what do we have to worry about?

made an interesting team. Both men were scholars and theologians, but Melanchthon was more careful than his blustery colleague. Luther had huge ideas; Melanchthon organized them. Luther was the bull in the proverbial china shop, making brash statements and challenging the authorities; Melanchthon scurried around, picking up after him and deciding which pieces were worth gluing back together. Luther himself wrote, "I am rough, stormy, and altogether warlike. I am here to fight innumerable monsters and devils . . . but Master Philippus comes along softly and gently, sowing and watering with joy."

While Luther stared down church councils and faced excommunication, Melanchthon was back home writing down the reasons for the

Reformation. In 1521 he published *Loci Communes Theologici* (Theological Common Places), exploring the issues of law and grace, the good news of Christ, and justification by faith. Martin was a master of the fiery challenge; Philipp served up sweet persuasion.

Melanchthon also did most of the writing of the Augsburg Confession, setting out the basics of their faith. When they got flak for this, Melanchthon wrote another work explaining the Augsburg Confession. This was the pattern throughout his career—filling in the gaps in Luther's writings, answering his critics, systematizing his views.

When Luther died in 1546, the movement looked to Melanchthon for leadership, but he seemed to lack the fire of his late associate. Without Luther leading the way, Melanchthon had no one to pick up after. Some Lutherans accused Melanchthon of being too soft, too wishy-washy, compromising Luther's positions.

This ineffectiveness later in life was certainly a sad chapter, but it speaks volumes about the unique teamwork between these two men. Luther needed Melanchthon to rein him in; Melanchthon needed Luther to coax him out. After all, it was Melanchthon who received Luther's famous advice: "Sin boldly." Of course Luther wasn't promoting sin, but he wanted his young friend to get past guilt and worry in order to step out strongly for God.

Perhaps it was to overcome those worries that Melanchthon adopted Romans 8:31 ("If God be for us, who can be against us?" [KJV]) as a kind of theme verse. He had gained many enemies throughout his career, so he needed the assurance that he still had one friend, the only friend who really mattered. Someone even stronger than Martin Luther.

Today you can visit Philipp Melanchthon's home in Wittenberg, the place where he quietly wrote the documents that helped to change the world. Carved over the doorway in German are these words: "If God is for us, who can be against us?"

The Anchor Holds

JOHN KNOX (1514-1572)

In Scotland he isn't as beloved as the poet Robert Burns or as the novelist Walter Scott. In the sixteenth century he wasn't the theologian that Luther or Calvin was. But more than anyone else he transformed the faith and character of the Scottish nation. You may have read novels and seen movies about the romantic Mary, Queen of Scots, but it was John Knox, not Mary, who had the most dynamic impact on the nation's history. Carlyle wrote, "What Knox did for his nation was a resurrection as from death." Before Knox, Scotland was on the edge of civilization. After Knox, it produced some of the finest thinkers, inventors, and writers in all Europe.

> ### John 17:3
>
> *And this is life eternal, that they might know thee the only true God, and Jesus Christ, whom thou hast sent* (KJV).
>
> John 17 is often known as Jesus' "high priestly" prayer, because he speaks to God on behalf of his people. He starts by focusing on his disciples, but later the prayer includes those who will believe in Jesus through their message. That's us.

Motivating Knox's actions was a specific chapter of the Bible. On his deathbed Knox asked his wife to get his Bible and "read where [he] cast [his] first anchor." His wife knew exactly what to read, for the chapter had been read to him every day for the past week. One verse in this chapter reads: "And this is life eternal, that they might know thee the only true God, and Jesus Christ, whom thou hast sent" (John 17:3 KJV). This "first anchor" had been cast nearly three decades earlier, and what mind-boggling decades they had been.

He was only twenty-two when he was ordained as a Catholic priest. Because there were more Catholic priests than churches, Knox became a tutor in the home of a Scottish noble who had Protestant sympathies. Protestant ideas were beginning to infiltrate Scotland, and a Protestant preacher named George Wishart soon grabbed Knox's attention and ultimately his support. But Wishart was too popular for his own good.

His enemies set a plot to kill him. He was captured and imprisoned, and a month later was tied to a stake, strangled, and burned.

Knox was devastated, but he returned to tutoring. Soon his pupils were joined by others, gathering at a little chapel to hear the Bible read and commented upon. Knox read to them from John 17 and 18, Christ's Last Supper prayer for his followers. After the experience with Wishart, Knox understood how the disciples must have felt.

But what should he do now? Because he had been associated with Wishart, his life was in danger. The fathers of his pupils suggested that he flee to the castle in St. Andrews, which was in Protestant hands. He took their advice, and after arriving there he began teaching again from John 17 and 18. Soon he was chosen chaplain of the castle, and that was an even more perilous position for him. Now, more than ever, he would be a marked man. But he did not dare run away. The Gethsemane story stayed in his mind. "This is life eternal," Jesus had said. He knew he was dealing with eternal issues here. He must cast down an anchor.

Three months later the castle was attacked from the sea by the French navy and on land by English troops. The French captured the castle and gave Knox a life sentence as a galley slave. Later he was released, thanks to the efforts of the British government negotiating with the Catholic Scottish authorities.

When the Catholic Queen Mary took the throne in 1553, Knox fled to Geneva, where he became a disciple of Calvin for six years. But his heart was still in Scotland. At last, in 1559 he was able to return. Under his leadership, Scottish independence was secured, a presbyterian system was established throughout the kingdom, a Calvinistic confession was adopted, and the pope's jurisdiction was abolished. He arranged programs for public education for all children and relief for the poor in each parish. The verbal battles between Mary Queen of Scots and the man "that thundereth from the pulpit" are legendary, but when she abdicated in 1567, Knox had won.

On his deathbed Knox credited the verse that had anchored him all his life, but it was also the verse that propelled him all his life.

The Playboy of the Eastern World
FRANCIS XAVIER (1506-1552)

The year was 1533. Martin Luther was publishing his translation of the Bible in German. John Calvin had just been converted to Protestantism in Paris and was now a hunted man. And a young professor of philosophy at the University of Paris was wondering in which direction to go. His Spanish parents had wanted him to become a priest; instead he had become a playboy. Handsome, athletic, musical, and academically brilliant, he was spending his free time gambling and carousing in Parisian taverns. But it wasn't satisfying.

Then one day after giving a lecture, Francis Xavier was stopped by an old friend of his, Ignatius Loyola. They talked long into the night. Afterward, Francis couldn't forget the words of Scripture that Loyola had quoted: "For what shall it profit a man if he shall gain the whole world and lose his own soul?" (Mark 8:36 KJV). This verse changed the course of his life.

Mark 8:36

For what shall it profit a man, if he shall gain the whole world and lose his own soul? (KJV).

In Mark 8, Jesus asked his disciples what they thought of him. Peter came out with his classic confession, "You are the Christ," (v. 29), and Jesus honored him for it. Then Jesus started talking about the future. He would have to suffer and die. Peter tried to talk him out of that negative mind-set but earned a sharp rebuke from the Lord: "Get behind me, Satan!" (v. 33). This gave Jesus the opportunity to talk about true discipleship. His followers would have to take up the cross, to lose their life in order to find it, because nothing—not even the whole world—could equal the value of one's soul.

Francis became one of Loyola's six recruits, the core group of his new "Company of Jesus," later known simply as the Jesuits. The Jesuits were an elitist order, accepting only the brightest and best. The challenge appealed to Francis, so he quit his professorship, was ordained to the priesthood, and began evangelistic work in northern Italy.

It was the age of exploration, and Portugal asked for priests to go and evangelize new lands in the Orient. The Jesuits were happy to oblige. During the next ten years Francis traveled back and forth between India and Japan, ministering in Goa, Ceylon, and the Moloccas.

Although Francis picked up languages quickly, the fact that he wasn't fluent in a language didn't stop him from trying to make converts. He had the Apostles' Creed, the Lord's Prayer, the Ave Maria, and the Ten Commandments put in the Tamil language, memorized them, and then taught them in the streets. At first he felt there was no time for preaching. Instead he would administer the sacraments quickly. Once, he baptized an entire village in a single day. Of course, Francis soon realized that such missionary work was only skin-deep. So he began to instruct native workers and children, and he memorized whole sermons in the native languages.

Remembering Paul's words to "become all things to all men" in order that he might "save some" (1 Cor. 9:22), Francis ministered to India's lower caste by working in a torn cassock and a shabby cowl. But in Japan, where poverty was despised, he wore the most magnificent apparel he could find and drew upon his university education in order to explain how a good and powerful God could permit evil. Some six hundred Japanese professed Christianity in the first year of his two-year stint there. In the South Sea islands, he lived among cannibals, saying, "My life is in the hand of Providence." One of his biographers wrote that he "had entered one of the stinking backwaters of the world, but here . . . he comes and goes with laughter and singing."

One writer has declared, "For zeal and courage, ability and endurance, and a glorious harvest of ransomed souls, the Church has had no missionary . . . to compare with Xavier."

One hymn is attributed to him, and it tells his story:

> My God, I love thee: not because I hope for heaven thereby,
> Nor yet because who love thee not are lost eternally.
> So would I love thee, dearest Lord, and in thy praise will sing,
> Solely because thou art my God, and my most loving king.

No Way to Nineveh

JOHN CALVIN (1509-1564)

John Calvin was ready to throw in the towel—at least as far as preaching was concerned. He was a quiet, sensitive man who suffered from migraines, chronic asthma, and various digestive ailments. So it should have been obvious to everyone that God had made him to be a student and writer, not a preacher and teacher. What he longed for, he admitted, was a life of "literary ease, with something of a free and honorable station."

He had barely escaped from Paris with his life; he had been hounded out of Geneva; and now a man named Martin Bucer was urging him to become the pastor of a church in Strasbourg, Germany, that ministered to French refugees.

Calvin wanted to run the other way, but Bucer wouldn't let him. "God will know how to find you, just as he found Jonah, another rebellious servant." In order to avoid storms or hungry fish, John Calvin gave in and went to Strasbourg. It proved to be a turning point in his life.

> ### Jonah 3:1–2
>
> Then the word of the LORD came to Jonah a second time: "Go to the great city of Nineveh and proclaim to it the message I give you."
>
> ---
>
> Jonah was called to preach in Nineveh, the capital of the wicked Assyrian Empire, but he ran the opposite way. When a storm came up, Jonah volunteered to be tossed into the sea, where a great fish swallowed him and, three days later, spat him up onto the beach. When a second command came his way, Jonah obeyed, but he still wasn't happy about it. What he feared was that Nineveh would repent and thus escape the judgment they deserved. As it turned out, they did repent, and God spared them. And that's what happened in Calvin's Geneva too.

Of course, Calvin had seen a few turning points already. After training for the Catholic priesthood at the University of Paris, he switched to the University of Orleans to study law. Then at age twenty-four, he had a sudden conversion. "God subdued and brought my heart to docility," he wrote in his *Commentary on the Psalms*.

When some of his new Protestant friends were forced to flee Paris, Calvin found that he was a wanted man too. He left his Paris dwelling in the nick of time and was on the run for a year before relocating to Basel, Switzerland, where he lived under an assumed name. In Basel at the age of twenty-seven, he published the first edition of his *Institutes*, a book that became a classic in his lifetime.

Then, because a war was going on and military troops blocked other roads, Calvin had to take a detour through Geneva. There, he says, "God thrust me into the game." A fiery Protestant leader, William Farel, insisted that he stay in Geneva and help with the ministry there. Calvin said he had other plans, but Farel said, "If you do not help us in this work of the Lord, the Lord will punish you for seeking your own interests rather than his." Admittedly terrified, Calvin stayed. Another turning point.

Two turbulent years later, both Farel and Calvin were expelled from Geneva. Little wonder, then, that Calvin returned to peaceful Basel to resume his life as a scholar and writer, never wanting to be a pastor again. Never again, that is, until Martin Bucer called him another Jonah.

Well, Strasbourg wasn't Calvin's Nineveh. It was just a warm-up for Nineveh. After three wonderful years in Strasbourg, where he found a wife and had time to develop as a pastor, a delegation from Geneva asked him to move back there again. Calvin said that he would rather endure a thousand deaths than be tormented "in that chamber of torture." To a friend he wrote, "There is no place under heaven that I am more afraid of." Yet another turning point.

Calvin left Strasbourg and returned to Geneva in tears, saying, "I offer my heart a slain victim for a sacrifice to the Lord." But in Geneva he accomplished titanic feats, establishing the famed Academy of Geneva that soon had 1,500 students and revising his *Institutes* (which became the textbook of Protestant theology for the next three hundred years). Protestant refugees from England, Scotland, and France—six thousand of them—poured into the city and found support there. Calvin's view of church organization inspired not only Presbyterianism, but also the whole system of modern representative democracy.

The history of the world was dramatically affected, all because John Calvin refused to be another Jonah.

The Stargazer Who Wouldn't Stand Still

GALILEO GALILEI (1564-1642)

For more than 350 years, the works of Galileo had been condemned by the Roman Catholic Church because Galileo had dared to hold the notion that the earth revolved around the sun.

But 1992 was a better year for Galileo. The Roman Catholic Church acknowledged that it had made "errors" in his trial. The *New York Times* carried the headline: AFTER 350 YEARS, VATICAN SAYS GALILEO WAS RIGHT: IT MOVES. In 1989 NASA had sent the Galileo spacecraft into space toward Jupiter, and when the spacecraft's camera was turned on, people saw the truth of what Galileo had written in 1610: "I have never doubted that if our globe were seen from afar . . . the land regions would appear brighter and the watery regions darker."

Galileo wasn't just a stargazer; he was a versatile scientist. It was Galileo who gave modern mechanics and physics its first solid base. He invented a thermometer and conducted research in motion and gravity. When he secured a primitive telescope, he was able to confirm what he had suspected—that Copernicus's theory of the earth rotating around the sun was true.

Joshua 10:13

And the sun stood still, and the moon stayed, until the people had avenged themselves upon their enemies.

After their wilderness wanderings, the Israelites had stormed into the Promised Land, defeating Jericho and Ai and scaring Gibeon into a peace treaty. In response, five Canaanite kings attacked Gibeon, and Joshua honored the new treaty by rushing to Gibeon's defense. The Israelites apparently needed more daylight to chase down their fleeing foes, so God made the sun stand still. This story still causes problems for interpreters. Certainly God could suspend the laws of nature, but some believe that the text is poetically talking about a well-timed meteorological event—perhaps a sudden break in the clouds that gave the army more daylight than they expected.

What got him into hot water with the church authorities was his belief that Copernicus's theory was not opposed to Scripture but supported by Scripture.

One biblical passage that the Vatican set forth to disprove the idea of the earth's movement around the sun was the story of Joshua commanding the sun to stand still in Joshua 10:13. Galileo countered by saying that Joshua's day would have been shorter rather than longer if God stopped the motion of the sun alone. If God stopped only the sun and not the other celestial bodies, he would completely upset and confuse the order of the universe.

Church leaders were alarmed by the arrogance of an impertinent layman trespassing on the realm of theology. Galileo might have gotten away with his scientific view, but when he meddled in theology, he was in trouble.

"The primary purpose of the Holy Writ," he said, "is to worship God and save souls. . . . In disputes about natural phenomena, one must not begin with the authority of scriptural passages, but with sensory experience and necessary demonstrations." Then he quoted a clergyman who said that the Holy Spirit's intention in inspiring the Scriptures was to teach us how one goes to heaven, not how heaven goes. He also quoted St. Augustine on the need for Scripture to adapt itself to new discoveries.

In rebuttal, one Catholic friar cleverly chose Acts 1:11 as his text: "Ye men of Galilee [a play on the name of Galileo Galilei], why stand ye gazing up into heaven?" (KJV). Then he launched into the story of Joshua and the sun standing still.

In 1616 Galileo was summoned to Rome and forbidden to hold, teach, or defend his "heretical system." He stayed quiet for a while, but in 1630 he wrote the popular *Dialogue on Two Chief World Systems*. Published in 1632, the book brought down the wrath of the Catholic Church on Galileo's head. He was again summoned to Rome, tried by the Inquisition, and under threat of torture, was forced to recant and deny his theory. Galileo's writings were banned and placed on the Catholic list of books forbidden to the faithful. It was not until 1832, two hundred years later, that Catholics were allowed to teach with complete freedom the views of Galileo. And not until 1992 was he exonerated.

Nevertheless, Galileo's writings circulated around the world and established the basis for modern astronomy.

Language They Could Understand

JOHN ELIOT (1604-1690)

John Eliot had always had a knack for foreign languages. When he was a student at Cambridge in England, he was known for his ability to pick up Greek and Hebrew. But now across the Atlantic he was trying to communicate with the Algonquin tribe; that was a challenge.

When Eliot was twenty-seven, he had come to Boston with a group of other Puritans, only eleven years after the first Pilgrims arrived. Because of his education, he was called to become the teacher of the Roxbury congregation. Seeing the need for a psalm book for congregational singing, he and two others prepared the *Bay Psalm Book,* a metrical version of the Psalms, the first book to be published in America.

So Eliot was busy. He also had a large family, a growing congregation, and the desire to do more spiritual writing for the colonists. But Eliot saw a bigger need. He said that God had put into his heart a compassion for the Native Americans, and "a desire to teach them to know Christ."

Some friends advised him to teach the Native Americans English so they could read the Bible for themselves. Eliot didn't like the idea. He thought it would be better if he could learn the language of the Native Americans and get the Bible into their own language.

The Algonquin language was difficult, far more difficult than the Greek and Hebrew he had learned at Cambridge. The Algonquins com-

> ### Ezekiel 27:9
>
> *Veteran craftsmen of Gebal were on board as shipwrights to caulk your seams. All the ships of the sea and their sailors came alongside to trade for your wares.*
>
> ---
>
> In Ezekiel 27 the prophet laments the destruction of Tyre, "the gateway to the sea"(v. 3). He uses an extended metaphor, saying that Tyre is a beautiful merchant ship that ultimately suffers shipwreck because of its pride (v. 27). One curious detail that fits with Eliot's story: The city of Gebal on the Lebanon coast was also known as Byblos. Its chief export was papyrus, used to make paper. Hence, the Greek word for book was biblos, from which we get the word Bible. You might say John Eliot himself was a veteran craftsman of "Biblos."

pressed very complex ideas into extended single words. No one had ever before put a language like that into writing.

After two years Eliot had translated the Ten Commandments and the Lord's Prayer and was learning to speak the language himself.

Now came the test. He wanted to preach to the Algonquins. Would they listen and understand him, or would they just laugh and walk away? A peaceful Algonquin named Waban arranged for a meeting around a campfire a few miles upriver from the Puritan settlements. It would be the first Protestant sermon in a Native American language to be preached on the continent.

What was his text? Ezekiel 27:9. At first this may seem like a strange choice, but the Algonquins listened closely as he read, "All the ships of the sea and their sailors came alongside to trade for your wares." The Algonquins knew very well about the sailors who had come to trade with them. After reading the text, Eliot talked about the great God who made and loved the Algonquins just as much as he made and loved the English.

Soon some Algonquins were converted. Villages of "praying Indians" were established, and an Algonquin church was formed. Eliot continued his work, training converts to become teachers and evangelists. The Algonquins started their own schools and developed their own law codes.

Eliot prepared a catechism and taught the Indians to read their own language. With two of his sons, John and Joseph, he prepared an Algonquin grammar for use in the schools. In 1663 his complete Bible in the Algonquin language, the first Bible to be printed in America, was published. It was perhaps the earliest example in history of the translation and printing of the Bible as a means of evangelism.

In 1674 when John Eliot was seventy, there were 3,600 "praying Indians." Unfortunately, in the following year King Philip's War erupted and many of the "praying Indian" villages were ravaged by both hostile Native Americans and warring settlers. But, undaunted, Eliot continued his missionary work, no doubt thinking of that first sermon he preached to the Algonquins using the strange text of Ezekiel 27:9.

The Nasty Namesake

KING JAMES I (1566-1625)

Not many people thought well of King James I of England except King James I. The only son of Mary, Queen of Scots, he became the king of England when Queen Elizabeth died. As he journeyed south from Scotland to take the throne in 1603, he was met by Puritans who presented their grievances to him.

King James already knew more about the Puritans than he wanted to know. One of them had called him "God's silly vassal." The Puritans wanted to level the offices of the church, and King James understood where that would lead: no bishops, no kings. King James believed strongly in the divine right of kings. No one was going to tell him what to do.

> ## Exodus 1:17
>
> *But the midwives feared God, and did not as the king of Egypt commanded them, but saved the men children alive* (KJV).
>
> ---
>
> Scripture has many instances of civil disobedience, when people are praised for honoring God instead of the government. A number of prophets, notably Elijah, Jeremiah, and Daniel, ran afoul of their rulers. In the New Testament, Peter states the position clearly: "We must obey God rather than men" (Acts 5:29).

Since religious friction was rampant in England, he called a conference of religious leaders within the first year of his reign. His plan was to persuade the Anglican bishops to adopt the theory of the divine right of kings. In exchange, he would clamp down on the Puritans. All the Puritans would get out of the conference was a chance to air their grievances.

The conference went well for King James. It looked as if the Puritans would get nothing. But one suggestion from a Puritan intrigued James. This Puritan suggested that a new translation of the Bible be made. More than 130 distinct issues of Bibles and Testaments had been printed during Queen Elizabeth's reign, so the Anglicans saw no need of a new translation. Yet the Puritans considered the current translations inadequate. For once, King James agreed with the Puritans. He had a problem with the current translations too.

Many of the translations had interpretive notes attached to them. The Geneva translation, in particular, troubled him. Most troublesome was the note on Exodus 1:17, regarding the story of baby Moses in the bulrushes. The midwives disobeyed the Pharaoh's order, and the note in the Geneva Bible's margin pointed out that they did right in disobeying the king. You can see how that might bother King James, with his belief in the divine right of kings. That Bible also had other notes that the king felt were "partial, untrue, seditious, and savouring too much of dangerous and traitorous conceits." So he agreed "that a translation be made of the whole Bible, as consonant as can be to the original Hebrew and Greek, and this to be set out and printed without any marginal notes."

King James announced the signing of the agreement with a Sunday extravaganza, including a procession of coaches, a grand banquet with drinking and dancing, and an amphitheater spectacular with bears being baited by greyhounds, bulls goring dogs, rope-dancing, and exhibitions of horsemanship. Of course, this offended the Puritans, but they got their translation. A few weeks later, some fifty-four translators were selected, without regard to theological or ecclesiastical bias. The translators were divided into six groups, each having a section of Scripture to translate. When they finished, the final revision was done in London with two delegates each from Oxford, Cambridge, and Westminster; then six others who had not been involved in the translation reviewed the work. The first edition came off the presses in 1611.

The Authorized Version (which became known as the King James Version) was an instant success. Some Puritans and Scottish Presbyterians, however, complained that they "could not see into the sense of Scripture for lack of the spectacles of those Genevan annotations."

But undoubtedly the King James Version changed the world. For 370 years it was the dominant English translation, and it remains popular today. As one historian has stated: "Despite his vanity in theology, his absurdities in kingcraft, his profane oaths, and his drunkenness," we are profoundly grateful to King James for his "part in this noble work."

The Prodigal Artist

REMBRANDT VAN RIJN (1606-1669)

The greatest Dutch master of the seventeenth century and one of the greatest artists of all time was Rembrandt van Rijn. Known for his portraits, he also loved to paint biblical characters involved with emotional situations. Two of his early paintings were *The Martyrdom of St. Stephen* and *Pilate Washing His Hands.*

But his biographers describe him as a proud, vain man in his young life. An early painting shows him drunk in a brothel, with sexually greedy eyes. Like the prodigal son, Rembrandt sought money and fame, trying to impress the rich and famous. His paintings were filled with extravagant costumes and apparently his wardrobe was too.

Then misfortunes struck, one after another. Both of his parents died before Rembrandt was thirty-five; three of his children died in infancy. The most painful blow came when he was at the peak of his fame in 1642. Shortly after his son Titus was born, his beloved wife, Saskia, died from complications in childbirth. Criticism from the church caused him to give up religion. His friends deserted him, and an economic recession dried up the market for his paintings. To pay bills and avoid bankruptcy, he eventually auctioned off many of his works for a ridiculously small sum.

Rembrandt's only hope and joy was his son, Titus. With pride he watched the boy grow into manhood. His paintings from that era include *Portrait of Titus Reading, Portrait of Titus in a Hat,* and *Portrait of Titus Dressed*

Luke 15:20–21

When he was yet a great way off, his father saw him, and had compassion, and ran, and fell on his neck, and kissed him. And the son said unto him, Father, I have sinned against heaven, and in thy sight, and am no more worthy to be called thy son (KJV).

Luke 15 has three parables of Jesus, all about lostness. The shepherd seeks his lost sheep. A woman searches her house for a lost coin. And a father looks for his lost son. In each case there is great rejoicing over the return. Of course, the prodigal son story has the added element of the jealous older brother. It seems clear that this is a portrait of Jesus' opponents, the Pharisees and lawyers, who groused about the "sinners" who were returning to God through Jesus' ministry.

59

as a Monk. One of Rembrandt's biblical paintings at this time was *Jacob Blessing the Sons of Joseph;* undoubtedly it was his prayer that Titus would have children that he could bless.

When Titus married and had a daughter, Titia, joy came again to Rembrandt, joy that he had not experienced since before his wife had died. But then tragedy struck again when Titus unexpectedly died. Rembrandt went into depression, living on bread and cheese and rarely leaving his home. His isolation was finally broken when he received word that Titia was going to be baptized. He attended with tears flowing down his cheeks. The emotional scene is reflected in one of Rembrandt's last paintings, *Simeon with the Christ Child in the Temple.* As you view the painting, you can almost hear Simeon (and Rembrandt) saying the words, "Lord, now You are letting Your servant depart in peace" (Luke 2:29 NKJV) as he held the child in his arms.

But how could Rembrandt express all the emotions that swirled within? What Bible story would do it best? The artist turned to the parable of the prodigal son, a story that had always been a favorite of his. *The Return of the Prodigal Son* reflects the complex emotion that swirled in Rembrandt's life. You see him as a father who wished he could embrace his son, Titus, one more time. But you also see Rembrandt himself as the humbled prodigal at the end of his life, now longing for the warm embrace of his heavenly Father. He had been stripped of everything, and now all that was left was the sublime simplicity of his Father's love.

Without question, Rembrandt's realism changed the art world. But even apart from the world of art his influence was profound. Because he found in Christ's life and parables the subject matter that stirred his emotions, he was able to put on canvas a unique dimension of scriptural truth for all the world to experience.

Trouble in Paradise

JOHN MILTON (1608-1674)

Talk about a midlife crisis! When John Milton turned fifty, his world came crashing in around him. As a vocal supporter of Cromwell and the Parliamentary party, he had been given a post in the government. But when the monarchy stormed back to power in England, Milton lost his job. Now because of his writings supporting democracy, some royalists were out to get him.

His family life wasn't any better: His second wife had just passed away in childbirth, as had his first, and his oldest daughter was disabled. He was also going blind. Milton decided to retreat from public life, to spend his time quietly, and perhaps to write that epic poem he had always dreamed about.

Even if he had known from childhood that he would later go blind, Milton couldn't have prepared any better. Growing up, he crammed his brain with all the learning it could handle. His father passed on to young John a love of music and a knowledge of the Bible. He also learned many languages.

Romans 5:18

Therefore as by the offense of one judgment came upon all men to condemnation; even so by the righteousness of one the free gift came upon all men unto justification of life (KJV).

In a crisply argued presentation, Paul establishes that all people—Jews and Gentiles—are sinners, and that God had always declared people righteous by his grace through their faith. Even Abraham was justified by faith, not works. In chapter 5, as he explores how that justification works, Paul sets out a simple equation: Jesus is the second Adam. Adam dragged the human race into sin. Christ brings us back into righteousness.

As a young man, Milton got politically involved with the Parliamentarians and wrote several important works on social issues, including divorce. The divorce book, considered licentious by many, was widely bought but seldom praised. Perhaps because of difficulties with that book, Milton then wrote *Areopagetica,* which opposed government censorship of written material (this is still a key text on the subject). Milton's theme throughout his works was personal freedom.

People must be allowed to make their own decisions, he maintained. God gave us reason so that we can make choices. Sometimes our choices are wrong, and we suffer the consequences, but we must be allowed to choose.

Removed from public life, Milton was able to concentrate on his epic poem. At one point he had considered writing about King Arthur, but he now settled on a larger theme: original sin. The Bible says precious little about the fall of Lucifer and not much more about the temptation in the Garden, so Milton set about exploring these stories. For years he followed a strict writing regimen, getting up early, having the Hebrew Bible read to him, contemplating what was read, and then meeting with a secretary who would take dictation on the latest stanzas in the epic. Writing, exercise, music, entertaining visitors, and listening to the works of other poets—this was the "quiet life" Milton enjoyed.

He finished *Paradise Lost* in 1665, the year of a great plague in London, which was followed by the Great Fire of 1666. Milton managed to find a publisher whose buildings were spared by the flames, and he received five pounds for the manuscript.

As with many classic works, *Paradise Lost* received mixed reviews at first. Some criticized its vernacular style. Some wanted the lines to rhyme, but even there Milton insisted on personal freedom. His blank verse didn't have the singsong effect of rhymed couplets, but it was an example of "ancient liberty recovered to heroic poem from the troublesome modern bondage of riming."

When Milton handed the manuscript to a student helper for an honest critique, he got more than he bargained for. "Thou has said much here of paradise lost," said young Thomas Ellwood, "but what has thou to say of paradise found?" In response, Milton got back to work, writing about the temptation of Christ in *Paradise Regained*.

The sequel never matched the first book's reputation, but it provided an important thematic counterpoint. Along with Milton, we find the theme described by Paul in Romans 5. The first Adam had personal choice and succumbed to temptation, dragging us all into sin. The second Adam, Jesus Christ, used his freedom to withstand temptation, offering us an all-expenses-paid trip back to paradise.

The Pilgrims' Project

THE MAYFLOWER SETTLERS (1620)

July 22, 1620, was a historic day. The Pilgrims finally were ready to leave Delftshaven in the Netherlands and go to the New World. Obstacle after obstacle had confronted them as they planned their voyage, but their leaders told them that "all great and honorable actions are accompanied with great difficulties." They knew they would face perilous times once they arrived, but they were ready. As one of their leaders, William Bradford, wrote in his *History of Plymouth Plantation:* "The dangers were great, but not desperate; the difficulties were many, but not invincible."

Their beloved pastor, John Robinson, preached a farewell sermon from Ezra 8:21, an account of the exiled Israelites about to set out for their homeland, seeking the Lord's blessing. It was a sermon the Pilgrims would not forget. Ezra had led an unescorted caravan across a bandit-infested desert; the Pilgrims would be facing risks too. Robinson reminded the Pilgrims that they, like Ezra's band, were united by their faith, and that they, like Ezra, were in God's hands. After the sermon Robinson fell down on his knees and with watery cheeks commended them to the Lord and his blessing. "And then with mutuall imbrases and many tears, they took their leaves one of an other which proved to be the last leave to many of them."

Pastor Robinson had to stay behind and continue as the pastor for the remaining Pilgrims in Holland. He and others planned to come later.

> ### Ezra 8:21
>
> *Then I proclaimed a fast there, at the river of Ahava, that we might afflict ourselves before our God, to seek of him a right way for us, and for our little ones, and for all our substance* (KJV).
>
> The nation of Judah had been defeated by Babylon in 586 B.C., and many Jews were taken captive. About seventy years later some of them began to return and rebuild the temple in Jerusalem. Ezra, a scribe, led a later group. The dedication service in Ezra 8 took place before they left Babylon. They knew that the trip would be treacherous, and they would have to face many enemies, so they needed God to provide a "right way" (or safe passage).

The first stop was England, where they encountered difficult delays. When one of their ships, the *Speedwell*, proved unseaworthy, a few more Pilgrims had to stay behind in Plymouth. The others boarded the sturdier *Mayflower*. Then they set out across the Atlantic. The voyage was not easy; the sailors teased and taunted them at every opportunity, and there were storms and problems with the ship. Frequently they recalled the words of John Robinson.

On November 11 the *Mayflower* arrived at Cape Cod. Though a long winter and possible attacks by Native Americans lay ahead of them, William Bradford led the Pilgrims in thanksgiving to God for his goodness.

One of their first actions in the New World was to draft the Mayflower Compact, establishing the first democratic government in America. It read in part: "Having undertaken, for the glory of God, and advancement of the Christian faith, and honor of our king and country . . . [we] covenant and combine ourselves together into a civil body pollitic." Winston Churchill later called it "one of the remarkable documents in history, a spontaneous covenant for political organization."

After a severe winter, the Pilgrims felt that God had sent to them Squanto and Samoset, two natives who spoke English and taught them how to plant crops. Fifty-two of the original Mayflower settlers died during the first year, but when the first harvest came, the Pilgrims gave thanks to God and also to the Native Americans who had helped them. For three days the Pilgrims entertained and feasted together with the Native Americans. Eventually more settlers came, as more groups sought religious freedom in the New World.

"It was to the admiration of many and almost wonder of the world," William Bradford wrote, "that of so small beginnings so great things should insue. . . . So the light here kindled hath shone to many."

Truth and Dare

HARVARD UNIVERSITY (1636)

In 1636 the Puritan colonists in Massachusetts had more important things to worry about than teachers and books. They were engaging in regular skirmishes with local Indians, they had political disputes with leaders back in Great Britain, and there were religious factions developing. Still, in the midst of all this, they decided to start a college, funding it with their own taxes. "The Lord was pleased to direct the hearts of the magistrates," wrote one pastor in Cambridge, "to think of erecting a School or College, and that speedily to be a nursery of knowledge in these deserts."

Many of the settlers were ordained ministers; others had college degrees. One historian suggests that the early population of the Massachusetts Bay Colony had the highest concentration of educated people of any place in history. So it was understandable that they put such a premium on education. As a group they committed four hundred pounds of their own money to set up this school, in a town they later named Cambridge, after the alma mater of so many of them. But little happened until two years later when a young minister named John Harvard died, leaving half his estate to the school project. Naturally they named it after him.

The school soon adopted a set of "Rules and Precepts" that made its goals clear. The first had to do with reading and speaking Latin, but the next three had a decidedly spiritual sense:

> ### John 8:32
>
> *And ye shall know the truth, and the truth shall make you free* (KJV).
>
> This is the chapter in which Jesus makes the strongest claims about his identity as God's Son, saying, "Before Abraham was, I am" (v. 58). When Jesus talks about truth here, he is obviously talking about his truth—the truth about him and the truth he teaches. He had just challenged his followers to "continue in my word," and he goes on to promise freedom from sin. "If the Son therefore shall make you free, ye shall be free indeed" (John 8:36 KJV).

2. Every one shall consider the main end of his life and studies to know God and Jesus Christ, which is eternal life.
3. Seeing the Lord giveth wisdom, every one shall seriously by prayer in secret seek wisdom of him.
4. Every one shall so exercise himself in reading the Scriptures twice a day that they be ready to give an account of their proficiency therein, both in theoretical observations of language and logic, and in practical and spiritual truths.

Harvard adopted as its motto John 8:32: "Ye shall know the truth, and the truth shall make you free" (KJV). Freedom was important to these settlers. That was the main reason they made the dangerous journey to the New World. Yet as we can see by the priority they placed on education, they knew that their best freedom lay in the knowledge of the truth—God's truth.

Their assumption was that all truth came from God, beginning with the Scriptures but extending into all scholarly pursuits. The college was concerned with "all good literature, arts, and sciences," according to a 1650 charter. The Harvard seal shows an open book—perhaps the Bible—with the word *veritas* (Latin for "truth"). In some early versions the seal includes the words *pro Christo et Ecclesia* ("for Christ and his church").

In 1701 Connecticut colonists established Yale College, breaking Harvard's monopoly on higher education. Then the College of New Jersey was founded, which later took the name Princeton. These schools shared with Harvard a common vision: religious education and training for ministry. Throughout modern history Christians have seen education as an important part of their mission in the world, thanks largely to the biblical emphasis on truth.

Like its Ivy League companions Yale and Princeton, Harvard University has developed into a prestigious school. Many major leaders of society—in business and academia as well as in government—have graduated from these schools over the centuries and have gone on to change the world in various ways. But at the root of all this education is a simple saying uttered by a first-century Galilean: "The truth shall make you free" (John 8:32 KJV).

The Scientist Discovered the Savior

BLAISE PASCAL (1623-1662)

It was 1654. The famous French scientist, Blaise Pascal, was riding in a carriage pulled by a team of four horses. The scenery along the Seine was always refreshing, and he never knew where or when inspiration might strike. On this fateful October day, however, inspiration struck in a very odd way.

Suddenly the two front horses got spooked, whinnying and bucking, yanking the carriage every which way. Then they leapt over the stonework separating the road from the river and fell into the Seine. Pascal's carriage would have followed the horses, but the bonds connecting them to the carriage had snapped. The carriage was left suspended atop the stonework, inches from disaster.

> ### Jeremiah 2:13
>
> *My people have committed two sins: They have forsaken me, the spring of living water, and have dug their own cisterns, broken cisterns that cannot hold water.*
>
> Jeremiah was known as the "weeping prophet" because his message was sad—God was bringing judgment upon them—and because his people hated him for bringing this message. In chapter 2 God complains about being rejected by his people. Their two errors were turning from God and trying to find their own ways of salvation.

That's the sort of experience that gets a person thinking about God.

Pascal had always been somewhat religious. His family followed Jansenism, a reform movement within the Catholic Church, so he was familiar with the concepts of faith and grace. But his main focus in life was learning, especially science and mathematics. As a child he had worked out the principles of Euclidean geometry on his own. As a teenager he had written a groundbreaking scientific thesis. As a young man he had invented an adding machine, a kind of barometer, and possibly a wristwatch. He had come up with the basic elements of modern hydraulics. You can see how Pascal might have been distracted from spiritual things.

His sister urged him to put aside the distractions and give himself fully to Christ. But there was always some new thing to invent, some new principle to discover.

Then when his carriage nearly fell into the Seine, he began to fear what might happen if he *didn't* give himself fully to Christ. One sleepless night Blaise Pascal had a vision that changed his life. As you might expect from a mathematician, he recorded the exact time of the vision—Monday, November 23, 1654, from 10:30 P.M. to 12:30 A.M. Jesus appeared to him in some fiery way, resulting in euphoria and commitment. To commemorate the vision, Pascal wrote his response on a piece of parchment, which he sewed into his coat. It was found there after he died.

FIRE!
Certainty! Joy! Peace!
I forget the world and everything but God!
Righteous Father, the world has not known you, but I have known you!
Joy, joy, joy! Tears of joy!
Jesus!
Jesus!
I separated myself from him, renounced and crucified him!
"They have forsaken ME, the fountain of living waters."
I separated myself from him!
May I not be separated from him eternally!
I submit myself absolutely to
JESUS CHRIST MY REDEEMER.

The quote in the middle comes from Jeremiah 2:13. It's a warning but also a promise, and Pascal seems to take it both ways. He is terrified of the fiery consequences of rejecting Jesus but drawn to the fountain of living waters for relief. God berates his people for digging their own cisterns instead of turning to him. Wasn't that exactly what Pascal had been doing—almost literally, when you consider his work in hydraulics?

After his conversion Pascal continued to think and write and experiment. He began to collect his thoughts, setting forth Christian faith in response to the rationalism of Descartes and the skepticism of Montaigne. These ideas were gathered and published as *Pensees* ("Thoughts"), which remains a classic, brimming with faith and wisdom.

Pascal died at age thirty-nine, just eight years after his conversion. He had trusted his brilliant mind throughout his life, but in those last eight years he had let his heart lead him to a deeper purpose. Among the most profound of his *Pensees* is this one: "The heart has its reasons, which reason does not know."

Prisoner of Love

JOHN BUNYAN (1628-1688)

Written when John Bunyan was in prison, *Pilgrim's Progress* is one of the best-selling books of all time. While its sales are amazing, it's just as amazing that the book was written at all.

Born near Bedford, England, Bunyan had practically no education and learned his father's trade of repairing pots and pans. As a youth he was foul-mouthed and mischievous. "I went on in sin with great greediness of mind," he wrote in his autobiography, *Grace Abounding to the Chief of Sinners.*

Bunyan tried to reform himself but couldn't. Discouraged about reformation, he decided "to take my fill of sin, still studying what sin was yet to be committed, that I might taste the sweetness of it." After his first child was born blind, he tried again to live an upright life, but he "was nothing but a poor painted hypocrite." When he went to church, he felt even worse. "I was more loathsome in my own eyes than was a toad. . . . I fell deeply into despair." Every time he thought of God, some blasphemous thought would enter his mind instead.

Then Bunyan began to hear some positive Scriptures, some in sermons, some as he tried to read the Bible himself: "Him that cometh to me I will in no wise cast out" (John 6:37 KJV); "The blood of Jesus Christ his Son cleanseth us from all sin" (1 John 1:7 KJV); and "My grace is sufficient for thee" (2 Cor. 12:9 KJV). God used these and other Scriptures to draw Bunyan to himself. Yet other verses frightened him. Finding it

---

1 Corinthians 1:30

But of him are ye in Christ Jesus, who of God is made unto us wisdom, and righteousness, and sanctification, and redemption (KJV).

The best way to settle an argument is to throw some humility around, and that's what Paul is doing as he begins his first epistle to the Corinthians. There were factions in the Corinthian church, with people fighting over which leader was wisest, most righteous, and closest to God. Paul makes it clear that all wisdom and righteousness comes from God, and that humans have no cause for boasting. All we are, we owe to Jesus.

hard to believe that God could love him, Bunyan felt "it was more easy for heaven and earth to pass away than for me to have eternal life."

One day Bunyan asked God to show him that he loved him, and he seemed to hear as an echo, "I have loved thee with an everlasting love." But when temptation struck, he doubted his salvation again. "I should sometimes be up and down twenty times in an hour."

And then as he was walking through a field, the words "Thy righteousness is in heaven" came to him. As he thought about the words, he began rejoicing; he felt freed from bondage. When he got home he searched the Bible for the quotation but couldn't find it. The closest he could come to it was in 1 Corinthians 1:30, which says that Jesus Christ has become our righteousness, and since Jesus is in heaven, then it is true that our righteousness is in heaven as well.

Before long Bunyan was telling his story and preaching in Baptist meetings. Two years later he was called to be the pastor of a church, even though he had practically no education. His fame as a Nonconformist preacher soon grew. But then a new government came to power, cracking down on the Nonconformists, and Bunyan was imprisoned for twelve years.

Prison wasn't a total waste for this preacher, however. He used his time there to write books: *Grace Abounding to the Chief of Sinners,* an account of his own spiritual pilgrimage, and *Pilgrim's Progress,* the classic allegory based on Bunyan's spiritual life. In this book the main character, Christian, meets such characters as Evangelist, Faithful, Pliable, and Giant Despair. His journey takes him from the City of Destruction through the Slough of Despond, to the foot of the cross, and then on through the Valley of the Shadow, Vanity Fair, Doubting Castle, and ultimately to the Celestial City.

There was no more doubt about his relationship with God. He preached with assurance, even as he wrote with assurance. Hundreds of millions have read his books in the past three centuries, because John Bunyan recognized that he had to trust in the righteousness of Jesus Christ.

Falling Apples and Secret Treasure

ISAAC NEWTON (1642-1727)

Isaac Newton, the man who supposedly discovered gravity when an apple fell on his head, was certainly the greatest scientist of his time and maybe of all time. He formulated the binomial theorem, developed the differential calculus, discovered the composition of light, invented the reflecting telescope, discovered the law of universal gravitation, and wrote *Principia mathematica,* which has been termed the "greatest work in the history of science."

Newton was also a devoted student of the Bible. He wasn't an orthodox Christian, because he didn't believe in the Trinity and didn't accept Jesus Christ as the Son of God. Nevertheless, he loved to study Bible prophecy.

He did believe in God as the Creator, and he felt that there were secrets and mysteries in both science and Scripture that could be deciphered by careful research. That's why he liked Isaiah 45:3. He believed God was giving him "the treasures of darkness, and hidden riches of secret places" (KJV).

Isaiah 45:3

And I will give thee the treasures of darkness, and hidden riches of secret places, that thou mayest know that I, the Lord, which call thee by thy name, am the God of Israel (KJV).

This section of Isaiah is addressed to Cyrus, the king of Persia. Verse 1 calls Cyrus God's "anointed"—the Hebrew word is the same as Messiah—pretty strong stuff for a Gentile. But the point is that God had a plan for his people, and he was empowering King Cyrus to accomplish it. Cyrus defeated the Babylonians, who had taken the Jews captive, and then Cyrus authorized the return of the Jews to their homeland. God promises to pave the way for Cyrus's conquests and to give him secret treasures—but it's ultimately for the glory of God, not of Cyrus.

Newton believed that only when natural and divine knowledge were harmonized and shown to be one could events have full significance. As he put it, "The mechanics manifested in natural phenomena served as windows through which man could catch fleeting and imperfect glimpses of the higher reality and ultimate purpose of creation." The universe, in other words, was a "cryptogram set by the Almighty." Hence, there was no place for warfare between science and Scripture.

Rene Descartes's philosophy of science was quite different. He believed that God had created the universe and had established its laws but then left it to run under those laws. Newton believed that God never abandoned his creation. While nature is governed by an inviolable system of physical laws, an omnipotent God continues actively to express his will within his system of matter and motion. Descartes separated God from his creation; Newton did not.

In his Bible study Newton loved to figure out puzzles. He tried to reconstruct the temple, working mostly from Ezekiel's description of it, but he was especially drawn to the prophecies of Daniel in the Old Testament and the Book of Revelation in the New. What sparked his interest was that "the language of prophetic writings was symbolic and hieroglyphical and their comprehension required a radically different method of interpretation."

Newton was so fascinated by the prophets that he compiled a catalog containing the lives of seventy biblical prophets and discussed what their individual prophecies meant. For instance, Newton said that the Book of Revelation showed the abandonment of apostolic faith for the worship of the Beast (which he viewed as Trinitarianism). Newton interpreted the Book of Revelation to say that the Antichrist would reign for 1,260 years. Those years, he felt, began in 607 when Trinitarianism had reached its peak in the Catholic Church. So the Beast would fall, according to Newton's interpretation, in 1867. Newton was undoubtedly better at interpreting apples falling from trees.

Perhaps Isaac Newton, in all his brilliance, was too intrigued by "treasures of darkness." He should have been satisfied with the light that shines in darkness, the true Light, the Word who was with God and was God (John 1:1, 5).

A Holy Experiment Pays Off

WILLIAM PENN (1644-1718)

At age twenty-two, William Penn had everything. The son of a British admiral, he had gone to Oxford, traveled throughout Europe, and had become an expert dueler. Besides that, he was handsome, aristocratic, charismatic, and was gaining training for a career in law. Not a bad start!

In addition, Penn's family was rich. His father sent him to Ireland to manage the family estates that he would some day inherit. In Ireland he faced a mutiny, and he enjoyed putting down the rebels so much that he felt he might become a military man.

About that time he heard Thomas Low, a Quaker evangelist. His sermon was entitled "The Faith That Overcomes the World," and the text was 1 John 5:4: "And this is the victory that overcometh the world, even our faith" (KJV). Penn said later that "the unspeakable riches of God's love" visited him, and he was led away "from the dark practices, wandering notions, and vain conversation of this polluted world."

> ## 1 John 5:4
> *And this is the victory that over-cometh the world, even our faith* (KJV).
>
> Jesus had told his disciples, "In this world you will have trouble, but take heart! I have overcome the world" (John 16:33). The world is a major theme in John's Gospel and Epistles. The world is the collection of human structures and attitudes that oppose God. But Jesus' followers, marked by love, obedience, and faith (also major themes of John), find victory. And that is what William Penn found too.

Joining the Quakers brought inner peace to William Penn but not outer tranquillity. The Quakers were the least understood and the most despised of the dissenters in England. They refused to take oaths, and that meant that they refused to swear allegiance to the king and to the country.

Some Quakers adopted a passive faith and bore persecution quietly. Not so William Penn; he was an activist. And as far as the Quakers were concerned, his conversion had come at just the right time. His training at Oxford, his social position, and his legal experience were assets to the Quaker cause. He was arrested and imprisoned several times, but each time, speaking in his own defense, he challenged the British legal system. In more than fifty tracts he pointed out to the English authorities that persecution of religious groups was counterproductive to a nation.

Unable to convince the British, he decided to try his ideas in America. Since the British crown owed William Penn's late father a substantial sum of money, Penn asked for a grant of land in America on which to resettle the Quakers and other religious dissenters. In the middle of the colonies there was some land that seemed to King Charles II like a worthless wilderness, so it was a painless way for the king to pay off a debt. That land became known as Pennsylvania.

To Penn this settlement was a "holy experiment," a way to show that faith really could overcome the world. Pennsylvania and its chief city, Philadelphia, "the city of brotherly love," would be a model of what people of goodwill could do, especially when guided by the inner light of God's Spirit.

One of his first actions was to make a treaty with the Algonquin chiefs in the area. He told them that he wanted nothing but their friendship, and that he and his friends would never injure them or their property. While neighboring colonies were drenched in the blood of raids and warfare, no drop of Quaker blood was ever shed by a Native American. Later the French skeptic Voltaire said, "It is the only treaty that was ever made without an oath, and the only treaty that never was broken."

Penn's active faith seemed to overcome the world, but this did not last. His dream for "a blessed government, and a virtuous, ingenious and industrious society" seemed doomed when Quakers started fighting with each other, when pacifism didn't seem to work on the frontier, and when civil authority grew corrupt.

Yet while his utopian dream was collapsing, religious freedom was catching on, finding its fullest expression in Pennsylvania. And because it was working in Pennsylvania, the idea was adopted in America's Bill of Rights a century later—signed in William Penn's own Philadelphia.

Singing a New Song to the Lord

ISAAC WATTS (1674-1748)

Young Isaac Watts was bored out of his skull. The psalms that his church sang in its services were so dull. In 1688 most Anglican churches were locked into old patterns of psalm singing. The deacon would sing a line, and then the congregation would repeat it. That might not be so bad, but their ancient psalter was filled with awful translations and singsong rhymes. Young Isaac just could not wrest any meaning from the psalms they sang. How could he keep a straight face when they sang the metrical arrangement of Psalm 133:2?

> 'Tis like the precious ointment down
>   Aaron's beard did go;
> Down Aaron's beard it downward went,
>   His garment's skirts unto.

"I could write better hymns than that," he told his brother one day. His father overheard this and said, "If you are so dissatisfied with the psalms we sing in church, why don't you see if you can do better."

Isaac enjoyed challenges. He had begun to learn Latin (thanks to his father) when he was only four. By the time he was in his early teen years, he was doing quite well with French, Greek, and Hebrew as well.

So Isaac didn't need more encouragement from his father than "see if you can do better." First he decided that Bible hymns didn't all have to be paraphrases of the Psalms; why not do some on New Testament

Revelation 5:9

And they sang a new song: "You are worthy to take the scroll and to open its seals, because you were slain, and with your blood you purchased men for God from every tribe and language and people and nation."

Of course, young Isaac Watts didn't have to go to the Book of Revelation to find the phrase "a new song." This phrase appears most often in the Psalms, but it is in Revelation that its full meaning is seen. Throughout the Old Testament new songs celebrated acts of God's intervention in history. So it's appropriate that in John's magnificent vision in Revelation of the beasts and elders around God's throne, a new song is sung to celebrate God's supreme act of intervention in history—the sacrifice of the divine Lamb.

75

passages? He liked Revelation 5:9, which begins, "And they sang a new song."

So the teenager wrote:

> Behold the glories of the Lamb,
> amidst His father's throne;
> Prepare new honors for His Name,
> and songs before unknown.

The following Sunday Enoch Watts introduced his son's hymn to the Southhampton congregation. The people liked it so much that they asked him to do another for the following Sunday. Then for 222 consecutive weeks, young Isaac prepared a new hymn for the congregation.

When Isaac began putting psalms into hymn form, he felt he should write them as if David were writing after Christ instead of before Christ. So he rendered Psalm 72 as "Jesus shall reign where'er the sun," Psalm 90 as "Our God, our help in ages past," and Psalm 98 as "Joy to the world, the Lord is come."

His first collection of original hymns was published when he was thirty-one, and soon the Watts hymnals became best-sellers. Many churches refused to use any other hymnal than *Watts Psalms and Hymns*. In the American Revolutionary War, when colonists ran out of the paper wadding needed to hold the powder and balls in their muskets, soldiers were given Watts hymnals, told to tear out the pages, and admonished, "Put Watts into 'em boys! Give 'em Watts." This wasn't exactly what Watts had in mind when he wrote "Am I a Soldier of the Cross?" and "We're Marching to Zion," but it does show the popularity of his hymnals on both sides of the Atlantic.

While Watts became one of London's most significant preachers and writers, he was best known for his "new songs," some of which don't seem very new now. But because this brash seventeenth-century teenager thought he could write better hymns, he opened the door for future writers of new songs—like Charles Wesley in the eighteenth century, Fanny Crosby in the nineteenth century, and a host of Christian musicians today.

Standing Up for the Messiah

GEORGE FREDRIC HANDEL (1685-1759)

Around the world when the "Hallelujah Chorus" is sung, the audience rises to its feet. Some stand because it's a custom; some stand because they are moved by the music or the performance; but others stand to honor the King of kings and Lord of lords.

Many stories have grown up around Handel's *Messiah*, and some of them are apocryphal, but this one is historically documented. King George II of England attended a concert of the *Messiah* at the Covent Garden Theatre on March 23, 1743. "When Handel's Messiah was first performed," an observer recorded about that performance, "the audience were exceedingly struck and affected by the music in general." And when the Hallelujah Chorus began, "they were so transported, that they all, together with the King (who happened to be present), started up, and remained standing till the chorus ended."

However, despite King George's enthusiastic response, most London concertgoers were not enthralled. In its first season the *Messiah* was met with "chilling apathy and stolid indifference," and within two years, Handel was driven into temporary bankruptcy.

But then Handel's life was always full of dramatic ups and downs. Born in Halle, Germany, he wrote operas for three years in Italy before

Revelation 11:15; 19:6, 16

And there were great voices in heaven, saying, "The kingdoms of this world are become the kingdoms of our Lord.... And I heard as it were the voice of a great multitude ... saying, Alleluia: for the Lord God omnipotent reigneth.... And he hath on his vesture and on his thigh a name written, KING OF KINGS, AND LORD OF LORDS" (KJV).

For centuries people have been paging through Revelation for clues about the end times. To be sure, the book is packed with tantalizing symbols. What do all those images mean? The overarching theme of the Bible's final book is simply this: "God wins." If you're struggling through hard times—as Christians were in John's day, are now, and will in the end times—remember that Jesus Christ emerges victorious. After all the struggles of this world are over, the multitude rises to sing an eternal Alleluia to the King of kings.

going to England when he was twenty-five. He achieved immediate fame, but when London tired of hearing Italian operas, he went bankrupt. He slowly rebuilt his reputation by writing biblical oratorios, but he was never without a host of critics.

Perhaps Handel's harshest critic was Charles Jennens, a pompous man who supplied the words for many of Handel's oratorios, including the *Messiah*. Jennens, never shy about expressing his feelings, once wrote, "Mr. Handel's head is more full of maggots than ever. . . . His third maggot is a Hallelujah which he has trumped up at the end of his oratorio. . . . This Hallelujah, grand as it is, comes in very nonsensically, having no manner of relation to what goes before."

Despite Jennens' inflated impression of his own opinions, his selection of passages from the Old Testament prophets, the Gospel writers, Paul's epistles, and the Book of Revelation is remarkable. While Handel's music is classic, Jennens' selection of texts is a work of art itself. The drama of human redemption through Jesus Christ the Messiah is treated as an epic poem, and the libretto is a capsule of the Christian faith. It is not just a story of what happened to Jesus; it is a story of what happens to humankind because of Jesus. One commentator said that the masterpiece should be entitled *Redemption,* because it celebrates the idea of redemption even more than the life and personality of Christ.

Handel composed the music in twenty-four days in the front room of his residence in London. Afterward he supposedly said of those days, "Whether I was in my body or out of my body as I wrote it I know not," and also, "I did think I did see all Heaven before me and the great God Himself." How could he help but be enraptured as he wrote music to match that majestic text from Revelation: "Alleluia: for the Lord God omnipotent reigneth . . . King of kings and Lord of lords."

Although Handel faced various reactions during his lifetime, after his death this German-born composer was proclaimed the father of British music, the greatest musician in British history. And his *Messiah* is hailed as the "greatest monument of musical genius in the world."

The Count of Jesu Christo

NICHOLAS VON ZINZENDORF (1700-1760)

In the early 1700s a new awareness was spreading through European Christianity. Historians call it pietism, but it resembles the evangelicalism of the mid–twentieth century. Pietist writers like Philipp Jakob Spener challenged believers to go beyond church attendance and make their faith a personal commitment. Spener's book *Pia Desideria* remains a classic of spiritual devotion.

Nicholas von Zinzendorf was born both into nobility and piety. The nobility came from his father, the piety from his godly mother and grandmother. But a decisive moment occurred when he was about twenty. Touring the art museum at Dusseldorf, Nicholas saw the painting *Ecce Homo* ("Behold, the man") by Domenico Feti. The work, which shows Jesus wearing a crown of thorns, bears the inscription: "I have done this for you; what have you done for me?" Zinzendorf was smitten. "I have loved him for a long time," he said to himself, "but I have never actually done anything for him. From now on I will do whatever he leads me to do."

> ### Acts 8:30–31
> *Then Philip ran up to the chariot and heard the man reading Isaiah the prophet, "Do you understand what you are reading?" Philip asked. "How can I," he said, "unless someone explains it to me?" So he invited Philip to come up and sit with him.*
>
> When persecution came to the early church in Jerusalem, Christians became missionaries elsewhere. Acts 8 tells of Philip, one of seven "deacons" of the early church, preaching in Samaria. Then he was directed by an angel to go to a desert road southwest of Jerusalem. There Philip found an Ethiopian government official trying to understand the prophecies of Isaiah. What a great way to introduce the gospel to a foreign country! Zinzendorf thought so too.

But what? He had a large family estate. Could his family property somehow be used for God's purposes? He had an apartment in Dresden where he held interdenominational religious services with a growing circle of worshipers. Was he meant to be ordained as a minister to lead this flock? Since childhood he had been writing poems and songs of devotion. Was he destined to be a hymn writer?

The answer came with a knock at his door, and a man was asking whether his group of Moravian believers might settle on the Zinzendorf estate. For nearly two centuries Moravians had been bounced around while Lutherans, Catholics, and Calvinists redrew the map of Europe. Various treaties had created a tenuous peace for the major groups, but Moravians and other smaller groups were left out. Often they were forced out of their homes. Now this group of Moravians needed shelter, and they had heard of a kindhearted Lutheran noble named Zinzendorf. Would he welcome them?

Yes, of course. Ten Moravians arrived that December. Then more refugees came, some Moravians and some from other oppressed groups. Soon Zinzendorf became involved with their worship services. They called their settlement Herrnhut—which could mean either "under the Lord's watch" or "on the watch for the Lord." By 1726 there were three hundred in the community. When arguments arose, the count stepped in to make peace.

Basic to the Moravian mind-set was missions. Catholic orders had sent out missionaries, and a few Protestants had gone to distant lands, but never before had a whole church accepted the task of spreading the gospel. On a trip to Denmark in 1731, Zinzendorf met a black man from the West Indies who had become a Christian. This man pleaded for someone to go back to the West Indies and tell the black slaves there—including his brother and sister—about Jesus. The count brought the plea back to Herrnhut, and several young men responded. The first young missionaries went to St. Thomas; within a few years nearly thirty had gone to St. Croix. Then Greenland, Lapland, Georgia, Surinam, the Guinea Coast of Africa, South Africa, Algeria, and elsewhere. Between 1732 and 1742, Zinzendorf's Moravian community of six hundred sent seventy missionaries to foreign shores.

A fine organizer, Zinzendorf developed some basic strategies for Moravian missions: Missionaries should focus on neglected people, such as the slaves; they should preach Christ rather than theology; they should work together with other denominations; and they should support themselves.

One foundational principle came from the story of Philip and the Ethiopian official in Acts 8. "You are not to aim at the conversion of whole nations," Zinzendorf declared. "You must simply look for seekers after the truth who, like the Ethiopian eunuch, seem ready to welcome the gospel."

Turning Heads
and Touching Hearts

JONATHAN EDWARDS (1703-1758)

Jonathan Edwards has been called the greatest mind ever produced in America, the most powerful preacher in American history, a brilliant philosopher, a key player in the Great Awakening, and America's greatest theologian.

He was a precocious child, beginning to learn Latin, Greek, and Hebrew when he was five years old. When he was eleven he wrote a treatise on flying spiders. When he was thirteen he entered Yale, and four years later he graduated as valedictorian.

But Jonathan had a problem, and he talked to his father about it. He rebelled against the doctrine of God's sovereignty. He couldn't understand how a good and loving God could leave people "eternally to perish and be everlasting tormented in hell."

He found the resolution to his problem in 1 Timothy 1:17, and this changed

1 Timothy 1:17

Now unto the King eternal, immortal, invisible, the only wise God, be honor and glory for ever and ever. Amen (KJV).

Near the beginning of this epistle Paul feels compelled to give a personal testimony. He acknowledges that he had been a "blasphemer and a persecutor and a violent man" (1:13)—the worst of sinners. Fortunately, Christ Jesus came into the world to save such sinners. After presenting this basic theology in a personal way, Paul concludes his introduction with a benediction to his eternal King. Though he was about to give several chapters of important advice to young Timothy, Paul didn't base it on his own expertise, but rather on the "only wise God."

his life. In his *Personal Narrative* he writes: "As I read the words, there came into my soul, and was as it were diffused thro' it, a sense of the glory of the Divine Being; a new sense, quite different from any thing I ever experienced before. Never any words of scriptures seemed to me as these words did. I thought with myself . . . how happy I should be, if I might enjoy that God, and be wrapt up to God in Heaven, and be as it were swallowed up in Him. I kept saying, and as it were singing, over these words of scripture to myself; and went to prayer, to pray to God that I might enjoy Him, and prayed in a manner quite different from what I used to do; with a new sort of affection. . . . From about that time, I began to have a new kind of apprehensions and ideas of Christ, and the work of redemption, and the glorious way of salvation by Him."

In 1734 when he was thirty-one years old and the pastor in Northampton, Massachusetts, Edwards preached a series of sermons on justification by faith. More than three hundred people united with the church, and the Great Awakening was starting. Said Edwards: "There scarcely was a single person in the town, young or old, left unconcerned about the great things of the eternal world."

Perhaps the most famous sermon ever preached in America was his message "Sinners in the Hands of an Angry God," delivered in 1741 in Enfield, Connecticut. At times the message could barely be heard because people were crying so loudly. Some clung to the pillars of the church, afraid they might slip into hell. Yet in his preaching, Edwards did not raise his voice and spoke without gestures; he did nothing to excite his audience.

All of this might make you think of Jonathan Edwards as a cold-hearted Puritan preacher. But he wasn't. He was concerned about people having a personal relationship with God; he centered on the experience of the heart. In *Victorious Christians You Should Know,* Warren Wiersbe writes that "it was this conviction that brought him many spiritual blessings as well as many spiritual battles."

In 1750, after twenty-three years as pastor of the Northampton church, he was dismissed by the congregation because he would not receive as new members those who had not given evidence of salvation. For the next eight years he served as a missionary to the Native Americans in western Massachusetts, and at the same time wrote some of his most profound works. In 1757 he was chosen as president of Princeton College, but only a few months after he took office, he died after a smallpox inoculation. His last words were "Trust in God, and you need not fear."

Forty years earlier a Bible verse in Paul's first epistle to Timothy had assured him that God was indeed someone who could be trusted.

Strangely Warmed by Freedom

JOHN WESLEY (1703-1791)

The storm was raging outside the ship. Inside, passengers were tossed about in their crowded quarters. John Wesley wondered why God would send him as a missionary to America just to let him be lost at sea. He had tried to live a good life, but now he was terrified that he would die in his sins.

Then he heard them. A band of Moravians was *singing hymns*. In the midst of the tempest, they were filled with joy and peace. Why didn't he have that? More than ever, he felt something was missing in his life.

John Wesley's story is different from most conversion testimonies, and yet it's the sort of tale that many can identify with. By all appearances, Wesley had been righteous all his life—perhaps too righteous.

> ### Romans 8:1–2
>
> *There is therefore now no condemnation for them which are in Christ Jesus. . . . For the law of the Spirit of life in Christ Jesus hath made me free from the law of sin and death* (KJV).
>
> Paul has just finished a powerful confession, expressing the frustration of wanting to do right, but continually doing wrong. Romans 7 ends with a cry for help and a prayer of thanksgiving. Then this message: no condemnation. As John Wesley discovered, the law can only tell us how sinful we are—it can't make us righteous. Only Christ can do that.

He was the fifteenth of nineteen children born to Samuel and Susanna Wesley. Samuel was an Anglican minister who longed for revival in the church and in England. Susanna was one of the most remarkable women in church history, a pretty good Bible teacher as well as a busy mom. John went to Oxford to train for the ministry. There, along with his brother Charles and other friends, he formed what became known as "The Holy Club." The group wanted to study the Bible and live out its teachings in a methodical way (hence they also were called "Methodists"). Driven by an awareness of his own sinfulness, John was trying very hard to live up to God's standards.

But as a minister, John was not doing well. So when the opportunity came to serve the church in America, he grabbed it. After three years in

America and not much to show for it, John skulked back to England. There he met up with some of his Moravian friends. On May 24, 1738, he was invited to a Moravian meeting on Aldersgate Street in London. The preacher was reading from Luther's commentary on Romans. This was exactly what the troubled John Wesley needed to hear.

"About a quarter before nine, while he was describing the change which God works in the heart through faith in Christ, I felt my heart strangely warmed," Wesley wrote in his journal. "I felt I did trust in Christ; Christ alone, for salvation; and an assurance was given me, that he had taken away *my* sins, even *mine,* and saved *me* from the law of sin and death." This event he regarded as his conversion experience. Despite his efforts to live the Christian life methodically, despite being a minister and even a missionary, John Wesley hadn't wholly trusted Christ to pay for his sins. He had the methods, but he'd missed the most important element—God's grace.

Though not a hymnwriter like his brother Charles, he did translate some Moravian hymns into English shortly after his conversion. One of these ("Jesus, Thy Blood and Righteousness") was written by Nicholas von Zinzendorf; its second stanza, a loose paraphrase of Romans 8:1–2, became John's testimony.

> Bold shall I stand in thy great day,
> For who aught to my charge shall lay?
> Fully absolved through these I am,
> From sin and fear, from guilt and shame.

Now everything he had been doing with worry and weariness was infused with joy and love. That wasn't just what John Wesley needed, it was what all of England needed. This vibrant commitment sparked the revival his father had dreamed of.

Seeing himself as "an apostle to the nation," Wesley traveled throughout England, preaching wherever anyone would listen. He paid special attention to the lower classes, often ignored by established churches. But Wesley wasn't just a fiery revivalist; he was a meticulous organizer as well, setting up a small-group structure that provided for the discipleship of new converts. Methodism was sneered at, and Wesley was jeered by traditionalists, but the movement caught on like wildfire.

In the late 1700s class warfare broke out in France, ending in a bloody revolution. Why not in England? Some historians suggest that the Methodists made it unnecessary. Sure, there was still economic injustice, but John Wesley had given the common folk a much more valuable franchise: an eternal inheritance.

The Preacher of the New Birth

GEORGE WHITEFIELD (1714-1790)

George Whitefield has been called the greatest evangelist since the apostle Paul, "the Demosthenes of the pulpit." He started the British revival and preceded the Wesleys in preaching rebirth and justification by faith. When he came to America, he spread the Great Awakening wherever he went.

Noted actor David Garrick said, "I'd give one hundred guineas to say 'oh' like George Whitefield." The skeptic David Hume came to hear him preach and later said he was so taken by the sermon that he forgot to sneer. Whitefield became a close friend of Benjamin Franklin, staying in his home, joking with him, corresponding with him, and regularly trying to convert him.

George Whitefield, the son of an innkeeper in Gloucester, England, was not always so secure in his faith. As a student at Oxford, he searched for spiritual answers and tried to earn salvation by good works. Then he read a book given to him by his friend Charles Wesley, and this changed his thinking. The key to unlock heaven's door, the book said, was not one's own personal goodness or holiness. Astonished, Whitefield prayed, "Lord, if I am not a Christian, for Jesus Christ's sake show me what Christianity is." As he read on, he discovered something he hadn't noticed before. It was something about new birth.

Ten days later as he was walking near a bridge, he found a woman on the verge of committing suicide. He read John 3 to her, including

> ### John 3:7
>
> *Marvel not that I said unto thee, Ye must be born again* (KJV).
>
> ---
>
> In Jesus' day a man named Nicodemus was a seeker, much like the young George Whitefield. Nicodemus came to Jesus at night to avoid damaging his reputation as a religious leader. Jesus led off with his cryptic comment about rebirth. Thinking literally, Nicodemus was puzzled. There was no way a person could return to the womb! But Jesus went on to talk about this spiritual "birth" that would occur when someone trusted in the only Son sent by a loving God. It's possible that Nicodemus was reborn that night or some time later. Later he spoke up for Jesus among the Pharisees and he assisted in Jesus' burial.

the verse that said, "Ye must be born again" (v. 7 KJV). She cried out, "I believe! I believe! I am born again! I'm saved." Again Whitefield was amazed. Was it that easy to be born again?

Six months later, still struggling to understand how to be born again, he read a book that spoke of the new birth as being a gift. Then Whitefield read the words of Christ: "If any man thirst, let him come unto me and drink" (John 7:37 KJV). He threw himself on his bed and cried, "I thirst, I thirst." And then he thought he heard someone say, "George, you have what you asked. You simply believed—and you are born again."

After that experience, he talked about new birth wherever he went. Ordained as a minister of the Church of England, he became known as the Boy Preacher. Crowds came to hear him, and his theme was always the same: "Ye must be born again." In one church he was told he could speak as long as he said nothing about new birth. He declined. Instead he preached in the fields, and two thousand coal miners and their families came to hear him. His subject: new birth. The next week he returned to find ten thousand there. The climax came when twenty-three thousand gathered on a nearby hill to hear the Boy Preacher talk about new birth.

Wherever he went, revival fires broke out. He preached to whites, blacks, and Native Americans; to rich and poor; to business leaders in private drawing rooms, and to prisoners in their cells.

To his friend Benjamin Franklin he once wrote, "As you have made such progress in investigating the mysteries of electricity, I now humbly urge you to give diligent heed to the mystery of the new birth." In one of the last sermons before his death, he said, "I am more than ever convinced of the truth of the new birth and that without it you can never be saved by Jesus Christ."

When a friend asked him why he preached so much about new birth, he simply quoted his theme verse, John 3:7: "Ye must be born again" (KJV).

Thirsting for God

DAVID BRAINERD (1718-1747)

It is not surprising that a Bible verse made an impact on David Brainerd. After all, he was a sensitive, introspective young man who tried so hard to become more godly that he put extra stress on his already weak physical frame. But what is surprising is that he made an impact on others!

Brainerd, a pioneer missionary to Native Americans in the mid-eighteenth century, was only moderately successful in his efforts. So what made Brainerd memorable?

It is *Brainerd's Journal*, a classic of Christian devotion.

William Carey, the father of the modern missionary movement, pointed to *Brainerd's Journal* as his inspiration. John Wesley distributed a biography of Brainerd to all his ministers, saying, "Let every preacher read carefully over the life of David Brainerd." As a student at Cambridge, Henry Martyn discovered Brainerd and wrote, "I long to be like him," then went to Persia and India to translate the Bible into Hindustani and other languages. Jim Elliot, martyred by the Auca Indians of South America in 1956, was also profoundly influenced by David Brainerd.

Growing up in Connecticut, Brainerd admitted, "I was from my youth somewhat sober and inclined to melancholy." His father died when he was nine, his mother when he was fourteen, and their deaths left him "exceedingly distressed." In his later teen years, he says he "sometimes envied the birds and beasts their happiness."

John 7:37

Jesus stood and cried, saying, If any man thirst, let him come unto me, and drink (KJV).

Jesus spent his early career in the northern area of Galilee, but in John 7 he heads for Jerusalem to celebrate the Feast of Tabernacles. On the last day of the feast, probably during a closing assembly, Jesus stands and makes this announcement. In his Gospel, John is fond of the metaphors Jesus uses to describe himself. Jesus is the Bread of Life, the Light of the World, the Good Shepherd, the True Vine, the Door, etc. His role as the supplier of living water (see also John 4:14) was especially refreshing in Israel's arid climate. And how do we respond to water? By drinking. By accepting. By taking it into ourselves. By making it a part of us.

At twenty-one he struggled to understand the verse, "If any man thirst, let him come unto me and drink" (John 7:37 KJV). Instead of finding comfort in it, Brainerd wrote, "I was irritated, through not being able to find out what faith was. What was it to believe? What was it to come to Christ?"

Then on July 12, 1739, after realizing that all his previous efforts to please God were only self-worship, he suddenly experienced a new relationship with God. "Unspeakable glory seemed to open to . . . my soul. . . . It was a new inward view of God, such as I never had before. . . . I stood still, wondered, and admired!" He said he was "so captivated and delighted with the excellency, loveliness, greatness and other perfections of God, that [he] was even swallowed up in him. . . . [he] was amazed that [he] had not dropped [his] own contrivances and complied with this lovely, blessed, and excellent way before." In short, Brainerd was converted.

After studying for the ministry at Yale, he was asked by two churches to become their pastor. But he felt called to preach the gospel where it hadn't been preached before, and so at the age of twenty-four he was appointed a missionary to the Native Americans. Though he worked first in New York and Pennsylvania, his greatest success was in New Jersey. A frequent theme of his preaching was John 7:37. In addition to John 7:37 Brainerd loved Isaiah 55:1 ("Ho, everyone that thirsteth, come to the waters" [KJV]) and Revelation 22:17 ("And whosoever will, let him take of the water of life freely" [KJV]).

Day in and day out, he rode horseback from one village to another, sharing the gospel despite declining health. At times his journal contains entries like "Rode about twenty miles. . . . Was extremely overdone with the heat and showers this day, and coughed up considerable blood." He died of tuberculosis at the age of twenty-nine, but the honest passions of his *Brainerd's Journal* have continued to influence fellow thirsters for generations.

Amazing Grace

JOHN NEWTON (1725-1807)

No doubt about it, John Newton had done a lot in his long life. A former slave trader, he was the author of "Amazing Grace" and other great hymns, a beloved pastor, and eventually an activist in the movement to abolish the slave trade. What was more important to him was not what he had done, but what God had done for him. And he never wanted to forget it.

When Newton entered the Christian ministry, he printed in bold letters portions of Isaiah 43:4 and Deuteronomy 15:15 over the fireplace in his study. The banner read: "Since thou wast precious in my sight, thou hast been honorable. . . . Thou shalt remember that thou wast a bondman in the land of Egypt, and the LORD thy God redeemed thee" (KJV).

> ## Deuteronomy 15:15
>
> *Thou shalt remember that thou wast a bondman in the land of Egypt, and the LORD thy God redeemed thee* (KJV).
>
> This verse appears in a section of Israel's law that covers treatment of servants. Slavery was a common practice in the ancient world, but the Old Testament law protected slaves. In this chapter it says that Hebrew slaves are to be given freedom after six years and given some supplies to start their new lives. All this is based on the experience of the Israelites, who had been slaves in Egypt.

The only child of a British sea captain, John had been introduced to the sea when he was eleven. His father wanted to make a first-class mariner out of him, and by the age of eighteen he was serving in the British navy on a man-of-war, fighting the French. After one naval battle he left the navy to be with his girlfriend. Arrested for desertion, he was taken back aboard the ship in irons. Then a month later he was exchanged to a slave ship where he "let lust run unchecked." He wrote, "I not only sinned with a high hand myself, but made it my study to tempt and seduce others upon every occasion."

John went ashore in Africa. At first he managed a slave warehouse, but soon everyone turned against him. He became a "servant of slaves." Like other slaves, he was made to work nearly naked in the fields. Eventually Newton was released to another slave trader. Once again he fouled the ship with his presence, shocking even the roughest of sailors with his language.

Then a storm struck. Everyone on board feared the ship would sink. Newton shocked himself by saying, "The Lord have mercy on us." Trying to remember Bible verses from his youth, he recalled that Jesus had died for the sins of others, and he wondered whether he was too sinful to be included. But it was the only hope he had.

Newton marked that date: "That tenth of March is a day much to be remembered by me; and I have never suffered it to pass unnoticed since the year 1748. For on that day—March 10, 1748—the Lord came from on high and delivered me out of deep waters."

Newton went on to become a minister of the gospel, preaching first in the town of Olney. Here he wrote hymns like "Amazing Grace" and "Glorious Things of Thee Are Spoken." He befriended the famous poet William Cowper, and they wrote hymns and enjoyed jokes together. His first sermons were done very shyly and hesitantly, but soon he became known for his warmth and caring. He offered Sunday dinner to anyone who came more than six miles to church.

Moving to London, Newton helped establish the London Missionary Society and encouraged young evangelicals to get involved with social problems. When William Wilberforce wanted to resign his seat in Parliament and become a clergyman, Newton persuaded him to stay in politics and fight slavery. As the only Abolitionist leader who had firsthand experience with slavery, Newton wrote a pamphlet about the horrors of the slave trade.

At the age of eighty-two Newton lay on his deathbed a few days before Christmas. He joked about being like a Christmas package all "packed and sealed" and ready to be mailed. And then he whispered as he gasped for breath: "My memory is nearly gone. But I remember two things: that I am a great sinner . . . and that Christ . . . is a great Savior."

What Do You Know?

NOAH WEBSTER (1758-1843) AND MICHAEL FARADAY (1791-1867)

Two men who shaped the world because of their precise knowledge—one with words, the other with scientific ideas—were both shaped by a Bible verse that begins with "I know."

As a New York schoolteacher during the Revolutionary War, Noah Webster was disturbed because he had to rely on British schoolbooks for instruction. So he prepared a speller, a grammar, and a reader, all focusing on things American. A stickler for accuracy, he was the first American to promote state and federal copyright laws. You could also call him one of the first American trivia buffs—he liked to keep statistics and to track weather patterns.

But while his head was crammed with facts, he struggled spiritually. He had always respected religion and had tried to live his moral life with "scrupulous exactness." But then he had a midlife crisis. He wasn't sure that his "scrupulous exactness" was good enough for God. So he began a meticulous study of Scripture, and soon he realized that the secret of salvation was not in knowing facts about God but in knowing him personally through Jesus Christ. One day when he was in his late forties, Noah Webster knelt down, confessed his sins, and asked for God's grace through the merits of Jesus Christ alone.

2 Timothy 1:12

I know whom I have believed, and am persuaded that he is able to keep that which I have committed unto him against that day (KJV).

Paul was writing this from prison, a dank dungeon that would probably be his final earthly home. He was suffering in prison because he had been preaching the gospel of Jesus. Some in that day (as in ours) assumed that people brought suffering upon themselves, and thus Paul was a failure. But Paul urges Timothy not to be ashamed of him or of the gospel. Paul had never been shy about admitting his past sins, but he would not dwell on the past, because his eternal destiny rested not on his own behavior but on the one whom he believed.

When Webster was forty-five he had begun spending most of his time on lexicography, and in 1828 his master work, *An American Dictionary of the English Language,* was published.

As he was dying, he quoted to a friend the verse that had meant so much to him: "I know whom I have believed, and am persuaded that he is able to keep that which I have committed unto him against that day" (2 Tim. 1:12 KJV). Webster loved words, but he found salvation only when he came to know God's incarnate Word.

Scientist Michael Faraday also quoted that verse on his deathbed. Visitors were trying to discover if he had any scientific theories in his mind that hadn't been published yet. So they asked, "Dr. Faraday, what are your speculations?"

"Speculations? Speculations? I have none," he responded. "I am resting on certainties. I know whom I have believed, and am persuaded that he is able to keep that which I have committed unto him against that day."

Faraday started life as a bookbinder's apprentice and taught himself science by reading the books he was binding. The article on electricity in the *Encyclopaedia Britannica* turned him on to electrical experiments. He took careful notes at scientific lectures and then printed and bound them to give back to scientific associations. Soon he himself was regarded as a scientist, and by the time he was twenty-five, Faraday was giving lectures in inorganic chemistry at the London Philosophical Society.

Faraday became the most famous scientist of his day, inventing the electric motor and the generator, without which modern society could not function. He also laid the foundations for the modern scientific theory of fields, providing us with the basis of understanding not only gravitational force, but also the forces within the nuclei of atoms.

Though he interacted daily with the speculations and theories of other physicists and chemists, on Sundays Faraday faithfully attended a tiny fundamentalist church associated with a small group called the Sandemanians. His church never had more than twenty members, but it dealt with certainties, not speculations.

In science he was both a brilliant inventor and an amazing scientific theorist. But when it came to spiritual matters, he didn't have time for speculations. For Faraday, it was "I know whom I have believed. . . ."

Apostle of Another Pentecost

WILLIAM CAREY (1761-1834)

William Carey seemed to be an average youngster in Paulersbury, England. He became apprenticed to a shoemaker as a teenager and married before he was twenty. Though he had only a basic education, he soon became a lay preacher in a small nonconformist church eight miles from his home.

He didn't appear to be talented. He couldn't manage his shoemaking business, and he didn't seem gifted as a preacher. When the local schoolteacher quit, Carey volunteered. But he didn't do well at teaching either. "He would frequently smile at his incompetency," his sister wrote later.

Then Carey discovered his true talent: He could learn languages easily. And he also loved maps. Hanging in his room was a large map to which he attached sheets of paper containing information about each country.

William Carey couldn't understand why Christians weren't trying to preach the gospel in all those countries that he saw on his map. One Baptist leader tried to put him in his place by saying, "Young man, sit down. When God pleases to save the heathen, he can do it without your aid or mine." Carey spoke up at a meeting of Baptist ministers, but the chairman rebuffed him: "You are a miserable enthusiast. . . . Nothing can be done before another Pentecost."

Once he was ordained, Carey decided to keep pressing his concern. In 1792 he wrote a paper entitled "An Enquiry into the Obligation of

Isaiah 54:2

Enlarge the place of thy tent, and let them stretch forth the curtains of thine habitations: spare not, lengthen thy cords, and strengthen thy stakes (KJV).

In this chapter the Lord encourages the barren woman to sing, because she's going to have many children. The shame of childlessness will then be erased, and the tent will have to be enlarged. Isaiah is, no doubt, speaking of Israel, offering hope to souls feeling barren in a time of exile. In the New Testament, Paul hints at a another fulfillment of this text. Abraham's wife, Sarah, is the once-barren mother who will gain multitudes of children—all those who come to God in faith (Galatians 4:27). In this sense, William Carey not only interpreted this prophecy but also helped to fulfill it.

Christians to Use Means for the Conversion of the Heathen." Three weeks later he preached a breakthrough sermon to his fellow ministers on Isaiah 54:2–3 ("Enlarge the place of thy tent" [KJV]), urging them to catch a wider vision, to develop bolder programs, to dwell in the bigger world. Then he said, "Expect great things from God; attempt great things for God."

The ministers took no action on Carey's appeal. Toward the end of the business meeting, Carey grabbed the arm of the pastor next to him and said in too loud a voice, "Is nothing again going to be done?" That got action. Before the meeting was adjourned, a motion was passed "forming a Baptist Society for propagating the Gospel among the Heathens." The "place of thy tent" was being enlarged.

Soon Carey himself was set apart for missionary work in India. A fellow pastor said, "There is a gold mine in India, but it seems almost as deep as the center of the earth." Carey responded, "I will venture down, but remember that you must hold the ropes."

Carey arrived in India in 1793 and served there until his death in 1834. He supported his family by raising indigo. Because he mastered languages easily, he made possible the translation of the entire Bible into six languages, parts of the Bible into twenty-nine more, and the development of seven grammars and three dictionaries. Under his direction the Serampore Press "rendered the Bible accessible to more than three hundred million people," he claimed. Carey also stimulated the formation of many mission societies and boards in subsequent decades, so it is little wonder that he is known as the father of modern missions.

But Carey did more. He served as professor of Oriental languages at Fort William College in Calcutta. He became one of the outstanding amateur horticulturists of his time and was given an honorary doctorate by the Horticultural Society of London. In 1829, after protesting the practice for years, he helped end the burning of widows and the drowning of children in India.

William Carey, the seemingly untalented cobbler of Paulersbury, England, had enlarged the place of his tent and made it big enough for India to climb inside.

The Unlikely Battler

WILLIAM WILBERFORCE (1759-1833)

Before the slavery battle was fought in America, it was fought in England, where it was bloodless but also long and arduous. In the thick of the fighting was a champion named William Wilberforce. He was an unlikely battler, because at five feet tall he didn't scare anyone.

Probably because of his size Wilberforce enjoyed being the life of the party, the class clown, the quick wit, the happy-go-lucky guy. When he was twenty-one he was elected to Parliament because he outspent his opponents, because he had no enemies yet, and because no one thought he would make any waves.

About four years later Wilberforce realized how empty his life was, and after a friend convinced him to read a Bible, he was converted. But as a new Christian he didn't know what to do with his life. He thought maybe he should withdraw from the world, but he decided to ask a respected Christian for advice. He chose John Newton, the former slave trader, by this time a sixty-year-old London pastor. Newton surprised the young politician by urging him to stay in the political arena. "The Lord has raised you up for the good of His church and for the good of the nation," he said. Newton also inspired him to fight the slave trade.

Afterward, Wilberforce wrote in his journal: "Almighty God has set before me two objectives: the abolition of the slave trade and the reformation of manners." In 1787 he launched his crusade. For two decades

---

Galatians 6:9

Let us not be weary in well doing: for in due season we shall reap, if we faint not (KJV).

In the last chapters of his epistles, Paul often includes many different nuggets of teaching, as well as personal comments from himself and others. Here, in Galatians, he adds a paragraph about reaping what we sow. Perhaps he was concerned (as in Romans 6:1) that people would abuse their freedom in Christ. If you don't have to be good to be saved, people might say, why be good at all? In Galatians 6:7–10 he reminds readers that our actions have natural consequences. Bad actions destroy, while good actions ultimately reap blessing. But what if you're still waiting for those blessings? Don't grow weary, he says. Your "due season" is coming.

he proposed the abolition of the slave trade, but over and over again businesspeople backed up their position with money and defeated the proposals. Once an opponent argued, "Abolition would instantly annihilate a trade which annually employs upwards of 5,500 sailors, upwards of 160 ships, and whose exports amount to 800,000 pounds sterling."

Wilberforce endured defeat after defeat, sometimes coming so close to victory that he could almost taste it. Those repeated losses left Wilberforce feeling depressed, wondering if he could keep up the fight much longer. At such a time he received a letter from Methodist leader John Wesley. It was probably the last letter Wesley, then in his eighties, ever wrote. "Unless God has raised you up for this very thing, you will be worn out by the opposition of men and devils," Wesley wrote. "But if God be for you who can be against you? Are all of them together stronger than God? Oh, be not weary of well-doing. Go on in the name of God."

"Be not weary in well-doing." Those were the words that Wilberforce needed to hear. And so he continued to make resolutions each year until finally, in 1807, the tide turned. When the votes were counted, the House voted 283 to 16 in favor of abolishing the slave trade. As biographer John Pollock tells it, "The House rose almost to a man and turned towards Wilberforce in a burst of Parliamentary cheers. Suddenly, above the roar of 'hear, hear,' . . . three hurrahs echoed and echoed while he sat, head bowed, tears streaming down his face."

Wilberforce stayed in Parliament until 1825, still pushing various reforms: relief for boy chimney sweeps, help for the poor, encouragement of education, and alleviation of prison conditions. Even after he left Parliament, he was still the "conscience of England." A few days before he died, his prayers were fully answered when the House of Commons voted to emancipate all slaves in British territories. "Thank God," he said, "that I have come to witness the day."

The little battler who was not weary in well doing had won his final fight.

The Course of Human Events

JOHN WITHERSPOON (1723-1794)

In the 1700s America was waking up in a lot of ways. With the fiery preaching of George Whitefield and the heart-pounding theology of Jonathan Edwards, the colonies had experienced a Great Awakening in a spiritual sense. Faith wasn't just a matter of belonging to an organization; it meant joining a cause.

Historians have debated how much this spiritual revival contributed to the political revolution of the 1770s. Certainly some Christians stayed loyal to the crown, but you can see how an emphasis on individual faith might lead to a concern for individual rights.

It was a society well-grounded in the Bible. As a result, public discourse was sprinkled with quotations and allusions to the stories, ideas, and characters of the

---

Ephesians 5:16

Redeeming the time, because the days are evil (KJV).

Paul has told the Ephesians about the theology of new life in Christ, and now he answers the question "So what?" Chapter 5 describes the Christian way of life—not only love (v. 2) but wisdom. We should avoid the deeds of darkness and expose them (v. 11), walking carefully (v. 15). Our wisdom should be based on "what the Lord's will is" (v. 17). You can see why Witherspoon used this text to challenge his hearers to know and do the right thing at the critical moment.

Bible. Preachers weren't shy about commenting on current events, and they often wrenched verses out of context to do so. (When the Stamp Act was repealed in England, some American preachers used the verse "As cold waters to a thirsty soul, so is good news from a far country" [Prov. 25:25 KJV].)

One scriptural phrase often bandied about was Micah 4:4, which contains a vision of a happy future in which everyone will be sitting "under his vine and under his fig tree; and none shall make them afraid" (KJV). That's not too far from the inalienable right to "life, liberty, and the pursuit of happiness" that found its way into the Declaration of Independence. The fact that "there is no respect of persons with God" (Romans

2:11 KJV) might have led Thomas Jefferson and others to the truth that all of us are created equal.

While many signers of the Declaration were sons of ministers, there was only one member of the clergy in the group: John Witherspoon. He was a solid Presbyterian who had been a leader in the Church of Scotland before taking the presidency of the College of New Jersey (later known as Princeton) in 1768. Early in his career he felt that pastors shouldn't get involved in politics, but apparently he changed his tune. He fervently supported the revolution, and the citizens of New Jersey elected him to the Continental Congress in 1776 and kept sending him back through 1782.

As the revolution developed, Witherspoon often preached on Ephesians 5:16: "Redeeming the time, because the days are evil" (KJV). American patriots didn't have to be reminded of the "evil" of the British monarchy—taxation without representation and other oppressive policies. But the question for many was timing. When was the right time to rebel? Witherspoon urged them to seize the moment.

As the Continental Congress met in Philadelphia in July 1776 to argue this point, Witherspoon played a key role. After John Adams presented the arguments for freedom, Witherspoon jumped up in support, saying, "New Jersey is plump for independence."

"The oratory is fine," said John Alsop of New York, "but the facts show we're not ripe for it."

"We are more than ripe for it," Witherspoon responded. This veteran preacher knew how to swing a metaphor. "And some of us are in danger of rotting for want of it."

A trial vote that day went 9–2 for independence with two still on the fence, so they kept debating. On July 4 when they had a draft of the Declaration before them, Witherspoon rose and addressed the Congress. "There is a tide in the affairs of men," he said. "We perceive it now before us. To hesitate is to consent to our own slavery." He urged that the document be signed "by every pen in the house." And it was.

Witherspoon was interested in redeeming the time. He saw a critical moment at hand, and he wanted to make the most of it. In light of that, it's interesting that the Declaration begins with a sense of timing— "When, in the course of human events, it becomes necessary . . ."

Ringing the Changes

THE LIBERTY BELL (1751)

The third time was the charm for the hunk of metal that became the Liberty Bell. In 1751 the Pennsylvania State Assembly ordered the bell from the Whitechapel Foundry in London. The bell was to hang in the steeple of the State House in Philadelphia (later known as Independence Hall).

The specifications were set out in detail. The bell's inscription was to read: "Proclaim LIBERTY throughout the Land unto all the inhabitants thereof. Lev. XXV,X. By order of the ASSEMBLY of the Province of PENSYLVANIA for the State House in Philada." Isaac Norris, a Quaker Assemblyman, made the order, misspelling Pennsylvania and abbreviating Philadelphia.

No one knew at the time how prophetic the inscription would be. The verse probably was chosen to honor the freedoms granted in Penn's charter on the fiftieth anniversary of that charter signed in 1701. The Leviticus passage has to do with the Year of Jubilee—every fiftieth year in which slaves were freed.

The bell didn't arrive in Philadelphia until August 1752, and it wasn't installed until the next March. Isaac Norris had written a quick note to the foundry saying that it looked great. But then he had to send another message: "I had the mortification to hear that it was cracked by a stroke of the clapper without any other violence as it was hung up to try the sound." Yes, the bell cracked in its first ring.

Two workers, John Pass and John Stow, then melted down the metal, added some more copper to strengthen it, and recast the bell. But when this bell was tested, no one liked its sound. Pass and Stow were "teased

> ### Leviticus 25:10
>
> *And ye shall hallow the fiftieth year, and proclaim liberty throughout the land unto all the inhabitants thereof* (KJV).
>
> Biblical law set up an ingenious system. Every fiftieth year was considered a Year of Jubilee. Land that had been sold reverted to its original family. Debts were forgiven. If people had sold themselves into slavery to pay debts, they were freed. Leviticus 25 offers details of this plan. It was a graphic way of remembering that all things ultimately belonged to God.

with the witticisms of the town," Norris wrote, and so they tried again. The third try was better, though Norris was still displeased with the sound and ordered a new bell from London. Still, the third bell was hung in the State House steeple, and people got used to it. When the fourth bell came from the Whitechapel Foundry, it didn't sound any better, so it was connected to the clock to toll the hours while the Liberty Bell stayed in the steeple to ring out special occasions.

The Liberty Bell tolled when Benjamin Franklin, a Philadelphian, was sent to England to present American grievances. It tolled when George III became king. It called citizens together to discuss the Sugar Act in 1764 and Stamp Act in 1765. Even though some neighbors complained in 1772 that they were "incommoded and distressed" by the loud ringing, it continued to peal. So it rang for the convening of the First Continental Congress in 1774 and the first revolutionary battles at Lexington and Concord in 1775.

But the most famous ringing of the Liberty Bell announced the first public reading of the Declaration of Independence on July 8, 1776.

Still, the bell hadn't become famous yet. When British troops took Philadelphia in 1777, it was hustled out of town and hidden, not for its symbolic value, but because the redcoats would have melted it down to make cannons.

And then it cracked. This probably happened in 1835 while it was tolling for Washington's birthday or mourning the death of Chief Justice John Marshall. By 1846 the crack had widened, making it unringable.

In the years leading up to the Civil War it was the abolition movement that claimed the bell as a symbol of freedom. It seemed to be perfect as an antislavery symbol. America had fought to win freedom, which this bell had celebrated, but now the nation was cracked and freedom was not available to all. Abolitionists boldly echoed the biblical phrase "Proclaim liberty throughout the land" (Lev. 25:10).

Did the Liberty Bell change the world? Maybe not, but it rang the changes as they occurred. From Penn's remarkable charter, to the Declaration and the Constitution, right up to the battle to free the slaves, the bell and its Bible verse had a valuable message to proclaim.

Healthy, Wealthy, and Especially Wise

BENJAMIN FRANKLIN (1706-1790)

People don't think of Ben Franklin as quoting Bible verses. If he quoted anything, it was proverbs like "Early to bed, early to rise, makes a man healthy, wealthy, and wise," or "A stitch in time saves nine."

But it's hard to think of anything Ben Franklin couldn't do. He was an inventor, a printer, a scientist, a civic leader, and a diplomat. He sponsored a city police force, a fire company, a circulating library, and a city hospital. He started an academy that evolved into the University of Pennsylvania. He was an advisor to General George Washington and a member of the committee that drafted the Declaration of Independence.

> **Psalm 127:1**
> Except the LORD build the house, they labor in vain that build it (KJV).
>
> This is one of the "psalms of ascent" that were probably sung by pilgrims climbing the hill to the temple in Jerusalem. This psalm is credited to Solomon, and so people might have been thinking of the "house" as Solomon's temple. But of course this could mean any structure—or even a family or a nation.

Following the American victory in the Revolutionary War, Franklin, along with John Jay and John Adams, negotiated the peace treaty with the British. If that weren't enough, when he was past eighty he was chosen as a delegate to the Federal Convention, to help prepare the United States Constitution. No one expected too much from him at his age, except that he might throw in a few proverbs now and then.

After two months of deliberating, few major issues had been settled. Instead it looked like the union would unravel. One delegate wrote home, "We are now in a state of anarchy and confusion bordering on civil war."

That was when Ben Franklin asked George Washington if he might speak. Leaning on his cane, he said: "How has it happened, sir, that we

101

have not hitherto once thought of humbly applying to the Father of lights to illuminate our understanding? In the beginning of the contest with Britain, when we were sensible of danger, we had daily prayers in this room for divine protection. Our prayers, sir, were heard, and they were graciously answered. All of us who were engaged in the struggle must have observed frequent instances of a superintending Providence in our favor. . . . And have we now forgotten this powerful friend? Or do we imagine we no longer need His assistance?

"I have lived a long time, and the longer I live, the more convincing proofs I see of this truth: 'that God governs in the affairs of man.' And if a sparrow cannot fall to the ground without His notice, is it probable that an empire can rise without His aid?

"We have been assured in the sacred writings that except the Lord build the house, they labor in vain that build it. I firmly believe this. I also believe that, without His concurring aid, we shall succeed in this political building no better than the builders of Babel; we shall be divided by our little, partial, local interests; our projects will be confounded; and we ourselves shall become a reproach and a byword down to future ages. And what is worse, mankind may hereafter, from this unfortunate instance, despair of establishing government by human wisdom and leave it to chance, war, or conquest.

"I therefore beg leave to move that, henceforth, prayers imploring the assistance of Heaven and its blessing on our deliberations, be held in this assembly every morning before we proceed to business."

The assembly was hushed, many of the delegates were sobered, and the meeting of the day was quickly adjourned without taking action on Franklin's motion.

Though Franklin's proposal was not accepted, it was a turning point in the Federal Convention. Compromises began to be made. Franklin himself helped draft the important compromise settling the question of representation between the large and the small states.

Three months later the Constitution had been written and was sent to the thirteen member states for ratification. Franklin died less than three years later. His main contribution to the Federal Convention had been to quote a Bible verse about how a house should be built.

By the Dawn's Early Light

FRANCIS SCOTT KEY (1779-1843)

Thirty-four-year-old Francis Key seemed to be in the wrong place at the wrong time—or maybe it was the right place at the right time.

Though the year was 1814, the War of 1812 was still being waged. The British had marched into Washington, D.C., almost unopposed, as the U.S. Army and government officials fled into Virginia. The White House, the Capitol, and most of the department buildings were in flames.

When a storm compelled the British to leave the city, they took with them a captive, a Maryland physician named William Beanes. He was being held on a warship in the Chesapeake Bay while the British were preparing to attack Baltimore and the nearby military post, Fort McHenry.

Key, a Georgetown attorney in his uncle's law firm, was a friend of Beanes. After consulting with his uncle, Key went to President James Madison, who okayed a rescue mission. In a small U.S. cartel ship, Key pursued the British fleet, and after boarding the admiral's ship, he negotiated his friend's release.

But not so fast! There was a war going on, and Key was now caught in the middle of it. The British admiral would not let Key or Beanes off the ship until the bombardment of Fort McHenry was completed. This certainly seemed like the wrong place at the wrong time. So Key watched the bombardment of Fort McHenry from a British ship. As the rockets lit up the sky, he could see the U.S. flag still flying over Fort McHenry. But would it still be flying in the morning?

> ## Psalm 143:8
>
> *Cause me to hear thy lovingkindness in the morning; for in thee do I trust* (KJV).
>
> This was quite an appropriate psalm for Key's perilous situation. In it David is crying out to God while being attacked by enemies. He remembers the good old days of peace and favor, even as his spirit is growing faint. In those days, warriors often had to wait for the sunlight of morning to reveal their situation. Had the enemy advanced or retreated? David, like Francis Scott Key, trusts God to bring him good news with the dawn.

Key was no hero and no battle-hardened soldier. He was a Washington attorney, a would-be poet, and most of all a staunch Christian, whose ultimate trust was not in armaments but in God. During the night he must have been reciting some of the psalms: "Some trust in chariots, and some in horses: but we will remember the name of the LORD our God" (Ps. 20:7 KJV), or "Cause me to hear thy lovingkindness in the morning; for in thee do I trust" (Ps. 143:8 KJV).

And in the morning the Fort McHenry flag was still flying. Later that day Key scribbled in abbreviated form the lyrics to "The Star-Spangled Banner" on the back of an envelope he had found in his pocket.

In the home of a Baltimore relative, Key wrote out the complete text. Within twenty-four hours, copies had been printed in handbill form and circulated on the streets. Seven days later the *Baltimore American* published it to the tune of a popular drinking song, *To Anacreon in Heaven.*

While the last stanza is not sung much any more, it is here that Key inserted his reference to Scripture:

> Then conquer we must, when our cause it is just;
> And this be our motto, "In God is our trust."

In his lifetime Francis Scott Key was known for many things. He became U.S. attorney for the District of Columbia. He was sent by President Andrew Jackson to negotiate a land dispute in Alabama. As a manager of the American Sunday-School Union, he spearheaded a drive to begin thousands of Sunday schools throughout the Mississippi Valley.

But he is best known for his writing of "The Star-Spangled Banner," which was named the United States national anthem in 1931. He is not as well recognized, however, as the father of the United States motto. When he wrote the line, "And this is our motto, 'In God is our trust,'" it seemed like wishful thinking. The United States had no motto. It wasn't until fifty years later that the words, "In God We Trust," first appeared on any U.S. coinage, and not until 1956 that it was declared the national motto.

In the wrong place at the wrong time? Not for the person who has as his motto, "In God we trust."

An Expansive Argument from an Eminent Leader

JOHN QUINCY ADAMS (1767-1848) AND MANIFEST DESTINY

To be honest, John Quincy Adams wasn't a very effective president—his four-year term was plagued by bitter partisan squabbling. Yet few men left more of a mark on the United States between 1800 and 1850 than he did. His vision did much to shape the young country, and this vision led America to claim the West.

Despite his background as the son of America's second president, Adams was not very presidential in his bearing. Short, stout, bald, and belligerent, he confessed in his diary that he was "cold, austere and forbidding." But Adams was very disciplined in his Christian devotion. Two hours before dawn he arose for prayer; then he read three chapters from the New Testament, usually in the King James Version, but sometimes in Latin, German, French, or the original Greek. After that he spent an hour reading the classics, followed by time to write in his diary.

> ### Psalm 2:8
> Ask of me and I shall give thee the heathen for thine inheritance, and the uttermost parts of the earth for thy possession (KJV).
>
> The second psalm has two levels of meaning. On its surface it's a coronation song, as the Lord installs his king on Zion (v. 6). But the word for Anointed One (v. 2) is the word for Messiah. So on one level the Lord promises to grant victory to Israel's king. But on another level he foresees the Messiah's rule over all nations.

Before his presidency he had served with distinction as a diplomat to the Netherlands, Prussia, and Russia, and had negotiated the treaty ending the War of 1812. He was secretary of state under President Monroe, and he has been called one of the nation's greatest secretaries of state. Adams wrote the key parts of the famed Monroe Doctrine, which stated that the Americas were off-limits to European nations. He was sixty-one when his White House term ended, but he didn't retire from public life. Instead he returned to the House of Representatives, fighting slavery and promoting America's expansion in the West. He was convinced that God had ordained the new nation to be fruitful and multiply across the continent.

This idea was nothing new. Back in 1631, Puritan leader John Winthrop called the Massachusetts Bay Colony "a shining city set on a hill." Thomas Jefferson spoke of the colonists as "the chosen people of God." Author Herman Melville wrote, "We Americans are the peculiar, chosen people—the Israel of our race. . . . God has predestined . . . great things from our race."

In 1838, as America was debating whether to fight England for the Oregon territory, John L. O'Sullivan, editor of the *Democratic Review*, wrote that America was "the nation of many nations . . . destined to manifest to mankind the excellence of divine principles, to establish on earth the noblest Temple ever dedicated to the worship of the Most High." Later he proclaimed that America had a legal right to Oregon "by the right of our manifest destiny to overspread and to possess the whole continent."

On Capitol Hill some lawmakers had doubts about the concept. Was it really America's manifest destiny to settle the West? They asked seventy-nine-year-old John Quincy Adams how he could be so sure that God had given Oregon to the United States.

Adams responded immediately, asking the clerk of the House to read two passages of Scripture. The first was Genesis 1:26–28, in which humankind is told: "Be fruitful and multiply, and replenish the earth, and subdue it: and have dominion" (v. 28 KJV). The second was Psalm 2:8: "Ask of me, and I shall give thee the heathen for thine inheritance, and the uttermost parts of the earth for thy possession" (KJV). None of Adams's colleagues dared argue with him about his interpretation of Scripture.

No doubt Adams had these verses in his mind for a long time, ever since he helped frame the Monroe Doctrine. So he called on Congress to authorize the continued westward expansion in obedience to God. He added: "We claim the country—for what? To make the wilderness blossom as the rose, to establish laws, to increase, multiply, and subdue the earth, which we are commanded to do by the first behest of God Almighty."

Soon Manifest Destiny became an American doctrine, and Oregon, Texas, and California were added to the country. And so by some Scripture-twisting the West was won.

The Woman Which Was a Sinner

ELIZABETH FRY (1780-1845)

Elizabeth Fry was full of surprises. Like the time she organized her sisters to stop a horse-drawn coach, pretending to be highwaymen robbing the passengers.

Like the time she decided that she would wear purple shoes with scarlet laces whenever she went to Quaker meetings with her parents, while every other woman in the meeting was wearing a slate-colored dress.

In her diary she wrote, "I am a bubble, a fool—idle, dissipated, stupid—all outside and no inside."

That's why everyone was surprised when she came home from a Quaker meeting in tears. "At this most critical period, the tender mercy of my God was marvelously displayed towards me," she wrote in her diary. She had opened her heart to Jesus Christ.

She married a wealthy Quaker merchant, and in the next thirteen years she gave birth to eight children (three more came later), became a Quaker minister, and gained renown for the way she could read Scripture. Ministers of other denominations came to hear her read, but she preferred reading to the sick, to the poor, and to gypsy camps.

But when she was thirty-three, this mother of eight surprisingly began another career. She asked the governor of London's Newgate Prison if she could pray and read the Bible with the women prisoners. He tried to dissuade her, because it was like a den of wild beasts in there. Three

---

Luke 7:37

And behold, a woman in the city, which was a sinner, when she knew that Jesus sat at meat in the Pharisee's house, brought an alabaster box of ointment, and stood at his feet behind him weeping (KJV).

The woman in this story wet Jesus' feet with her tears, wiped them with her hair, kissed them, and anointed them with the perfume. The term "sinner" here probably means she had been a prostitute, and thus you can understand the reaction of the Pharisee who was hosting this dinner. "If this man were a prophet, he would know what kind of woman she is" (v. 39). But Jesus did know, and he welcomed her expression of gratitude for her many sins that had been forgiven.

hundred women with children were crowded into four rooms without beds or bedding or extra clothing. Some women were nearly naked. The language was obscene and the odors foul.

Elizabeth Fry disregarded the warning. She walked in and told the women she hadn't come to condemn but to comfort. And then she took off her bonnet, sat in a low seat facing the women, and opened her Bible. The story of the woman who was a sinner in Luke 7 became a favorite. The fact that Jesus could say to this woman, "Her sins, which are many, are forgiven; for she loved much" (Luke 7:47 KJV) touched the hearts of some of the most depraved women.

Soon Elizabeth Fry turned one room into a classroom for the children of inmates; then she taught the women sewing and other handwork. She organized a committee to work for the improvement of conditions and to provide "clothing and employment, instruction in the Bible and other subjects." She invited prison authorities to her home and persuaded them to hire a female supervisor instead of a male supervisor. She also started a society for the care of criminals after their discharge from prison and a night shelter for the homeless in London.

An American congressman came and saw Westminster Abbey, the Tower of London, and the British Museum, but said, "I saw the greatest curiosity in London; I have seen Elizabeth Fry in Newgate, and I have witnessed there the miraculous effect of true Christianity."

Elizabeth Fry traveled through the British Isles and Europe, seeking to improve prison conditions. Soon prison reform societies were established in the Netherlands, Denmark, France, Prussia, Italy, and elsewhere.

When the king of Prussia came to England on an official visit, he asked to visit Newgate Prison with Elizabeth Fry. After reading the Scripture in her beautiful cadence, she knelt in prayer with the female prisoners. The Prussian king also knelt with the women.

Once at a drawing room meeting, she was asked if any one Scripture had proved especially useful in dealing with criminals facing death. She replied quickly, "I can have no hesitation in answering thy question; it is the story of the 'Woman which was a sinner.' The simple reading of that story has softened the stoniest hearts, and made eyes weep that never wept before."

Out of the Pits

ROBERT RAIKES (1735-1811)

What Bible verses were key in starting the Sunday school movement? You might expect it to be the one where Jesus bids the little children to come to him "for of such is the kingdom of heaven." But no, the most influential verses in the launch of Sunday schools were Matthew 12:11–12, in which Jesus is asked whether it is kosher to heal on the Sabbath and responds by talking about lifting a sheep out of a pit.

Here's how it happened. Robert Raikes, a newspaper editor in Gloucester, England, often editorialized about problems in society. He was concerned about prison reform and about poverty and especially about poor children.

Popular opinion said it was necessary to keep the "vulgar in their proper place." And the proper place for poor children was the factory where they worked all week. The problem came on Sundays when these children released all their pent-up energy. A woman once complained to Raikes, "The street is filled with multitudes of these wretches who, released on the Sabbath from employment, spend their time in noise and riot, cursing and sweating in a manner so horrid as to convey to any serious mind an idea of hell rather than any other place." Raikes had heard the children too, and their language shocked him. But what could be done?

Matthew 12:11–12

What man shall there be among you, that shall have one sheep, and if it fall into a pit on the sabbath day, will he not lay hold on it, and lift it out? How much then is a man better than a sheep? (KJV).

Observance of the Sabbath day was a major bone of contention between Jesus and his opponents. The Pharisees had developed some intricate rules about how to "remember the Sabbath," and they criticized those like Jesus who didn't follow them. In this chapter they've already reprimanded Jesus for letting his disciples pluck a few ears of grain to snack on during the Sabbath. That was harvesting, they said, which was work, unlawful on that holy day. And healing a man with a shriveled hand was also work. They practically dared Jesus to do this healing—and he did. In response, the Pharisees began to plot Jesus' death.

One Sunday morning Raikes started a school in Sooty Alley and hired a woman to run it, paying her one shilling a Sabbath. He called it an experiment. Between 1780 and 1783 he opened seven or eight schools with about thirty youngsters in each.

After the three-year experiment, he decided to publicize the schools and encourage others to try it. That's when the opposition struck. Members of Parliament were aghast at the idea. A bill was suggested for the suppression of Sunday schools. Clergymen objected because Raikes was putting women to work on the Sabbath in violation of one of the Ten Commandments. The archbishop of Canterbury called a group together to see how Sunday schools could be stopped.

Raikes responded: "Our Savior takes particular pains to manifest that whatever tended to promote the health and happiness of our fellow creatures were sacrifices peculiarly acceptable on that day." He pointed out passages in both Matthew and Luke where Christ says that it is okay to help an animal if one of them falls into a pit on the Sabbath. Raikes said that children of the cities had fallen into a pit.

At first he too had doubts of what Sunday schools could do, because these youngsters were wild and vile. But he began getting clothes for some of them and treating them to beef and plum pudding. He was amazed at the results. "I cannot express the pleasure I often receive in discovering genius and innate good dispositions, among this little multitude."

In Raikes's county the crime rate dropped dramatically. People started thinking that maybe Raikes wasn't so crazy after all. John Wesley encouraged Methodist societies to try it. Within four years 250,000 youngsters were in Sunday schools all across England.

The idea was picked up in America. The American Sunday-School Union evangelized the West with it, and by 1900 America had eight million Sunday school students with an equal number elsewhere in the world. In the twentieth century the numbers continued to multiply.

No doubt about it, Robert Raikes's idea of finding lost sheep and lifting them out of the pit has changed millions of lives in the past two centuries.

A Star Goes East

ADONIRAM JUDSON (1788-1850)

The first foreign missionaries from America were an impetuous, brilliant, and sometimes moody young man named Adoniram Judson and his bride of two weeks, Ann Hasseltine. They set sail in 1812 on a ship loaded with chicken coops and pig pens. They planned to serve in India but ended up as missionaries in Burma.

Four years earlier Judson had been a skeptic. When he was twenty years old he went to New York City to begin a theatrical career. There he had joined a traveling dramatic troupe that led "a reckless, vagabond life, finding lodgings where [they] could and bilking the landlord where [they] found opportunity." After a few weeks, disillusioned and heartsick, he headed home to Massachusetts. On the way he stopped at a wayside inn, but he couldn't get to sleep because a man in the next room was moaning and groaning in pain. This man, who was evidently dying, caused Judson to think about death and whether he was prepared to die. The next morning he asked the innkeeper about the man and learned that the man had died during the night. The man's name, the innkeeper revealed, was Jacob Eames. Judson was stunned; Eames had been his close friend at college. In fact, it was Eames's skepticism that had turned Judson away from Christianity.

Back home Judson continued to wrestle with spiritual questions, but three months later he wrote that he "began to entertain a hope of having received the regenerating influences of the Holy Spirit." On December 2, 1808, he "made a solemn dedication of himself to God."

Matthew 2:2

For we have seen his star in the east, and are come to worship him (KJV).

Theories abound about the star that the wise men saw. What sort of heavenly event was it? We may never know for sure. Yet we know that these magi came from "the east," possibly from Persia, where Daniel might have established a God-fearing tradition among the stargazers. Perhaps that's why they came to Jerusalem, Daniel's hometown, to inquire about the newborn king.

111

What then should he do with his life? The answer came the following year when he read a printed sermon on Matthew 2:2: "For we have seen his star in the east, and are come to worship him" (KJV). The author of the sermon, a chaplain for the East India Company, said that the time was ripe to spread Christianity in the East. Just as the wise men had come from the East to worship the infant Jesus, so now it was time for Christian missionaries to go back to the East with the gospel. Missionaries had already gone from England and from Germany, but none had gone yet from America.

Later Judson recalled that time: "For some days, I was unable to attend to the studies of my class and spent my time wondering at my past stupidity, depicting the most romantic scenes in missionary life and roving about the college rooms declaiming on the subject of missions." He read whatever books he could find about the East, including one on Burma.

In the next two years Judson raised his financial support, became engaged to Ann Hasseltine, and graduated from seminary.

The Judsons went first to India, but British authorities ordered them to be deported to England. Instead they hitched a ride on another vessel to the French island of Mauritius, and from there to Burma. In Burma they worked seven years before they had their first convert. Judson learned the Burmese language, completed a Burmese grammar in three years, and after twenty-one years, finished a translation of the Bible in Burmese. When war broke out between England and Burma, Judson was suspected of being a spy; he was imprisoned and tortured for seventeen months. When released he served as the interpreter in peace negotiations.

By the time of Judson's death in 1850, seven thousand Burmese had professed faith in Christ and sixty-three churches had been established. And in the following years, thousands of other American men and women have followed the Judsons into foreign missionary service. Nearly two centuries after they first set sail, there are more than thirty thousand full-time American missionaries from more than six hundred mission boards working in more than one hundred countries around the world.

Up to Code

SAMUEL F. B. MORSE (1791-1872)

One obscure Bible verse from the Book of Numbers might have been forgotten if Samuel F. B. Morse had not invented the telegraph and quoted the verse as his first wired message. For Morse it was no happenstance that he chose "What hath God wrought!" (Num. 23:23 KJV) as the first message. Later he wrote, "No words could have been selected more expressive of the disposition of my own mind at that time than these: to ascribe all the honor to whom it truly belongs."

When you realize that the modern communications network, with faxes, modems, e-mail, and the Internet, had its beginnings with the telegraph, you can see how much Morse really changed the world. It is not surprising that he is known today as the "Father of American Telecommunications."

How Morse became an inventor is a surprising story in itself. The well-known artist Gilbert Stuart encouraged Morse's father to send Samuel to Europe to study art. Stuart was very impressed with the young man's talent. So Morse went to England, studied under Benjamin West, and exhibited some of his work in London's Royal Academy.

When he came back to America, however, Samuel Morse faced a series of problems. His young wife, his father, and his mother all died within a brief period, and he found himself unable to make a decent living as a painter in America. So he returned to Europe.

Aboard ship he heard some men discussing new experiments with something called electromagnetism. Morse picked up on the idea quickly: "If the presence of electricity can be made visible to any part

> ### Numbers 23:23
> *What hath God wrought!* (KJV).
>
> This phrase appears in the odd story of the prophet Balaam. The king of Israel's enemy, Moab, offered to pay Balaam to put a curse on Israel. Balaam said no at first, then yes, then his donkey said no—well, we said it was odd. Anyway, Balaam finally utters a prophecy, but it turns out to be a blessing on Israel. In this verse he says Israel cannot be cursed because people looked at the great events of Israelite history and said, "See what God has done!"

of the circuit, I see no reason why intelligence may not be transmitted by electricity." Before the ship landed in Europe, he had developed a plan. In 1837 he applied for a patent on the American Electromagnetic Telegraph and created the Morse Code with letters communicated by dots and dashes.

Morse tried to get financial backing in America and then in Europe to support his new invention. But his efforts were unsuccessful. No matter what Morse tried, he met with failure. He was an outstanding artist, but he couldn't make a living at it. He had developed a revolutionary new invention, but he couldn't find any backers for it. "The only gleam of hope," he said, " is from confidence in God. When I look upward it calms any apprehension for the future, and I seem to hear a voice saying, 'If I clothe the lilies of the field, shall I not also clothe you?' Here is my strong confidence, and I will wait patiently for the direction of Providence."

In 1843 he went to the U.S. Congress for support, but many laughed at him. However, just before Congress adjourned late in the evening, they awarded him thirty thousand dollars to erect a telegraphic line between Baltimore and Washington. Morse built the line within a year and then sent that first message: "What hath God wrought!"

Before long, telegraphic communications were sweeping the nation. Businesses, newspapers, railroads, and government agencies were all depending on Morse's invention. Indeed his invention had revolutionized communications.

Though Morse is best known as the inventor of the telegraph, he was also the founder of the National Academy of Design, was appointed the first chair of fine arts in America at New York University, made the first photographic portrait in the nation, and introduced the daguerreotype in America.

Four years before his death, Morse wrote: "The nearer I approach to the end of my pilgrimage, the clearer is the evidence of the divine origin of the Bible, the grandeur and sublimity of God's remedy for fallen man are more appreciated, and the future is illumined with hope and joy."

Familiarity with God

CHARLES G. FINNEY (1792-1875)

As a young schoolteacher, Charles Finney was called a "splendid pagan." He was, after all, about six foot two, blue-eyed, a good dancer, and was good at music and athletics. Later, as a young lawyer, he confessed he was "as ignorant of religion as a heathen."

He had never owned a Bible. However, because many lawyers quoted the Bible, he decided to buy one, and because all the right people went to the Presbyterian church, so did he, even volunteering to lead the church choir.

He later wrote about one autumn evening when he was twenty-nine: "I made up my mind that I would settle the question of my soul's salvation." However, for the next two days, he wrote, "it seemed as if my heart grew harder. I could not pray. . . . I became very nervous, and . . . a strange feeling came over me as if I were about to die. . . . I felt almost like screaming."

As Finney started for his office the next morning, an inner voice seemed to say to him, "What are you waiting for? Are you trying to work out a righteousness of your own?"

So instead of going to his office, he walked into the woods to be alone. He climbed a small hill, saying to himself, "I will give my heart to God, or I will never come down from there." But he still had trouble praying. He was afraid that one of the townspeople would see him on his knees, talking to himself. Then an overwhelming sense of his own sinfulness came over him.

> ### Jeremiah 29:12-13
> *Then shall ye call upon me, and ye shall go and pray unto me, and I will hearken unto you. And ye shall seek me, and find me, when ye shall search for me with all your heart* (KJV).
>
> Jeremiah had the unpopular task of telling his people that they would be defeated by their enemies and carried off to captivity. But God also gave Jeremiah a word of hope. After seventy years things would turn around. They would prosper again. But most of all, as these verses indicate, their relationship with the Lord would be renewed.

Just then, two verses from Jeremiah came to his mind: "Then shall ye call upon me, and ye shall go and pray unto me, and I will hearken unto you. And ye shall seek me, and find me, when ye shall search for me with all your heart" (Jer. 29:12–13 KJV). "I do not think I had ever read it," he said, "but I knew it was God's word." So he responded, "Lord, I take you at your word. You know that I am searching for you with all my heart, and you have promised to hear me."

Almost immediately he quit his law practice and accepted a call to preach. Within the next year, sixty-three people were converted through his preaching in the little town of Adams, New York. Soon Finney was speaking throughout western New York, and revival fires broke out wherever he went.

He faced criticism on many fronts. He was charged with encouraging "familiarity with God in prayer," with encouraging new converts to become church members too quickly, with allowing women to pray in public and saying that any member of the church could serve in the ways he or she was capable of serving, and with praying for people in public by name.

But the carping didn't dampen the response to Finney's message. Soon he was invited to New York, Philadelphia, and later to England. Finney's greatest revival meetings were in Rochester, New York, where one hundred thousand were added to local churches after a six-month crusade. Lyman Beecher commented, "That was the greatest work of God, and the greatest revival of religion, that the world has ever seen in so short a time." America's Second Great Awakening had begun.

In 1835 when Finney became president of Oberlin College near Cleveland, he insisted that no one would be denied admission because of race or sex. The school became the first coeducational college in America, and one of the first schools to accept people regardless of race.

But Finney is known primarily for his revival ministry. His innovations—prayer meetings for revival, public invitations to receive Christ, the personalizing of the salvation message, the counseling of inquirers, and the use of buildings other than churches for evangelistic meetings—became standard practice for later evangelists.

Cathedrals and Candlesticks

VICTOR HUGO (1802-1885)

For more than a dozen years, Broadway audiences have been enthralled by *Les Miserables*, a story of forgiveness and redemption first penned by a nineteenth-century Frenchman. In the last five years, children of all ages have flocked to movie theaters to see a story created by that same French master. *The Hunchback of Notre Dame* has the classic Disney animation, but the original characters are complex—the homely Quasimodo risks his life out of love for the misunderstood Esmerelda.

What is it about this French novelist that dazzles audiences more than a century after his death? It might be that he explored a theme that never seems to grow old: the power of love in action.

Victor Hugo always knew that he would be a writer. At the age of fifteen he wrote a poem that was honored by the French Academy, and when he was twenty he published his first book of poetry. In the plays, poems, and novels that followed, he began to challenge the accepted forms of French literature. Spearheading a new Romantic movement, Hugo wrote in a more emotional, free-flowing style than the French were used to. The style caught on.

In 1831 Hugo published his greatest work, *Notre Dame de Paris* (translated into English as *The Hunchback of Notre Dame*). Set in the fifteenth century, it features some of the outcasts of Parisian society—a gypsy girl and a deformed bellringer. In one key scene the hunchback is strung up by an angry mob, and he cries out for water, only to be mocked. Suddenly the crowd parts, and the gypsy girl walks forward with a container of water, which she gives to the suffering man.

> ### Matthew 10:42
>
> *And if anyone gives even a cup of cold water to one of these little ones because he is my disciple, I tell you the truth, he will certainly not lose his reward.*
>
> Matthew 10 contains Jesus' instructions to his disciples as he sends them out to minister in his name. He tells them what to say, what to take with them, and what to watch out for. If people don't welcome them in certain towns, they are to shake the dust off their feet and move on. But those who receive them kindly will be greatly rewarded.

117

Such acts of kindness are portrayed powerfully in Hugo's work, calling to mind Jesus' teaching about giving a cup of cold water in his name. Though Hugo is not known as a religious writer, several of his characters seem to operate in Jesus' name. At the beginning of *Les Miserables*, a desperate Jean Valjean, just out of prison, finds lodging in a bishop's home but runs off with the bishop's silver candlesticks. Valjean is arrested and hauled back to the bishop, who refuses to press charges. In fact, the bishop offers the candlesticks as a gift for Valjean to use to build a better life. Throughout the novel we see Valjean as a recipient of mercy but also extending mercy—cups of cold water (sometimes literally)—to Fantine, Cosette, and Marius. Even when he has the opportunity to kill Javert, the police inspector who has refused to show him mercy, Valjean lets him go.

The personal and political trials of Jean Valjean seem to mirror Hugo's own experience. In 1843 his daughter and her new husband were killed in a boating accident. Hugo grieved deeply. Though he wrote some melancholy poems ("I shall not look on the gold of evening falling..."), he didn't publish another book for ten years. He did get involved in government, however, and was elected to the Assembly. When Louis Napoleon led a coup in 1851, Hugo led a resistance effort but then fled. *Les Miserables* was penned in 1862 while he was in exile. He returned to France in 1870, and at his death in 1885 he was hailed as a national hero. His body lay in state under the Arc de Triomphe, and his funeral procession lasted six hours.

Through his writing Victor Hugo shows the transforming power of love. "The supreme happiness in life," he wrote, "is the assurance of being loved; of being loved for oneself even in spite of oneself." This is the cup of cold water that this great novelist offers to all his readers.

The Poor Man Who Opened a Filling Station

GEORGE MÜLLER (1805-1898)

It had not been a good year for George and Mary Müller. Throughout much of 1835, thirty-year-old Müller had been struggling with poor health. In June Mary's father died, and four days later their fifteen-month-old son was stricken with pneumonia and died. Mary was in depression. Müller wrote in his diary, "Our taxes are due . . . and we have no money to pay them." In August severe stomach problems plagued him. In September he couldn't find the strength to speak in public. That's the way the year was going.

But through all of Müller's emotional and physical pain, one image kept recurring—the faces of the children on the streets, the orphans begging for bread. These children either begged in the streets, were sent to workhouse dungeons, or became city prostitutes. Ever since he and Mary had moved to Bristol three years earlier, these children had been on his mind, and no one was doing anything to help them.

In November he wrote in his diary: "Today I have had it very much impressed on my heart, no longer merely to think about the establishment of an orphan house, but actually to set about it." A few days later he wrote: "I . . . am more and more convinced that it is of God." But still later in November, thinking about how ridiculous it was that he, who could hardly provide for his own family, was dreaming of starting an orphanage, he added, "I have been . . . entreating the Lord to take away every thought concerning it out of my mind if the matter be not of him."

> ### Psalm 81:10
>
> Open thy mouth wide, and I will fill it (KJV).
>
> Psalm 81 recalls God's care for the Israelites during their wanderings in the wilderness. While Müller's faith focused on the last part of verse 10, the first part says, "I am the LORD your God, who brought you up out of Egypt." Even as the Lord provided his people with manna in the wilderness, so the Lord would continue to provide for them if they remained faithful.

On December 5 as he was still wrestling with the strange idea of starting an orphanage when he had no money at all, he opened his Bible and read Psalm 81:10: "Open thy mouth wide, and I will fill it" (KJV). Until that day he had prayed about whether God wanted him to start an orphanage. After that day he began asking God to supply the funds and the personnel to staff the orphanage. Two days later he received the first gift for the orphanage—a single shilling. Then came another shilling, and then a large wardrobe. The Müller Orphanages had begun.

Müller resolved never to ask anyone—except the Lord—for money. Didn't the psalm say that the Lord would fill the hungry mouths? On December 13 "a brother and sister offered themselves, with all their furniture, and all their provisions which they have in the house, if they can be usefully employed in the concerns of the orphanage." Four months later Müller opened his first orphanage, and within a year he was housing sixty youngsters in it.

It was still a year before Charles Dickens wrote *Oliver Twist,* drawing the attention of the public to the plight of the orphans. According to Dickens, "Orphans were despised by all and pitied by none." Despised by all? Pitied by none? No, George Müller was doing something about it; all he needed to get going was Psalm 81:10.

In time, Müller founded five orphanages in Bristol, housing two thousand orphans, and he never asked anyone for funds. He simply asked the Lord; he opened his mouth and let the Lord fill it. Supplies always seemed to arrive just in the nick of time. Once the orphans were seated at an empty breakfast table; no food was available. George Müller prayed as usual, thanking God for his provision. Before the prayer was ended, there was a knock at the door. A bakery wagon had broken down outside the orphanage, and the driver wondered if Müller could use the bread he was carrying. In his lifetime Müller received about eight million dollars (not counting gifts of bread and furniture) and cared for a total of about ten thousand orphans.

Because of Psalm 81:10 George Müller was a pioneer in caring for England's orphans, whose open hearts and open mouths needed to be filled.

From One Warrior to Another

ROBERT E. LEE (1807-1870)

In some ways Robert E. Lee, the famous Confederate general of the Civil War, was the perfect soldier. The son of a Revolutionary War hero, he graduated from West Point when he was twenty-two, fought and was wounded in the Mexican War, served as a West Point superintendent, and then became a cavalry officer in the 1850s.

He was also a godly man, believing that God was in charge of human affairs in times of war just as he was in times of peace. He loved the psalms of David and he had memorized many of them. Psalm 144 was a favorite. It begins, "Blessed be the LORD my strength, which teacheth my hands to war, and my fingers to fight" (KJV).

In 1861 Lee was asked by President Lincoln to take command of the Union volunteer army. Knowing that it was organized to invade the southern states that were seceding from the Union, Lee refused the appointment and resigned from the U.S. Army. Though he owned no slaves at the time, and though he was not committed to the cause of slavery in the South, he was loyal to the state of Virginia, and when Virginia left the Union, Lee left too.

Lee was made general of the Confederate Army of Northern Virginia, and although he fought against larger numbers, he was victorious in battle after battle. After victories at Fredericksburg and Chancellorsville, he moved north into Pennsylvania, trying to take control of Gettysburg. Fierce fighting followed, but Lee could not penetrate the Union lines. After suffering heavy casualties, he and his army retreated south.

> ## Psalm 144:1
>
> *Blessed be the LORD my strength, which teacheth my hands to war, and my fingers to fight* (KJV).
>
> David, who is credited with writing this psalm, was much like Robert E. Lee. David was a noted warrior who was also a man of culture and deep spirituality, and all of these elements appear in Psalm 144. This psalm is clearly a prayer for victory, and military images abound, but David also talks about singing new songs on his ten-stringed lyre (v. 9). Like Lee, David knew both victory and defeat, but he maintained a strong faith in the Lord's power and goodness.

Discouraged by the losses, Lee submitted his resignation to Confederate President Jefferson Davis, but his resignation was not accepted.

Lee spoke to his soldiers after this defeat as they observed a day of fasting, humiliation, and prayer. "We have sinned against Almighty God," he said, "We have forgotten his signal mercies." And after exhorting his troops to holy living, he closed by saying, "Our times are in his hands," (paraphrasing Psalm 31:15) and "we have relied too much on our own arms for the achievement of our independence."

When Ulysses S. Grant was placed in charge of the Union forces, he pursued Lee's troops into the South. As decisive battles were looming, Lee recalled Psalm 144. He often quoted from memory the first verse and then, as a prayer, the sixth and seventh verses: "Cast forth lightning, and scatter them: shoot out thine arrows, and destroy them. Send thine hand from above; rid me, and deliver me" (KJV). Maybe Lee thought that God had not wanted him to invade the North, but now that he was defending the South, encouraged by Psalm 144, he was determined to fight on.

But two days after he prayed this verse to God, Lee's troops suffered heavy casualties in the Battle of the Wilderness. A month later at Cold Harbor they again suffered great losses. Eleven months later at Appomattox Court House, with fewer than 30,000 men compared to Grant's 115,000, Lee surrendered to the Union forces, ending the Civil War.

Lee died in 1870, five years after the war ended, and on his desk was found the motto: "God disposes; this ought to satisfy us." This was no doubt a faithful response to the age-old saying, "Man proposes, God disposes." Lee knew that people may throw themselves into various pursuits, including war, but God determines the outcome. One of Lee's biographers wrote, "Good people can lose wars. . . . Virtue exists independently of victory." Yet it's apparent that General Lee wasn't trusting in his own virtue, but (like the psalmist) in God's strength.

Women's Work

PHOEBE PALMER (1807-1874)

Phoebe Palmer may have started the Third American Awakening; she undoubtedly was a major force in the nineteenth-century discussion of women's role in the church.

In her book *Promise of the Father*, Phoebe Palmer asks, "Who were in the Upper Room when the Holy Spirit descended at Pentecost?" Included among the followers were "the women, and Mary the mother of Jesus." And Scripture says, "They were all filled with the Holy Ghost, and began to speak with other tongues, as the Spirit gave them utterance" (Acts 2:4 KJV). That, combined with Peter's quotation of Joel's prophecy in Joel 2:28 ("Your sons and your daughters shall prophecy" [KJV]), was all the authorization that Phoebe Palmer needed to preach the gospel.

Married at the age of twenty to Walter Palmer, Phoebe Palmer was the mother of six children, only three of whom survived infancy. In the 1830s Phoebe Palmer and her sister opened their homes to a gathering called the Tuesday Meeting for the Promotion of Holiness. The members of the group sought "Christian perfection" and "entire sanctification." After studying the Bible and the writings of John Wesley and others, Palmer claimed her entire sanctification in 1837. While Wesley believed that sanctification was a lifelong process, Phoebe Palmer believed that it could be instantaneously received by faith in God's promises. It was during the Tuesday Meeting that Phoebe Palmer first began to preach and teach,

Joel 2:28

I will pour out my spirit upon all flesh; and your sons and your daughters shall prophesy (KJV).

When this verse was written, locusts were plaguing Israel, so the prophet Joel took the opportunity to warn the Israelites of God's judgment. Those nasty insects were just a hint of the judgment that would befall the nation unless they got right with God. (Some think this army of locusts was a metaphor for the Assyrians or Babylonians, but locusts themselves could do nearly as much damage.) After calling for repentance, Joel presented a brighter vision of that coming "day of the LORD" (Joel 2:31 KJV). In a renewed relationship with his people, God would pour out his Spirit on them all.

and soon the attendance exceeded two hundred. The Palmers had to move twice to larger houses that could accommodate the crowds. The Tuesday Meeting group continued for sixty years, and its teachings about holiness paved the way for denominations like the Church of the Nazarene, the Church of God, and the Pentecostal Holiness Church.

Phoebe Palmer never asked for ordination or a Methodist preaching license, but she and her husband took preaching assignments for about six months out of the year, and she did most of the speaking. In October of 1857, the Palmers were conducting revivals and camp meetings in Quebec and Ontario. When invited by a Methodist pastor in Hamilton, Ontario, to speak at his church, the Palmers thought it would be for a day. But when twenty-one people were converted, the couple was asked to stay for a bit longer. In the next few weeks six hundred people were converted. Wherever Phoebe Palmer and her husband went, crowds came and many were converted. The Third Awakening had begun.

Although the Palmers had strong views on Christian perfectionism, the Third Awakening was not sectarian. Revivalist chronicler Timothy Smith writes, "Distinctions between the sects and between ministers and laymen were ignored. The joyous liberty of the camp meeting 'love feast' was thus transferred to an urban setting." Methodists, Baptists, Lutherans, Congregationalists, Presbyterians, and Episcopalians all worked together.

Immediately after revival fires were ignited in the eastern United States, Walter and Phoebe Palmer went across the Atlantic to spread them in England, where they spent four years preaching and teaching. It has been estimated that perhaps twenty-five thousand were brought to Christ under the direct ministry of Phoebe Palmer in both North America and Great Britain.

Within a decade or two after Phoebe Palmer's death, many denominations were formed that wrote into their constitutions that women had the right to preach. No doubt about it, Phoebe Palmer had started something . . . or maybe it was the prophet Joel who actually started it.

Holding the House Together

ABRAHAM LINCOLN (1809-1865)

A tall, lanky man stood up in the 1858 Illinois Republican Convention and began to speak, saying, "If we could first know where we are, and whither we are tending, we could better judge what to do, and how to do it." The people of Springfield knew this man well. They had heard him offer his witticisms in courtrooms, in front of various civic groups, and down at the general store. When Abe Lincoln took the floor, his listeners were in for a treat—even if he did start out with some rather obvious observations.

> ### Mark 3:25
>
> And if a house be divided against itself, that house cannot stand (KJV).
>
> ---
>
> The enemies of Jesus had a problem. It was hard to discredit Jesus when he backed up his teaching with miracles. When he exorcised demons, didn't that prove he had spiritual power? But then someone had a brainstorm: Maybe Jesus used demonic power to cast out demons! Jesus dismissed that challenge quickly. Why would Satan fight against himself?

He was referring in this speech to the Missouri Compromise, which was supposed to settle the slavery dispute but only made things worse. "A house divided against itself cannot stand," he intoned, quoting from the Bible (Mark 3:25), which he had been reading since childhood. "I believe this government cannot endure permanently half slave and half free. I do not expect the Union to be dissolved; I do not expect the house to fall; but I do expect it will cease to be divided. It will become all one thing, or all the other." Lincoln's words were prophetic, but he did not foresee the national tragedy and personal heartache that would unfold in just a few years' time.

Born in a log cabin to uneducated parents, Lincoln learned to read from a handful of books in his home: the Bible, *Robinson Crusoe*, *Pilgrim's Progress*, Aesop's *Fables*, and a few history volumes. As a young man, he moved to New Salem, Illinois, near Springfield, where he ran a store and a mill, split rails, surveyed, and served as the town postmaster. He also fought in a local conflict against the Black Hawk Indians and studied law. At age twenty-five he was elected to the state legislature, where he served for seven years, then had a two-year stint in Congress. In between his governmental responsibilities, he worked as a circuit lawyer and public speaker. He was a popular figure in Illinois, but few people outside that region knew who he was.

In the 1850s Lincoln joined the new Republican party, and its newness helped him rise quickly through the ranks. In 1856 he received a substantial number of votes for the vice-presidential nomination. And when he stood up to speak in that 1858 convention in Springfield, he won the party's nomination to run for the U.S. Senate.

Lincoln was running against a Democrat named Stephen Douglas, and the two appeared throughout the state in a series of debates. Lincoln repeated the "house divided" line because it capsulized his position on the critical issue of slavery. He lost that election but yet he was seen as a rising star within the party. In the next two years he continued to speak around the country about slavery, secession, and other issues. At the national convention in 1860, Lincoln won the nomination of his party for the presidency, and in November he was elected the sixteenth U.S. president.

When Lincoln was elected president, southern states began to secede from the Union, forming the Confederate States of America. The U.S. Army fought to keep the nation intact, and Lincoln himself was driven by the notion that the nation must not be divided. On November 19, 1863, Lincoln looked out over the battlefield of Gettysburg and gave the most famous speech of his life. Later he said, "When I left Springfield, I asked the people to pray for me; I was not a Christian. When I buried my son—the severest trial of my life—I was not a Christian. But when I went to Gettysburg and saw the graves of thousands of our soldiers, I then and there consecrated myself to Christ."

The Confederacy surrendered in 1865, ending four brutal years of fighting. Five days later, having succeeded in holding the house together, President Lincoln was assassinated.

Without a doubt Abraham Lincoln ranks among America's greatest presidents. The crux of his greatness was his commitment to that simple Bible verse: "And if a house be divided against itself, that house cannot stand" (Mark 3:25 KJV).

The Little Lady with a Big Book

HARRIET BEECHER STOWE (1811-1896)

When Abraham Lincoln shook hands with Harriet Beecher Stowe in the White House, he said, "So this is the little lady who made this big war?" He was talking about the Civil War, of course, and no one had done more to rouse the North to the plight of the slave than Harriet Beecher Stowe, author of *Uncle Tom's Cabin*.

When the Emancipation Proclamation was signed, Stowe was quietly enjoying a concert at the Boston Music Hall. In the middle of the concert, a telegram bearing the news was read, and the auditorium erupted with shouts. When the audience realized that Harriet Beecher Stowe was in attendance, everyone shouted "Mrs. Stowe, Mrs. Stowe." Perhaps she, just as much as Lincoln, had caused the Proclamation to be written.

> ## John 15:15
>
> *Henceforth I call you not servants . . . but I have called you friends* (KJV).
>
> This section of John's Gospel records Jesus' Last Supper discussion with his disciples. It is deeply personal, with a strong sense of Jesus' impending death. He warns his friends about the trials ahead but he also invites them to draw strength from him and from the Spirit he will give them. It is the end of one era, but the beginning of a new one, and Jesus lifts these followers into a new kind of relationship with him.

In the nineteenth century everyone knew the Beecher family. Harriet's father, Lyman Beecher, was a famous preacher in Connecticut. But as a girl Harriet was not impressed with her father's spellbinding preaching style. "Most of my father's sermons were as unintelligible to me as if he had spoken in Choctaw," she said.

One Sunday's sermon was different, perhaps because her father couldn't decipher the crumpled notes he had stuffed in his pocket and so spoke extemporaneously. His text was taken from John 15:15: "I call you no longer servants. . . . Instead I have called you friends," and the next verse: "You did not choose me, but I chose you." Stowe listened as she never had before, and that afternoon she fell down on her knees in her father's study. With tears she confessed, "Father, I have given myself to Jesus and He has taken me."

When Stowe was twenty-one she moved with her family to Cincinnati, where her father became president of Lane Theological Seminary. The Beecher home was on a bluff overlooking the Ohio River, and across the river was slave territory. Some Cincinnati ministers hung lamps in their windows to let slaves know that their houses were a safe haven for those successful in crossing the river. In the middle of winter, some slaves struggled to get across on cracking ice; sometimes when Stowe heard the ice cracking at night, she wondered if a slave had fallen into the river. Once Calvin Stowe, whom she married in 1836, rescued a black maid whom kidnappers were trying to sell into slavery. Stowe would never forget the stories she heard from this woman.

In 1850 Stowe moved to Maine with her husband and children. Here she decided to use the long winter months to write. Her inspiration came one Sunday morning as she was taking communion. In her imagination she began to see an old, white-haired slave being whipped. Despite the torture, he was praying for those who were beating him. Using that vision as her inspiration, she began writing her novel, chapter by chapter, to be serialized in a national magazine. The saintly old slave in her vision she called Tom; his overseer she called Simon Legree.

The success of *Uncle Tom's Cabin* in the magazine prompted a publisher to print five thousand copies of the book. These sold out in two days, so the publisher went back to press, printing twenty thousand. This printing sold out in three months. By the end of the year, the book had sold three hundred thousand copies, and the presses couldn't keep ahead of the demand. Stowe had become a celebrity throughout America.

Soon the book was printed in England, France, Germany, Italy, and Portugal. When someone cautioned her that fame might go to her head, Stowe responded, "You do not need to be afraid of that. You see, I did not write the book."

"What do you mean?" the person asked.

"I was only the instrument. The Lord wrote the book."

Someone said that with one book Harriet Beecher Stowe had created two million abolitionists. And yet the book was not strident in tone. She treated all the characters—including slaveowners—with sympathy. Historian Allan Nivens praised the book's compassion, saying, "It attuned itself to the spirit of Him who died for all who were weary and heavy-laden."

Or as Harriet Beecher Stowe might say, "It was written in the spirit of Him who said, 'I call you not servants . . . but I have called you friends.'"

Into the Heart of Africa

DAVID LIVINGSTONE (1813-1873)

Early in his life David Livingstone, Scottish missionary and explorer, was driven by the first part of Matthew 28:19—"Go ye therefore" (KJV). Later in life he relied heavily on the last part of Matthew 28:20—"Lo, I am with you alway" (KJV).

Livingstone went to Africa as a medical missionary and ended up as a world famous explorer. "I am a missionary, heart and soul," he wrote his parents. "God had an only Son, and he was a missionary and physician. A poor, poor imitation of Him I am, or wish to be. In this service I hope to live, in it I wish to die." How successful he was as a missionary is questionable, but his remarkable explorations opened up an entire continent to thousands of future missionaries. No one, Christian or otherwise, has exercised a greater influence on the history of central Africa than he.

Livingstone loved to explore God's creation. He once wrote: "Missionaries ought to cultivate a taste for the beautiful. We are necessarily compelled to contemplate much moral impurity and degradation. . . .

> ## Matthew 28:19–20
>
> *Go ye therefore, and teach all nations, baptizing them in the name of the Father, and of the Son, and of the Holy Ghost: Teaching them to observe all things whatsoever I have commanded you: and, lo, I am with you alway, even unto the end of the world. Amen* (KJV).
>
> Matthew ends his Gospel with these words. Known as the Great Commission, these verses have become a favorite of mission-oriented Christians in the last few centuries. The word "teach" in verse 19 carries the meaning "make disciples." According to church tradition, Jesus' disciples carried out this command, with Thomas going to India, Matthew to Ethiopia, and others to Asia Minor and elsewhere. And thousands of missionaries today continue to claim this command and the promise that goes with it.

See the green earth and blue sky, the lofty mountain and verdant valley, the glorious orbs of day and night and the starry canopy with all their celestial splendor, the graceful flowers so chaste in form and perfect in coloring." After discovering a large inland lake, Livingstone was impressed with the "immense region before [him]. Thousands live and die without God and without hope, though the command went forth of old, 'Go ye into all the world, and preach the Gospel to every creature'" (Mark 16:15 KJV).

Two years later he began to explore farther northwestward in order to find an alternative route that missionaries could use to enter the heart of Africa. His exploration took him west to the Portuguese settlement of Luanda on the Atlantic Ocean, and then east 2,500 miles across the continent to the mouth of the Zambezi River on the Indian Ocean. He was awed by the great Victoria Falls and took careful notes that would prove helpful in botany, geology, astronomy, geography, medicine, and trade.

When people expressed concerns about his safety in going where no white man had ever gone before, he tried to calm their fears by quoting Bible verses back to them. "Lo, I am with you alway, even unto the end of the world" (Matt. 28:20 KJV). But in 1856 when he encountered hostile tribes, Livingstone knew he was in danger. Writing long entries in his diary, he talked out his worry: "Felt much turmoil of spirit. . . . All my plans knocked on the head by savages tomorrow?" But then he quoted the command and promise of Matthew 28:19–20.

The year 1871 proved to be one of the darkest times in Livingstone's life. All his supplies were gone; he had received no mail for five years; he was presumed dead. He wrote in his diary: "I felt in my destitution as if I were the man who went down from Jerusalem to Jericho, and fell among thieves; but I could not hope for priest, Levite, or good Samaritan to come by on either side." But a good Samaritan did come by. Henry Stanley, a writer for the *New York Herald*, found him in the heart of Africa and uttered the famous line, "Dr. Livingstone, I presume." Stanley unsuccessfully tried to persuade Livingstone to return to England.

The good doctor died about a year later, and he was found kneeling beside his bed. His heart was buried in Africa, but his body was taken to London and buried in Westminster Abbey, and he is said to be the only pauper buried there with full state honors.

Many Christians have followed where Dr. Livingstone has led. He would be surprised and delighted to know that there are now more Christians in Africa than there are in North America.

The Dour Dane Finds a Reason to Smile

SØREN KIERKEGAARD (1813-1855)

The great Danish philosopher Søren Kierkegaard is described as being many things—
brilliant, eccentric, iconoclastic, melancholy, dour—but never joyful.

Joy was not something Kierkegaard
had much experience with as a child. His
stern, brooding father believed his family had been cursed and that his children
would die before they were thirty-four
years old. Kierkegaard, the youngest of
seven children, had witnessed the death
of five brothers and sisters.

When he went to the university, Kierkegaard rebelled against his father's stern-
ness and led a wild life. At the age of
twenty-two he wrote in his journal, "What
I really lack is to be clear in my mind what
I am to do, not what I am to know . . . to
find the idea for which I can live and die."
The following year he wrote, "I have just returned from a party of which
I was the life and soul; wit poured from my life, everyone laughed and
admired me—but I went away . . . and wanted to shoot myself."

The year after that he wrote, "It must be terrible, on the day of judgment, when all souls come back to life—to stand there utterly alone,
alone and unknown to all, all."

Then the next year, early in 1838, he wrote, "Sometimes, there is
such a tumult in my head that it feels as though the roof had been lifted
off my cranium, and then it seems as though the hobgoblins had lifted

> ## Philippians 4:4
> *Rejoice in the Lord always. I will say it again: Rejoice.*
>
> ---
>
> Joy is a major theme of Paul's epis-
> tle to the Philippians, so it's no sur-
> prise that he returns to it in his clos-
> ing chapter. He has discussed his
> own impending death, a friend's ill-
> ness, the fierce opponents of the
> gospel, and some infighting within
> the church—but none of that should
> dampen the Philippians' joy. The fol-
> lowing verses (vv. 6–8) speak of
> anxiety giving way, through prayer,
> to the "peace of God, which tran-
> scends all understanding" (v. 7).

up a mountain and were holding a ball and festivities there—God preserve me."

In the next couple of months he reconciled with both his earthly father and his heavenly Father. His journal contains this surprising entry: "May 19. Half-past ten in the morning. There is an indescribable joy which glows through us as unaccountably as the Apostle's outburst is unexpected: 'Rejoice, and again I say, Rejoice.' Not a joy over this or that, but full jubilation 'with hearts and souls and voices.' I rejoice over my joy, in, by, at, on, through, or, and, with, my joy—a heavenly refrain which suddenly breaks in upon our ordinary song, a joy which cools and refreshes like a breeze."

Kierkegaard had experienced the joy of conversion but he was still plagued with melancholia. It was another ten years before he experienced a sense of forgiveness. God, he realized, had not only forgiven his sins but had also forgotten them. Kierkegaard finally felt free, and the last seven years of his life were his most productive.

Much of his writing focuses on the question, "What does it mean to be a Christian in a society that claims to be Christian, in a country where everyone belongs to the state church and professes to believe?" Kierkegaard believed that becoming a Christian was too easy; in fact, it was the easiest thing to do in an environment like that. When Christianity becomes so attractive that nearly everyone accepts it, then, said Kierkegaard, you can be sure it is not Christianity at all.

Because he spoke against the Church of Denmark, he was not popular in his homeland. He said the church had departed from New Testament faith and had reduced the clergy to mere civil servants. Although he despaired of Christendom, he found hope in Christ. He prayed: "Lord Jesus Christ! A whole life long you did suffer that I too might be saved, and yet your suffering is not yet at an end; but this too you will endure, saving and redeeming me, this patient suffering of having to do with me."

After collapsing on a street in 1855, he was hospitalized, his legs paralyzed. When a friend tried to encourage him by telling him how well he looked, Kierkegaard responded, "The only trouble is, I can't walk. But indeed there are other means of transportation. I can be lifted up . . . and sit astride a cloud and sing, 'Hallelujah.'"

To See Thee More Clearly

FANNY CROSBY (1820-1915)

One day a Scottish minister told Fanny Crosby, the blind hymn writer, that it was too bad God did not give her the gift of sight. She responded, "If I had been given a choice at birth, I would have asked to be blind . . . for when I get to Heaven, the first face I will see will be the One who died for me."

One of her best known gospel songs, "Saved by Grace," echoes that same thought:

> Some day the silver cord will break,
> And I no more as now shall sing;
> But O, the joy when I shall wake
> Within the palace of the King!
>
> And I shall see Him face to face,
> And tell the story—Saved by grace.

1 John 3:2

Beloved, now are we the sons of God, and it doth not yet appear what we shall be; but we know that, when he shall appear, we shall be like him; for we shall see him as he is (KJV).

John's first letter draws sharp distinctions between light and darkness, love and hate, righteousness and sin. It reflects a persecuted, embattled church that needs the blessed assurance that John offers them. As God's children, we face a glorious future.

Another one of her songs, "My Savior First of All," expresses it this way:

> When my lifework is ended and I cross the swelling tide,
> When the bright and glorious morning I shall see,
> I shall know my Redeemer when I reach the other side,
> And His smile will be the first to welcome me.

When she was only six weeks old, Crosby developed a minor eye infection; the doctor recommended hot poultices, which destroyed her sight. Her father died before she was a year old, and she was raised by her mother and grandmother.

When she was eight she wrote her first poem:

> O, what a happy child I am,
> Although I cannot see!
> I am resolved that in this world
> Contented I will be.

And she was content. By the age of ten she could recite entire books of the Bible, including the four Gospels. She learned to play the guitar and soon was putting her poems to music. When she was fifteen she entered the School for the Blind in New York City and stayed there for eighteen years as a student and a teacher. At the school she met Alexander Van Alstyne, whom she married when she was thirty-eight.

Crosby did not always write hymns, as one might think. Although she had been writing songs since childhood, these were popular songs, with little or nothing to do with Christianity. But in 1864 when she was forty-four, she met hymn writer and publisher William Bradbury, who encouraged her to write gospel songs. And did she ever! Over the next half-century, she penned more than eight thousand hymns and gospel songs. Many of these have become favorites in evangelical churches.

Two of Fanny Crosby's gospel songs were revived by evangelist Billy Graham and used frequently in his crusades. "Blessed Assurance," which became almost synonymous with Graham, refers to "visions of rapture" that "burst on my sight." The other hymn, "To God Be the Glory," was well known in Great Britain but largely forgotten in the United States until the first Graham Crusade in London heard it. The last stanza closes with the words "But purer, and higher, and greater will be Our wonder, our transport when Jesus we see."

For Fanny Crosby, the blind writer of gospel songs, the essence of heaven was always "When he shall appear, we shall be like him; for we shall see him. . . ."

The Lady with the Lamp
FLORENCE NIGHTINGALE (1820-1910)

She was given the name Florence because she was born in Florence, Italy. But Florence was not the place where Nightingale was meant to be.

She was given the name Nightingale because her father, a banker, had inherited the estates of Peter Nightingale. Florence Nightingale lived the high-society life and was waited on by maids, footmen, valets, and coachmen. But British society was not the place for her.

She was a brilliant girl, and her father had taught her Greek, Latin, German, French, and Italian. She could read the Bible from the Greek text. But teaching and academia were not the areas for Nightingale.

She turned down several offers of marriage, one to a man who later became a member of Parliament, a poet, and an associate of Tennyson and Thackeray. A comfortable married life was not the place for Nightingale either.

> **Matthew 17:4**
>
> *Then answered Peter and said unto Jesus, Lord, it is good for us to be here* (KJV).
>
> ---
>
> Unfortunately, Peter wanted too much of a good thing. He and James and John had accompanied Jesus up a mountain, where Jesus suddenly was transfigured before them. Moses and Elijah appeared with Jesus, and Peter was ecstatic. He said, "It is good for us to be here," but then suggested that they put up three tents for the three shining figures, presumably shrines where they could be worshiped. A voice from heaven interrupted Peter's plans, identifying Jesus as God's beloved Son, and urging the disciples to listen to him.

As a teen she said, "I craved for some regular occupation, for something worth doing, instead of frittering time away on useless trifles." At the age of twenty-two she wrote, "My mind is absorbed with the idea of the sufferings of man. It besets me." Two years later she recognized her destiny was to serve the sick and the dying.

Of course, her parents didn't understand, and to tell the truth, Nightingale herself wasn't always single-minded about her direction in life. She loved people's attention; she danced well; she could be the life of the party; she enjoyed fine clothes and the glitter of society.

Nevertheless, she wrote in her diary, "I am thirty, the age at which Christ began his mission. . . . Now, Lord, let me think only of thy will." As she was traveling through Germany, she happened to visit the Institute of Protestant Deaconesses in Kaiserwerth, and the nurses there impressed her. Their life, though simple, was meaningful. "Now I know," she wrote.

When she returned to London, she took a position with the Institution for the Care of Sick Gentlewomen in Distressed Circumstances. Previously this organization had opened its doors only to women associated with the Church of England, but Nightingale insisted that the doors be open to other Protestants, Catholics, and Jews as well.

When a cholera epidemic erupted in London, Nightingale was appointed to coordinate the nursing of the disease. Every day she took great risks as she ministered to cholera patients, and her fame spread throughout the nation. When the Crimean War broke out, she went to superintend the volunteer nurses at the British military hospital near Scutari, Turkey. Within three weeks of her arrival, some three thousand patients were placed under her care. She had little time to do anything except tend to the sick and dying soldiers. But she wrote one letter, saying, "In the midst of this appalling horror there is good—and I can truly say, like St. Peter, 'It is good for us to be here'—though I doubt whether, if St. Peter had been here, he would have said so."

When others went to bed at night, Nightingale continued making the rounds, carrying her small lamp. A reporter wrote of her, "When . . . silence and darkness have settled upon those miles of prostrate sick, she may be observed alone, with a little lamp in her hand, making the solitary rounds." In a famous poem, Henry Wadsworth Longfellow immortalized her as "the Lady with the Lamp."

To a group of nurses she once said, "Christ is the author of our profession." Nightingale changed not only the field of nursing but also how people considered nurses, because she believed with the apostle Peter, "It is good for us to be here" (Matt. 17:4).

The Wages of Sin, the Promise of Death

FYODOR DOSTOEVSKY (1821-1881)

April 23, 1849, should have been the last day of his life. Arrested for subversive activities, along with fourteen other men, Fyodor Dostoevsky stood before a firing squad. Clothed in white burial shrouds, Dostoevsky and the other men were tied to posts upon a platform. A clerk read the charges and announced, "The wages of sin is death." A priest came by, allowing each condemned man to kiss the cross before dying.

"Ready! . . . Aim! . . ." Then a messenger rushed in with word from the czar that their lives were to be spared. Instead of being executed, they were sentenced to four years of hard labor in Siberia. "Now my life will change," Dostoevsky wrote to his brother. "I shall be born again in a new form."

Prison life was difficult, but Dostoevsky gained information he would later use in his books. This writing displayed a keen knowledge of the criminal mind and focused on issues of life and death, guilt and innocence. The only book he could read in prison was the New Testament, and this also had an impact on his later novels. Dostoevsky's wife once said, "He used to say that the Gospel was the only thing that kept hope alive in his heart. Only in that book did he find support; whenever he resorted to it, he was filled up with new energy and strength."

"There is a freeing of the spirit and joy to be had from reading Dostoevsky," wrote Nicholas Beryaev, "the joy that one gets from suffering. It is the path the Christian has to tread."

> **John 12:24**
>
> *Unless a kernel of wheat falls to the ground and dies, it remains only a single seed. But if it dies, it produces many seeds.*
>
> The drumbeats of crucifixion were beginning. Jesus had just had his triumphal entry into Jerusalem, but now he was preparing his disciples for what would happen next. He challenged them to greater commitment and used this simple analogy to hint about his death.

Released from prison, the author struggled to put his life together. He had developed epilepsy as a child, and in prison the attacks became more frequent. A magazine he edited was suppressed by the government (though he had given up his socialist ways). His first marriage failed. He developed a gambling habit. In order to pay off his creditors, he had to sign contracts to produce new books, often giving away valuable royalties.

In one such contract crunch, he had to finish a novel by a certain date or give up the rights to all of his books. This novel fittingly was called *The Gambler.* He hired a secretary to help him meet the deadline, and she also became his wife. Over the next decade and a half, with his wife's help, Dostoevsky produced perhaps the finest collection of fiction in Western literature, including *Crime and Punishment, The Idiot, The Possessed,* and *The Brothers Karamazov.*

Arts historian Daniel Boorstin notes that novels in the mid–nineteenth century were either moving outward or inward; in other words, some focused on major social issues while others took a microscope to the human soul. Dostoevsky's novels did both. Few novels have explored the thoughts and feelings of troubled human beings with such insight. In *Crime and Punishment,* a man rationalizes a murder, performs it, and then slowly goes mad—finding freedom only in confession. In *The Brothers Karamazov,* a man wishes the death of another and feels overwhelming guilt when he realizes that his hints caused someone else to do the deed.

And through all these plot twists and all this deep introspection is woven a thoroughly Christian sensibility. Jesus is there within the suffering, guiding the troubled souls to redemption.

Yet Dostoevsky avoided preaching to his readers—his characters preach to themselves as part of their own soul-searching. *The Brothers Karamazov* includes an extended story that one character tells, questioning how there could be a God who allows evil. The power of these questions indicates that the author himself pondered these same questions. In fact, Dostoevsky once said his faith was not the naïve acceptance of a child, "but [his] hosanna has come through a great furnace of doubt."

The dedication of that novel is a Bible verse—John 12:24. The same verse is found on Dostoevsky's tombstone. It bears witness to the conviction that faith is a life-and-death matter.

All Aboard!

HARRIET TUBMAN (1821-1913)

A railroad needs a conductor. And that's what Harriet Tubman was for the Underground Railroad, the secret network that rescued hundreds of slaves from the South prior to the Civil War. But Tubman preferred to be known as Moses— and that's appropriate. Between 1849 (when she escaped from slavery herself) and 1863 (when the Emancipation Proclamation was issued), she led between two hundred and three hundred slaves out of bondage.

Both whites and blacks risked their lives for the Underground Railroad, providing lodging, food, and clothing for the escapees. Their homes became known as depots. The slaves, of course, could not stay long in any one place but were passed along to other safe houses until they were out of danger. Quakers in the North were of particular help in providing depots, but when Harriet Tubman went South she was completely on her own.

> ### Exodus 15:1
>
> *Then sang Moses and the children of Israel this song unto the LORD, and spake, saying, I will sing unto the LORD, for he hath triumphed gloriously: the horse and his rider hath he thrown into the sea* (KJV).
>
> After centuries of slavery in Egypt, the Israelites were finally released by the Pharaoh. When they approached the Red Sea, they realized that Pharaoh's troops were chasing them. Miraculously, God opened a path through the water for his people and then closed it upon the pursuing Egyptians, drowning them. It was a glorious triumph, celebrated in song, with dancing and tambourines.

After escaping from slavery when she was about twenty-four years old, Tubman got a job in Philadelphia, where she earned enough money to go back across the Mason-Dixon line and rescue her sister and her sister's children. A few months later she went back to get her brother and two others. Then the trips became more frequent. The escapes were planned for a Saturday night so that the master could not start advertising for the missing slaves until Monday morning. Sometimes she would hire a black man to tear down posters giving information about

139

the missing slaves, and sometimes she would take her runaways farther south to confuse the pursuers.

Once in New York Tubman saw a freed slave being returned to his slavemaster under the Fugitive Slave Act. As the guards were taking him away, Tubman ran to the man, threw her arms around him, and made herself a hostage too. The guards beat her in an attempt to make her release him, but she wouldn't let go. Finally she was able to escape onto a boat, and on the other side of the river a wagon drove the ex-slave and Tubman to freedom. She was proud of her record of never having lost a slave that she took into her care. A lawyer who witnessed her bravery said, "How she came to be there is a mystery and where she hid herself afterwards is equally a mystery."

For Tubman it wasn't a mystery at all. God was in charge of her, just as he was in charge of Moses when he crossed the Red Sea. "Just so long as He wanted to use me, He would take care of me. . . . I always told Him: 'I'm going to hold on steady to You, and You've got to see me through.'"

She loved to sing Moses' songs, and her singing was her trademark. In fact, the song of Moses in Exodus 15 was part of her signal system for conducting her rescues. She also enjoyed discovering new spirituals as she went to different parts of the South. During the Civil War she joined the Union army as a laundress, cook, and nurse, but the job she most enjoyed was as a scout, spying behind Confederate lines. After the war she worked to establish schools for freedmen in North Carolina. Her biography was fittingly entitled *Harriet, the Moses of Her People.*

The Book That Led Its Own Author to Christ

LEW WALLACE (1827-1905)

By the time he wrote *Ben Hur: A Tale of the Christ,* General Lew Wallace had already achieved fame in several careers. He had served in both the Mexican War and the Civil War; he had practiced law; and he had been governor of the New Mexico territory.

Though he had a curiosity about religion, he was not a Christian. In his own words: "I was not in the least influenced by religious sentiment. I had no convictions about God or Christ. My ignorance of the Bible was painfully a spot of darkness in the darkness. I was ashamed of myself."

Once he had spent hours talking with the noted atheist Robert Ingersoll, and Ingersoll's arguments made Wallace determined to come up with some personal convictions of his own about religion. As Wallace started to read the New Testament, he was interested in the story of the wise men in Matthew 2. Who were they? Where in the East did they come from? After considerable research he wrote up his ideas thinking that someday he might develop them into a magazine article. Little did he know what would eventually develop from that research.

A few months later he spent an evening with friends, discussing religion, the Bible, and Jesus Christ. Wallace himself said very little that evening because he didn't have much to say. He had never thought religion was important, but after that discussion he considered the possi-

> ### Matthew 2:1
>
> *Now when Jesus was born in Bethlehem of Judea in the days of Herod the king, behold, there came wise men from the east to Jerusalem* (KJV).
>
> ---
>
> Many traditions surround these visitors from the East. People have long assumed that there were three of them, but Scripture only says that there were three gifts. Medieval tradition named them, but again the Bible does not. Some scholars think they followed a tradition Daniel had started in Persia, searching the skies for messages from Daniel's God.

bility that he had been wrong. Again, he suspected that the answers would be in the Bible.

Wallace felt that the best way to study something was to have a practical goal. So he told his wife he was going to write a book, and that the subject would be Jesus Christ. The first chapter would be derived from his research on the wise men, and the last chapter would be about the crucifixion. When his wife asked him what he would put in between, he replied, "I don't know yet."

His research and planning took seven years. In the middle of that time, he was appointed governor of the New Mexico territory. Occasionally his literary work would be temporarily disrupted by a war with Native American tribes or a death threat from the notorious outlaw Billy the Kid, but Wallace kept returning to his research and writing. Besides reading the Bible, he read every book he could find about the Bible. And as his research progressed, he more and more came to believe the Gospel accounts. By the time *Ben Hur: A Tale of the Christ* was completed, Lew Wallace was convinced that Jesus was indeed the Christ.

Wallace's story tells of Judah Ben-Hur, a patrician Jew whose enemy, Messala, causes him to be unjustly sentenced to the galleys and his family to be imprisoned. When Ben-Hur is freed, he enters a chariot race against Messala, and in the race Messala is defeated and maimed. Ben-Hur's mother and sister, freed by the new Roman procurator, Pontius Pilate, are cured of leprosy by Jesus shortly before his crucifixion.

The book quickly became a best-seller, with sales eventually passing the three million mark. In 1926 it was made into a silent film; its producers spent more than four million dollars to make it, a record up to that time. Then in 1959 it was remade as a three-and-a-half-hour epic blockbuster. Some critics have called it the greatest epic film ever made. The film, which cost fifteen million and took six years to make, was nominated for twelve Academy awards and won eleven.

And it all began because General Lew Wallace wanted to find out a bit more about the wise men.

A Novel Approach to Faith

LEO TOLSTOY (1828-1910)

Tolstoy is in a league with literary giants like Shakespeare. Best known for his realistic novels *War and Peace* and *Anna Karenina,* he also wrote short stories, plays, and essays. Tolstoy was also an important figure in Russia's social revolution and in religious reform. He changed the literary world, and he changed Russia.

At the age of eighteen he left college and scuttled his traditional faith. He spent four years enjoying Moscow society, another four years in the army, and about two years traveling in Europe. Then, after a brother's death, he began asking serious questions about the meaning of life. "Is there any meaning in my life which can overcome the inevitable death awaiting me?" he asked.

> ## Matthew 6:33
>
> *But seek ye first the kingdom of God, and his righteousness; and all these things shall be added unto you* (KJV).
>
> ---
>
> Jesus has just been discussing the importance of trusting God for the basic stuff of life—what you eat and what you wear. Worrying does no good, and we shouldn't serve money as our master. When we put God's kingdom first, "these things"—that is, basic provisions—will be supplied.

He wished he could ignore the question, but he couldn't. He had become Russia's most popular writer; he had become a leader, a guide, a teacher; yet he had to admit that he had no message to declare, no light to shed upon life, no clue to its mystery. He was in the prime of life with everything he had ever wanted, but he wasn't happy. "Thinking of the celebrity my books had brought me, I told myself, 'Fine, you will be more famous than Gogol, Pushkin, Shakespeare, Moliere, and all the writers in the world, and then what?'" He thought seriously about suicide.

One spring day when he was walking in the forest, Tolstoy took a big step of faith. God, like vodka, he said, was to be swallowed at a gulp without thinking. "As soon as man applies his intelligence and only his intelligence to any object at all, he unfailingly destroys the object," Tolstoy wrote in his notebook: "At the thought of God, happy waves of life welled up inside me. Everything came alive, took on meaning. I had only to know God, and I lived: I had only to forget Him, not to believe in Him, and I died. I only really live when I . . . seek Him. . . . Live to seek God and life will not be without Him. And stronger than ever rose up life within and around me, and the light that then shone never left me again."

Although Tolstoy rejected many of the doctrines of orthodox Christianity and was eventually excommunicated by the Russian Orthodox Church, he continued to search for truth. He loved the Gospels, but particularly the Sermon on the Mount. When he heard that the best version of the Bible was one used in the Netherlands, he started to learn Dutch, because he wanted to enjoy the Sermon on the Mount in a new language.

He confessed he would never know for sure why he was born or where he was going, as the Lord alone held the key to the mystery, but every day he prayed, "Lord, you who are within me, give me light, give me love."

In one of his later works, he asks: "What is the aim of human life? Why do I live? Only religion can answer that question. And this is the answer: Seek ye first the Kingdom of God and His righteousness, and all these things shall be added unto you. Living to ourselves, we seek happiness and do not find it; but seeking first the Kingdom of God and his righteousness, we obtain peace, freedom, and joy without seeking them. . . . You must understand that your life is not yours, not your property, but His who produced it for His own purposes."

When Two Are One

CATHERINE BOOTH (1829-1890)

Twenty-three-year-old Catherine Mumford was attracted to the new minister of the small Wesleyan church, and he was attracted to her. Yet it was obvious to Catherine that William Booth was not well educated and didn't know the Bible as well as she did. She was also bothered because his stand against drinking wasn't as firm as hers.

Catherine was not strong physically—as a child she had been rather sickly—but she was very forceful in expressing her opinions. One of her hobbies was to read theology books and then talk about them. In fact, one of her favorite books was Charles Finney's *Lectures on Revivals of Religion,* and she was delighted to discover it was a favorite of William Booth's as well.

William wanted to become engaged, but Catherine wasn't sure. She wrote to him, "I dare not enter into so solemn an engagement until you can assure me that you feel I am in every way suited to make you happy, and that you are satisfied that the step is not opposed to the will of God."

Two days later they spent time talking and praying together without coming to any conclusion as to whether or not they should be engaged. So they decided to use a method that they had heard John Wesley sometimes used: Take a Bible, balance it on its spine, and let it fall open; then be guided by the first passage you see. They tried it, and their Bible fell open to Ezekiel 37. The chapter is best known for its description of the

Ezekiel 37:19

Behold, I will take the stick of Joseph . . . and the tribes of Israel his fellows, and will put them with him . . . and make them one stick, and they shall be one in mine hand (KJV).

Ezekiel was a master of show-and-tell. Here God instructs him to take two sticks, write the names of Judah and Joseph on them, and tie them together. This symbolized how God would eventually reunite his divided people. Judah was the southern kingdom, which had recently been taken captive by Babylon. The two largest tribes of the northern kingdom were Ephraim and Manasseh, named after the sons of Joseph, and this kingdom had been annihilated centuries earlier. But through Ezekiel, God gives a vision of future glory and unity.

Valley of Dry Bones, not a typical passage for young lovers. But what William and Catherine saw were the last words of verse 19: "And they shall be one in mine hand" (KJV), and those were the words the couple wanted to read. Though their method of getting divine guidance is dubious at best, Catherine wrote to William: "The whirlwind is past and the succeeding calm is in proportion to its violence. . . . The more you lead me up to Christ in all things, the more highly I shall esteem you; and if it is possible to love you more than I do now, the more I shall love you."

She envisioned herself as the Old Testament judge Deborah, who accompanied her general, Barak, into battle. The analogy wasn't far off. Like the two sticks of Ezekiel 37, William and Catherine had become one in the Lord's hand. And like Deborah and Barak, they went together into battle.

Five years later she preached from her husband's pulpit and wrote a pamphlet defending the right of women to preach. After finding it difficult to work in Wesleyan denominations, the couple began their own Christian mission in London. Their work eventually grew into the Salvation Army. Revivalist evangelism was at the core of the Army's approach, but its concern for the social problems of the poor made it perhaps the only Christian movement of the nineteenth century to reach the masses.

Catherine also worked hard to improve the situation of women and children in a time when juvenile prostitution was on the rise in London. The age of consent was thirteen, and Catherine viewed this as a national disgrace. She and William initiated a petition that received 393,000 signatures, forming a stream of paper two and a half miles long. Among the things it petitioned was to raise the age of consent for girls to eighteen, to make the procuring of young people for prostitution or immoral purposes a criminal offense, and making men and women equal before the law, so that it would be just as criminal for a man to solicit a woman as for a woman to solicit a man. A new law was eventually passed, raising the age of consent to sixteen. This was not all that the Booths had asked for, but it was a victory nonetheless.

When Catherine died of cancer in 1890, an estimated fifty thousand people filed by her casket to pay their final tribute.

Have Faith in God

HUDSON TAYLOR (1832-1905)

People thought Hudson Taylor was a failure. He had gone to China in 1853 as an enterprising twenty-one-year-old, and all the other missionaries thought he made a fool of himself because he had some strange ideas about identifying with the people he served, wearing their clothes and using their language. He felt he had accomplished little, except to make himself a laughingstock. His frustration took a toll on his health, and, severing his ties with his mission board, he returned home to England a beaten man.

Fortunately, Taylor didn't give up. "I am quite willing to fail if you wish me to," he prayed, and he pressed on with his groundbreaking ideas. Within a few years he had founded the China Inland Mission, based on his principles of ministry. This would be a "faith mission"—missionaries would trust God for support and not ask people for money. It would also be interdenominational, "a voluntary union of members of varying denominations agreeing to band themselves together"—quite unusual for that day.

> ## Mark 11:22
>
> *And Jesus answering saith unto them, Have faith in God* (KJV).
>
> This saying comes from a puzzling event that occurred during the week before Jesus' crucifixion. As Jesus and his companions were walking along, they saw a fig tree with no figs. Jesus cursed the tree, saying it would never bear fruit again. The next day the disciples saw that the tree had completely withered and they were amazed. This verse is Jesus' response to their amazement, and he goes on to say the familiar words about moving mountains with one's faith. Interpreters have suggested all sorts of symbolic meanings for that tree, but the simplest meaning is that Jesus was demonstrating the power of faith in God, a lesson that Hudson Taylor learned well.

This was a gutsy act by a man who struggled with the fear of failure. "God chose me because I was weak enough," he said. "God does not do his great works by large committees. He trains somebody to be quiet enough, and little enough and then he uses them."

Taylor's faith-mission concept was based on three points. The first point was the Scripture verse "Have faith in God" (Mark 11:22 KJV), which was inscribed over one of the entrances to his London office. The second and third points were two Hebrew place names, Ebenezer and Jehovah-Jireh, which he translated into Chinese and painted in ideographs on a scroll.

The name Ebenezer comes from a story in 1 Samuel in which the prophet Samuel erected a memorial stone and called it Ebenezer, meaning "Hitherto the Lord has helped us." Taylor could be enthusiastic about his faith, but in times of discouragement the Chinese ideograph reminded him of what the Lord had done for him in the past.

The name Jehovah-Jireh was also painted on a scroll in Chinese ideographs. This place name comes from a story in Genesis in which God stopped Abraham from slaying his son and provided a ram as a substitute sacrifice. This name means "The Lord will provide."

Taylor also took the promises of the Bible and tested them. "I believe it means just what it says," he announced. For instance, the Bible says, "Pray ye therefore the Lord of the harvest, that he would send forth labourers into his harvest" (Luke 10:2 KJV). So he started to pray for more missionaries.

At times Taylor's faith faltered, but ultimately he realized, "If we are obeying the Lord, the responsibility rests with Him, not with us." A few years later he wrote back from China, "How to get faith strengthened? Not by striving after faith, but by resting on the Faithful One."

Apart from the faith-mission concept, Taylor also introduced several missionary innovations. He accepted candidates without college training; he required his missionaries to identify with the Chinese by wearing Chinese clothing; and he insisted that the control of the mission operation be from the field, not from a London headquarters. Women, both single and married, received official appointment as well as men, and all missionaries were to share financially in what was received. Taylor said, "It is always helpful to realize . . . that the work of God does not mean so much man's work for God, as God's own work through man."

In 1890 the China Inland Mission reported 641 missionaries, 462 Chinese workers, and 260 mission stations. The concepts on which the mission was founded were soon adopted by other faith missions, and now there are more than 100 faith missions with more than 7,000 missionaries around the world.

Snow Job

CHARLES HADDON SPURGEON (1834-1892)

Despite a blizzard, fifteen-year-old Charles Spurgeon trudged off to church as he normally did on Sunday mornings. But the heavy snow kept him from going to his usual place of worship; instead he found refuge in a Primitive Methodist church.

The teenager knew all about Christianity but had never made a life-changing commitment to Jesus Christ. "It was my sad lot," he wrote later, "to feel the greatness of my sin without a discovery of the greatness of God's mercy."

The Primitive Methodist church almost didn't open that morning. But the caretaker thought that a few people might show up, and so he opened the doors and lit the stove. By 11:00 some twelve to fifteen people had come inside, but not the minister. He apparently had been unable to make it through the snow.

Isaiah 45:22

Look unto me, and be ye saved, all the ends of the earth (KJV).

This section of Isaiah contains several intriguing prophecies about the Messiah. It might also be characterized as God's wooing of his captive people because he keeps telling them of the plans he has for them. Times may be tough now, he says, but better times lie ahead. He also asserts his rights as the Creator, the source of their strength, and the one true God. "I am God, and there is no other," he says in this verse and elsewhere. And don't miss the fact that "the ends of the earth" are invited to receive salvation—not just his chosen people, Israel.

Finally one of the laymen of the congregation reluctantly agreed to take the pulpit. As he looked down, he could see the small congregation, a couple hundred empty seats, and a strange boy seated under the gallery. The text for the sermon was "Look unto me, and be ye saved" (Isa. 45:22 KJV), and after about ten minutes of repeating himself, the man was about to step down from the pulpit. But before he did, he addressed the teenager under the gallery. "Young man," he said, "you look very miserable, and you always will be miserable if you don't obey my text. But if you do obey now, this moment, you will be saved." He paused again, then shouted at young Spurgeon with more animation

149

than he had shown in his entire sermon. "Young man, look to Jesus! Look! Look! Look!"

This substitute preacher and his boring sermon was what the Holy Spirit used to bring Charles Spurgeon to Christ. "There and then the cloud was gone," Spurgeon recalled. "The darkness was rolled away."

After that, everything happened quickly. At age sixteen he preached his first sermon; at seventeen he became pastor of a church; and at twenty he was called to be the pastor of the prestigious New Park Street Church in London. Within a year the building had to be enlarged to accommodate the crowds. The congregation outgrew the enlarged building and moved into Exeter Hall, and from there to the Surrey Gardens Music Hall. In 1861 when Spurgeon was twenty-seven, the congregation moved into the Metropolitan Tabernacle, which seated six thousand, and the church was filled every Sunday for the next thirty years.

At first the boy preacher was a novelty. Other clergymen scoffed at this young man who had no college or seminary training. But soon it seemed that all of London was coming to hear his sermons, including mayors, sheriffs, lords, earls, and even royalty. He started Pastor's College to help young men who could not afford to pay tuition. He started an orphanage that housed five hundred children. He launched a colportage association with about one hundred book-and-Bible salesmen who went door-to-door, peddling gospel literature. Then there were satellite churches, Sunday schools, a magazine, and a stream of books that the public demanded. It is estimated that his writings could fill a twenty-seven-volume encyclopedia. During his thirty-four-year ministry, he preached to an estimated ten million people.

When he died in 1892, all of England, including the Prince of Wales and the British prime minister, mourned his death. A crowd of about one hundred thousand came to his funeral.

And it all started forty-two years earlier, when a caretaker opened the church doors on a snowy January morning, and a substitute preacher gave a bumbling sermon on "Look unto me, and be ye saved" (Isa. 45:22 KJV). The boy under the gallery looked to God, and that changed the world.

That Same Old Verse

DWIGHT L. MOODY (1837-1899)

Whenever Dwight Moody went anywhere, unexpected things happened. At the age of eighteen he went to Boston and got a job at his uncle's shoe store. It was in that shoe store that he found Christ. "It was the most delicious joy that I'd ever known," he recalled later.

When he was nineteen he went to Chicago to make a fortune selling shoes. He sold shoes, lots of them, but he enjoyed the Sunday school he had started more than his job. By the time he was twenty-three, the Sunday school attendance had grown to 1,500 students. Even President-elect Abraham Lincoln visited it one Sunday.

When he was thirty he went to England so his wife could regain her health. While there, he met Charles Spurgeon and George Muller, two Christian leaders he greatly admired, but what changed his life was when he happened to meet a converted pickpocket named Harry Moorehouse. Moorehouse followed Moody back to the States and invited himself to preach at Moody's church. Moody wasn't too sure of how good a preacher Moorehouse was, but he thought it would be safe to let him preach on Thursday and Friday night, when he himself would be out of town.

When Moody returned, he asked his wife how Moorehouse did. She was enthusiastic and told her husband that Moorehouse had preached both times on the same text: John 3:16. Moody asked Moorehouse to stay through Saturday night so he could hear him. Again Moorehouse's

> ### John 3:16
>
> For God so loved the world, that he gave his only begotten Son, that whosoever believeth in him should not perish, but have everlasting life (KJV).
>
> This is probably the best-known verse of Scripture, and it encapsulates the message of the gospel and essentially the meaning of the whole Bible. Jesus says this during his discussion with the inquiring Pharisee Nicodemus. Jesus had just told him he needed to be born again through God's Spirit. Then Jesus compared himself to the bronze serpent that Moses lifted up in the wilderness (Num. 21:8–9). Those who looked to it in faith were healed of their deadly disease.

text was John 3:16, and just as surprising to Moody was that most of the congregation had brought Bibles with them. Moody invited Moorehouse to speak on Sunday through the following Thursday. Each time Moorehouse spoke on John 3:16. The last night he apologized, saying, "I have been trying to find a new text, but I can't find anything better than the old one," so he spoke on John 3:16 again.

After the message, Moorehouse talked privately with his host. "Mr. Moody, if you will change your course and learn to preach God's words instead of your own, He will make you a great power for good."

Moody was uneducated, his pronunciation was atrocious (one listener commented that Moody was the only person who could pronounce the name Nebuchadnezzar in two syllables), and his vocabulary was limited, so he had never pretended to be a great Bible scholar or theologian. But Moorehouse told him merely to study the Bible. Moody described this approach later: "If a text of Scripture troubles me, I ask another text to explain it, and if this will not answer, I carry it straight to the Lord."

Moody's ministry changed in four ways: His preaching became more focused on Scripture; he used public Bible readings as an adjunct to his message; he encouraged his audiences to bring their Bibles "to check up on him"; and he preached more on the love of God as revealed in John 3:16.

Moody confessed later: "I used to preach that God was behind the sinner with a double-edged sword ready to hew him down. . . . I never knew . . . that God loved us so much. . . . I took up that word 'Love,' and I do not know how many weeks I spent in studying the passages in which it occurs, till at last I could not help loving people. This heart of mine began to thaw out; I could not hold back the tears. . . . If outsiders could find that people in them loved them when they came, the churches would soon be filled."

Moody's ministry kept expanding. He traveled more than a million miles and preached to an estimated one hundred million people. England and Scotland opened up to him, and his preaching produced a revival that the British Isles had not seen since the days of the Wesleys. In America he held crusades in all the major cities, and thousands responded to the message of God's love. Probably about 750,000 professed faith in Christ through Moody's ministry. He also began the Moody Bible Institute of Chicago, a literature outreach, a school for girls and another for boys, a Bible conference, and much more.

When the Spirit Says Move

THE PENTECOSTAL/CHARISMATIC
MOVEMENT (1906)

No branch of Christianity ever exploded around the world as the charismatic movement did in the twentieth century. At the beginning of the century, the number of Pentecostal believers was less than one hundred; now the number is in the hundreds of millions. The hallmark of the movement is speaking in tongues, a practice traced to the Day of Pentecost in Acts 2, when the disciples in Jerusalem amazed onlookers and three thousand people were converted.

Speaking in tongues had occurred in various parts of the country in the late 1800s, but until the dawn of the twentieth century the examples were isolated. Then in 1900 in Topeka, Kansas, Charles Parham encouraged his students at the Bethel Bible College to seek the baptism of the Holy Ghost, evidenced by speaking in tongues.

In 1905 Parham spread the Pentecostal message to a suburb of Houston, Texas, and the following year it burst upon a

> ### Acts 2:4
>
> And they were all filled with the Holy Ghost, and began to speak with other tongues, as the Spirit gave them utterance (KJV).
>
> ---
>
> "They" were the followers of Jesus—120 of them—gathered together seven weeks after his resurrection. Pentecost was a feast day for the Jews, so many people had made a pilgrimage to Jerusalem from foreign countries. These pilgrims were amazed to hear preaching in their own languages. Scholars disagree on the exact nature of these utterances. Was it an ecstatic language that people heard as if it were their own, or did God miraculously give the disciples the ability to speak various languages? And what relation does this tongues-speaking have to later instances in Acts and 1 Corinthians?

small African-American congregation in Los Angeles. Needing an assistant pastor, the congregation called William J. Seymour of Houston. When Seymour came, the text for his first message was Acts 2:4. The pastor of the church, who did not speak in tongues, was offended by the teaching and padlocked the church doors the following Sunday. Most of the congregation followed their new assistant pastor to a nearby house, however, and when the house could not accommodate the crowds—actually, the crowds caused the building to collapse—Seymour and his congregation moved to an old building on Azusa Street, in an industrial section of Los Angeles.

A humble, one-eyed man with a halting delivery style, Seymour was a surprising candidate to start a religious revival. He had "no more emotionalism than that post," one observer commented. Seymour took no offerings and he did no advertising, but during the next three years, people came from around the world to the Azusa Street Mission. The Pentecostal movement based on Acts 2:4 had begun.

It quickly spread across the United States and into Canada. Soon new denominations were formed, and while these denominations grew rapidly in the first half of the century, it wasn't until 1960 that the "tongues" movement broke through to the major denominations. This is often referred to as the second wave of the Pentecostal movement. An Episcopalian rector, Dennis Bennett, began speaking in tongues and told his congregation about it. Soon Episcopalians, Catholics, Presbyterians, and others began speaking in tongues.

The third wave began in the 1970s. New denominations like the Calvary Chapel movement, led by Chuck Smith, and the Vineyard church movement, led by John Wimber, began growing rapidly across the country. These newer groups accepted tongues-speaking as one of the gifts of the Spirit but did not place emphasis on the baptism of the Spirit as traditional Pentecostals did. The third wave emphasized the *charisma,* the gifts of the Spirit (Romans 12; 1 Corinthians 12, 14), and so the trend became known as the charismatic movement.

As denominational distinctives seemed less and less important to much of Protestantism and Catholicism, the dynamic approach of the charismatics was very attractive. Charismatics seemed to enjoy their worship and get more out of it. Soon worship styles from the third wave were infiltrating all branches of the Christian church.

The humble, one-eyed preacher on Azusa Street knew that God could do great things, but he probably never suspected how much his sermon on Acts 2:4 would change the world.

The Preacher and the Peasant Girl

ABRAHAM KUYPER (1837-1920)

Abraham Kuyper was a parish preacher in the little community of Beesd in the Netherlands, but he had nothing to preach about. The son of a minister, he had lost his faith when he attended the University of Leyden. Later he commented, "The inherited faith lost its root in my heart; it shriveled under the withering heat of unbelief. Of the old treasures I retained nothing."

Not only had he retained nothing of the Christian faith, but he also became hostile to the gospel. Yet when "life began to be an earnest thing, then [he] realized . . . how poor and empty, how devitalized and comfortless, the new religion of our time had left [him]."

In his parish there were some rather odd people; he tried to understand them, but it was difficult. He recalled:

> ### 1 Corinthians 1:27
> God hath chosen the foolish things of the world to confound the wise; and God hath chosen the weak things of the world to confound the things which are mighty (KJV).
>
> Wisdom is a major theme in the opening chapters of this epistle. The Corinthians prized human wisdom—after all, they were the philosophical heirs of Socrates, Plato, and Aristotle. But Paul challenged them, declaring that the foolishness of God is wiser than man's wisdom (1 Cor. 1:25), and "the wisdom of this world is foolishness in God's sight" (1 Cor. 3:19). The message of the cross seemed like nonsense to many erudite Greeks, but that was precisely the "foolish thing" that would confound them.

They had interest in spiritual matters. Above all, they knew something. I could not measure my impoverished Bible knowledge with that of these plain people. And not only in Bible knowledge. They had a consistent view of life. . . . But what vexed me most was their uncompromising spirit. Budge they would not, not an inch. I found myself at a fork in the road. Either I must take a sharp position against them or go with them without conditions.

A poor peasant girl named Pietje Baltus once talked with Kuyper, and he listened because she seemed to have something that he didn't have.

She told him that she had a hope within her, and that he too must have it or he would perish eternally. She also prayed for him every day. "I could not relax," she said, "until the Lord himself came and took him from my soul, and until I had the happiness of knowing that Christ had him in charge."

Kuyper was a brilliant graduate of a prestigious university; Pietje was an unschooled peasant girl. But God has chosen the foolish things of the world to confound the wise, the Bible says, and "the preaching of the cross is to them that perish foolishness." He later wrote that as Pietje Baltus continued to pray for him, "the warmth of the gospel began to drive out the freezing chill of philosophy. [He] came to the conviction that the foolishness of the cross was the highest and only wisdom, and with a heart of thanksgiving [he] ranged [himself] with those who fought under its banner."

And he certainly took up the banner. Kuyper became an ardent student of Scripture and wrote about two hundred books, including many commentaries. When he moved to Amsterdam he became the editor of a semireligious, semipolitical weekly paper. Soon he was regarded as the leading journalist of the Netherlands. In 1870 he founded the Free University of Amsterdam, where he served as professor of theology. His writings during this time offered Christians a consistent worldview and a clear way of understanding and interacting with a fallen culture. In 1874 he became a member of the Dutch Parliament and fought for the poor and disenfranchised. In 1901 he was elected prime minister of the Netherlands, and he served in that capacity for four years.

What he enjoyed most, however, was preaching the Word of God, and in his preaching he stressed both the sovereignty of God and the necessity of a deep devotional life. "Stress on creedal confession," he once wrote, "runs dry in barren orthodoxy, just as truly as spiritual emotion, without clearness in confession standards, makes one sink in the bog of sickly mysticism."

The great prime minister had learned a great lesson from unschooled little Pietje, and once again God was turning worldly wisdom and foolishness upside down.

The "Whatsoever" Woman

FRANCES WILLARD (1839-1898)

On the flyleaf of Frances Willard's Bible is this inscription:

FEBRUARY 17, 1877—On this sweet, eventful day in which, with every hour of study, my Bible has grown dearer, I take, as my life-motto henceforth, humbly asking God's grace that I may measure up to it, this wonderful passage from Paul: "And whatsoever ye do in word or deed, do all in the name of the Lord Jesus."

Frances Willard is known as a crusader for women's concerns, and it is largely because of her efforts that women got the right to vote. She also strongly influenced the Prohibition movement. Others were certainly involved in both battles, but the passage of the Eighteenth and Nineteenth Amendments owes a great debt to her.

> ## Colossians 3:17
>
> *And whatsoever ye do in word or deed, do all in the name of the Lord Jesus* (KJV).
>
> This verse caps a passage that is rich in Christian instruction. We are to clothe ourselves with compassion and other virtues, to bear with one another and forgive freely. Peace should rule our hearts, and the Word of Christ should live inside us as we sing songs of gratitude. Whatever we do should have the stamp of Christ upon it, and all of our words and deeds should reflect Christ.

As a youngster Willard was called a "little infidel" because she never accepted anything at face value. She was always asking *why* or *how do you know?* "They call me an infidel," she once said. "I consider myself an inquirer." At the age of nineteen she wrote, "If there is a God, a heaven, a hell, a devil, then I am undone." But a year later, after being stricken with typhoid fever and hearing a voice plead with her, "My child, give me thy heart," she finally surrendered to Jesus Christ.

She became a college president at the age of thirty-one, but a fire destroyed her plans for the school. Then she attended the first national convention of the Temperance Crusade in 1874 and became the corresponding secretary. But Willard's goals in life were bigger than just controlling the liquor traffic.

In 1876 she dropped out of temperance work because she began to feel that women's suffrage and prohibition had to go hand in hand—and the Women's Christian Temperance Union (WCTU) leadership disagreed. Willard also felt strongly about the "purely artificial limitations which prevented woman's participation in all the professions," but she wasn't making much headway on that front either.

So 1877 began with Frances Willard feeling quite discouraged. But then she read Colossians 3:17, which motivated her to do "whatsoever" in the name of Jesus Christ. Shortly after that the evangelist D. L. Moody asked her to hold "ladies meetings" every afternoon in his Boston evangelistic campaign, which she did very successfully.

Next she crusaded to give women the right to vote on temperance issues. Collecting 180,000 signatures in three months, she preached that "prohibition is the nail, but woman's ballot is the hammer that must drive it home." When she went to the national convention again in 1879, she was elected president, and for the next sixteen years she controlled the WCTU. She was no Carrie Nation, who went into taverns wielding an ax, but she was an organizer who mobilized women all across the country. Willard trained her leadership so well that they eventually led the women of America to secure the passage of the Nineteenth Amendment, guaranteeing women the right to vote.

But Frances Willard did not like to use the phrase "women's rights." "Not rights, but duties," she declared; "not her need alone, but that of her children and her country; not the 'woman,' but the 'human' question is stirring women's hearts and breaking down their prejudices today."

After her death, the U.S. Congress extolled Frances Willard as the "first woman of the nineteenth century, the most beloved character of her times."

The Winds of War . . . and Peace
WOODROW WILSON (1856-1924)

Woodrow Wilson, twenty-seventh president of the United States, winner of the Nobel Peace Prize in 1919, victor in World War I, and designer of the League of Nations, won many battles but lost the ones that really mattered to him. And Wilson was not a good loser.

As president of Princeton University, he once threatened to resign when he was rebuffed by his board of directors. The board compromised and Wilson stayed on. A few days later he spoke to the undergraduates on the text of Ecclesiastes 11:4 ("He that observeth the wind shall not sow; and he that regardeth the clouds shall not reap" [KJV]). He interpreted the verse this way: "The world is not looking for servants—there are plenty of these—but for masters, men who form their purposes and then carry them out, let the consequences be what they may." That was how Woodrow Wilson ran his life.

Ecclesiastes 11:4

He that observeth the wind shall not sow; and he that regardeth the clouds shall not reap (KJV).

Ecclesiastes is an odd book of the Bible. The author, possibly Solomon, often seems cynical and depressed. "Everything is meaningless!" he declares, after searching for meaning in wealth, work, pleasure, and other pursuits. And yet as the book draws to a close, there are some nuggets of wisdom. Chapter 11 notes a certain pattern in nature. Clouds bring rain, trees lie where they fall, and natural disasters will occur, but we never know when. So we shouldn't spend all our time watching the Weather Channel, or we'll never get around to sowing or reaping.

The son of a southern Presbyterian minister, Woodrow was raised in a family that practiced daily Bible reading and prayed on bended knee. From their strong religious faith, suggests one biographer, came "conviction, self-control, [and] determination," which later in life gave the impression of some kind of "secret understanding between Thomas Woodrow Wilson and his Creator. . . . It was his strength—and his weakness." Indeed, Wilson conveyed a sense of always knowing the right thing to do and scorned those who disagreed.

159

After two years as governor of New Jersey, Wilson was encouraged to run for the presidency. It took forty-six ballots before the Democrats nominated him as their candidate. Wilson told his campaign manager, "You know I am a Presbyterian and believe in predestination. . . . It was providence that did the work." Wilson was elected president a few months later only because Republicans split their votes between Teddy Roosevelt and William Howard Taft.

Not observing the wind of public opinion, Woodrow Wilson was a vigorous president and formulated precise proposals for Congress to enact. When war began in Europe during his first term, Wilson maintained neutrality. The slogan for his reelection campaign was "He kept us out of the war," and once again he eked out a victory.

However, after Germany sank three American ships, public sentiment demanded a military response. Wilson was slow to act; "We are not governed by public feeling. I want to do right whether it is popular or not," he said. Yet he had no choice. The United States entered World War I as Wilson declared, "The world must be safe for democracy."

But Wilson's primary concern was not necessarily to win the war but to make peace. With this objective in mind, Wilson put forth his Fourteen Points, which was a blueprint for world peace. Wilson went to Paris to push ahead peace negotiations and returned with not just the Versailles Treaty, which ended the war, but also a League of Nations proposal, which he believed was the only way future wars could be averted.

Wilson was awarded the Nobel Peace Prize for his efforts, but his unyielding stance on the details of the League of Nations antagonized the opposition. During a nationwide train trip to rouse support for the plan, Wilson collapsed and never fully recovered. Unable to carry on the fight, he had to sit back and watch others fight a losing battle for him. In 1921 he was succeeded as president by Warren G. Harding, who said, "We seek no part in directing the destinies of the world."

But there is no doubt that Woodrow Wilson helped establish America's role as peacemaker, and he did it by sowing regardless of the wind.

Base Paths to Sawdust Trails

BILLY SUNDAY (1862-1935)

The evangelist Billy Sunday was remarkable and transformed the world in more ways than one. It was said that he preached to more people than any other man in the history of Christianity. Of course, that was before radio, TV, and Billy Graham. But nevertheless, about a million people responded to Sunday's gospel invitation.

Sunday was remarkable not only in his popularity but in his rise to fame as well. Growing up in Iowa, he spent two years in an orphanage, where he got a grammar school education. He worked as an undertaker's assistant when he was twenty and played baseball for the local team. When his team won the state championship, he attracted the attention of "Pop" Anson, legendary manager of the Chicago White Stockings. Soon Sunday was playing in the major leagues, where he gained fame for his fielding and his ability to steal bases. Until 1962 only the legendary Ty Cobb exceeded Billy Sunday's record for base-stealing.

One day in 1886 Sunday and some teammates were invited to the Pacific Garden Mission. He went and was converted. Five years later he gave up baseball and began working with the YMCA and then worked as an assistant to the Presbyterian evangelist J. Wilbur Chapman. In 1895, when Chapman returned to the pastorate, Sunday decided to conduct evangelistic services on his own.

The first years were difficult. The separation from his wife and children was difficult for Sunday, and it affected his wife, Nell, even more;

> ## Psalm 34:9–10
>
> *O fear the LORD, ye his saints: for there is no want to them that fear him. . . . They that seek the LORD shall not want any good thing* (KJV).
>
> ---
>
> Psalm 34 is a psalm about God's goodness and testifies to the way that the Lord has met David's needs. Ironically, this psalm was written when David was on the run from the murderous King Saul. During one of the most trying times of his life, David found solace in writing this lovely psalm. "Taste and see that the Lord is good," he says (v. 8 KJV). Obviously these verses are talking about needs, not luxuries. Verse 19 warns that the righteous will have many problems, but that the Lord will provide a way out.

by 1907 she was facing physical and nervous exhaustion. And Sunday, who always liked Psalm 34, now gravitated toward verses 9 and 10: "There is no want to them that fear him. . . . They that seek the Lord shall not want any good thing" (KJV).

After a short rest Nell began accompanying her husband, serving as his administrator, and soon Sunday was a nationally recognized figure. The small towns of Iowa were in the past—now he was preaching in cities like Philadelphia, Kansas City, Detroit, Boston, and New York. Major newspapers and magazines were covering him, and he dined with big-city mayors and even presidents. When Woodrow Wilson asked him to help sell war bonds, he gladly did so. *American Magazine* put him on their "Greatest Man in America" list.

Unlike his predecessors John Wesley, Dwight L. Moody, and J. Wilbur Chapman, who never asked for money, Sunday became obsessed with it. When someone wanted Sunday's autograph, he frequently wrote Psalm 34 under his name. The Lord had blessed him, Sunday could say, and so there wasn't any good thing (v. 10) that he lacked as far as material goods were concerned. Local newspapers started to become critical; they questioned the extravagant amount that the Sunday family spent on clothing. While the Sundays gave generous gifts to charity, they added tens of thousands of dollars each year to their savings and investment accounts. Unlike some later evangelists like Billy Graham, who received a designated salary from his board of directors, the Sundays were their own board of directors. Largely because of the Sundays' attitude regarding money, evangelists became a laughingstock.

To be sure, Billy Sunday changed the world in good and bad ways. Many came to faith in Christ through Sunday's animated preaching, but many others have been turned off to the gospel by Sunday's emphasis on money.

Gathering Up
a Fragmented Society

EDGAR HELMS (1863-1942)

In thousands of communities in America and around the world, the work of Goodwill Industries is well known. But not too many people know the story behind Goodwill.

In one of his last letters, Edgar Helms explained, "I have often been referred to as the founder of Goodwill Industries. This is not strictly true. The originator of Goodwill Industries was the Master of men who spoke from a Galilean hillside and commanded his disciples to 'gather up the fragments . . . that nothing be lost.'"

Edgar Helms, a Methodist minister, had a mission church in Boston's slums. For some pastors, a mission church might be a satisfactory place to start a career, but they would never want to spend their

> ### John 6:12
>
> Gather up the fragments that remain, that nothing be lost (KJV).
>
> Jesus took a boy's lunch of five loaves and two fish and fed a multitude that numbered more than five thousand. After gathering up the leftovers, the disciples had twelve baskets of extra food. The fact that there were twelve baskets of extra food demonstrates that the miracle was no figment of the disciples' imagination. And, as he did in his first miracle when he turned water into wine, Jesus provided more than enough.

whole lives there. Not so for Helms. He had come from a poor family and never forgot what it was like to be poor.

As an adult Helms got a job with a newspaper and after sixteen years he was able to own the paper himself. As the publisher, he showed his concern for the poor and wrote strong editorials about those who mistreated the poor.

After his work with the newspaper, Helms felt that God wanted him to preach. He was given a mission church in Boston's slums, and shortly after he arrived, a group of residents came to him asking for food and clothing. Helms had been around underprivileged people much of his life, but he had never seen such need as these people had.

What could he do? Helms remembered the words of Jesus after he had fed the five thousand. Jesus had sent his disciples back to pick up the remnants "that nothing be lost" (John 6:12 KJV). And that's what Helms began doing. With a burlap sack over his shoulder, he went to the ritzy Beacon Hill section of Boston and told his story. Every day he filled his sacks and rode the streetcar back to his mission. When the streetcar conductor refused to give space to Helms's bulky bags, Helms borrowed a wheelbarrow to collect the old clothes.

When Helms got back to the mission, he spread the clothes out in the small auditorium and invited the poor to help themselves, but he was disappointed to see how they pushed and shoved, greedily grabbing everything they could. He learned that the poor must pay something for the clothing, and if they had no money, he put them to work to earn some. Some of the women mended the clothing; some of the men mended the furniture. These workers were paid and with their pay they bought what they needed. That is the way Goodwill Industries began.

The success of Helms's Goodwill project inspired others. It was not his idea to make a huge organization, but he found himself invited to many states and countries to explain the Goodwill plan. Soon there were hundreds of Goodwill Industries across the country, and nearly fifty affiliated groups in other countries.

Today the program provides disabled and socially disadvantaged people with employment, job training, job placement, and vocational evaluations. It is financed partly through the sale of donated clothing and household items. And God continues to multiply the "fragments" that are picked up.

Master of the Peanut

GEORGE WASHINGTON CARVER (1864-1943)

Born into a slave family, George Washington Carver became America's foremost agricultural scientist. His efforts helped to free southern farmers, both black and white, from the poverty that followed the Civil War. From the peanut he made milk, soap, salad oil, ice cream, and more than three hundred other products. From the sweet potato, he produced an egg yolk substitute, vinegar, soap, ink, and about 150 other things. He was always making something out of some ordinary object. The secret of his success? "Simple," he would say. "It is found in the Bible: 'In all thy ways acknowledge him, and he shall direct thy paths.'"

Proverbs 3:6

In all thy ways acknowledge him, and he shall direct thy paths (KJV).

Proverbs might be called a primer for life. It is clearly written in an educational mode, calling young people to listen and learn. Later chapters are collections of pithy aphorisms, but these early chapters present a clear example of how to live a life of wisdom, self-control, and absolute trust in the Lord.

When George Washington Carver died, Congress officially mourned his passing, and state legislatures eulogized him. Even President Franklin Roosevelt declared, "The world of science has lost one of its most eminent figures. . . . All mankind is beneficiary of his discoveries in the field of agricultural chemistry."

Of course, Carver hadn't always been so honored. Shortly after his birth, he and his mother were kidnapped by marauding nightriders from a Missouri plantation. His mother was sold to another slaveowner, but no one wanted the sickly baby. Eventually, the original slaveowners recognized the baby, traded a racehorse for him, and named him George Washington.

As a young man, George Washington Carver worked his way through Iowa State College of Agriculture and Mechanic Arts and two years later joined its faculty. When the noted black leader Booker T. Washington invited him to join the Tuskegee Institute in Alabama as its director of agricultural research, he accepted. He stayed there the rest of his life.

At Tuskegee, Carver became famous for his discoveries. He once said, "My discoveries came like a divine revelation from God. In half an hour after the idea was revealed to me, I produced the yolk of an egg from the Puerto Rico sweet potato. . . . Anything will give up its secrets, if you love it enough."

At the turn of the century, peanuts were a minor crop, but by 1923 a Montgomery newspaper reported that fifty-three million bushels of peanuts had been grown, making seven million pounds of peanut butter and three million pounds of oil. "All of this came from Carver," the paper said.

Carver told of a conversation he had with God early in his career.

"Dear Creator, please tell me what the universe was made for."
Said the Creator, "You want to know too much for such a little mind as yours. Ask for something your size."
"Dear Creator, tell me what man was made for."
Again the great Creator replied, "Little one, you are still asking too much."
Finally I asked, "Tell me then, Creator, what the peanut was made for."
After that, the great Creator taught me how to take the peanut apart and put it together again.

This scientist obviously enjoyed life and God's creation. "A personal relationship with the great Creator of all things is the only foundation for the abundant life," he said. "Walk and talk with God and let Him direct your path."

During his first years at Tuskegee, several students came into Carver's laboratory and asked him to teach them the Bible. The class continued every Sunday morning for three decades as more and more students came to hear him expound on God's Word. One student commented, "He knew the Bible thoroughly, and he made it a practice to illustrate his talks from the Word. Many times he brought objects from the laboratory."

"You see," Carver often said, "there is no need for anyone to be without direction, or to wander amid the perplexities and complexities of life. We are plainly told, 'In all thy ways acknowledge him, and he shall direct thy path.' So why go blundering along our poor, blind way when God has told us he will help us?"

Pennies from Heaven

J. C. PENNEY (1875-1971)

The Golden Rule has changed the world many times over, but J. C. Penney, the chain-store tycoon, made it the motto of his business. John Brooks, a writer for *The New Yorker,* characterized Penney in a tongue-in-cheek fashion. "If a novelist had invented him, the resulting character would surely have been ridiculed by critics as too typecast, too broadly drawn for belief. Even his name was too good to be true: J. C. (Jesus Christ?) Penney—the meeting of religion and money."

Born in Missouri, Penney made money as a boy by raising pigs and watermelons. Later he ran a butcher shop, but the business failed because he wouldn't deal with hotels that served liquor. He went out to Kemmerer, Wyoming, and worked at a dry goods store, buying a one-third interest in the store in 1902. This store developed into a chain of what he called the "Golden Rule Stores."

> ## Luke 6:31
>
> *Do to others as you would have them do to you.*
>
> ---
>
> The Golden Rule appears in Matthew 7:12 as part of Jesus' Sermon on the Mount, and also here in Luke's shortened version of that message. In Luke, this verse appears along with the challenge to love our enemies. We don't need a challenge to love those who love us; that comes naturally. But the power of the Golden Rule is that it applies to everyone—friends, enemies, strangers on the street, and business partners. We should treat them as we want to be treated.

In 1908 Penney operated four stores; by 1911 the number had jumped to twenty-two, and by 1916 there were 127 stores. One key element in Penney's success was that he made store managers partners in the business. In 1931 Penney wrote his autobiography and called it *The Man with a Thousand Partners,* because by that time he had one thousand J. C. Penney Golden Rule Stores, and each manager had a share in the company.

Penney became a multimillionaire before he was fifty years old. Not only did he control his one thousand Golden Rule Stores, but he also ran corporations and was the head of a large bank in Miami. He was known for his "Penney Principles," five simple statements that amplified the Golden Rule and expressed his desire to serve the public honestly.

But as the Great Depression struck, the real estate boom collapsed in southern Florida. At first Penney thought it was only a temporary recession, and so he poured more money into his Miami bank. His charities and foundations were also suffering, so Penney shored these up by selling some of the stock of his company. But when the Miami bank was forced to close, J. C. Penney lost millions, and so did other investors. Now the public began to doubt his Golden Rule philosophy; some even attacked Penney's character, calling him a hypocrite and a fraud that only used the Golden Rule to attract business. Penney said later, "It was the first time the honor of any of my dealings had been questioned."

Everything he had worked so hard for was unraveling. He went to the hospital for what doctors called emotional distress. He worried whether he would have enough money to pay the hospital bills if he survived. He even went so far as to write farewell notes to his wife and children because in his depression he expected to die before morning.

But in the morning he heard singing in the hospital halls. A Christian group was singing a gospel song: "Be not dismayed whate'er betide, God will take care of you." It was the message that Penney needed to hear. He prayed, "Lord, of myself I can do nothing. Will you take care of me?"

God did. After hitting that low point, Penney spent more time reading his Bible, more time depending on the Lord, and less time depending on his own abilities. And the J. C. Penney chain of stores grew back stronger than ever, still following the Golden Rule.

Later in life, when the chain had become the country's fifth largest merchandising operation, with annual sales in the billions, Penney said, "The company's success is due to the application of the Golden Rule to every individual, to the public, and to all of our activities."

Falling for the Savior

AMY CARMICHAEL (1867-1951)

Amy Carmichael made her mark on the century as a rescuer of India's temple prostitutes, and as a missionary, poet, and author. But what made a lasting mark on her were three Bible verses that came to her in her late teen years.

Carmichael's father died when she was eighteen, and during this time of grief her mother often quoted Nahum 1:7 to her children: "The LORD is good, a stronghold in the day of trouble; and he knoweth them that trust in him" (KJV). It was a verse that Carmichael would never forget.

A short time later, Carmichael and her brothers saw a shabbily dressed old woman burdened by heavy bundles and went to her rescue, carrying the load for her. At first Carmichael was embarrassed to be seen with such a disreputable woman, because respectable people passed by and gave the teenagers curious looks. "We plodded on," Carmichael wrote later, "a wet wind blowing us about, and blowing too the rags of that poor old woman, till she seemed like a bundle of feathers and we unhappily mixed up with them." And suddenly a New Testament verse came to her mind: "Every man's work shall be made manifest; for the day shall declare it." That afternoon Carmichael shut herself in her room and settled the pattern for her future life. Later she wrote, "I said nothing to anyone, but I knew that something had happened that had changed life's values. Nothing could ever matter again but the things that were eternal."

Jude 24

Now unto him that is able to keep you from falling, and to present you faultless before the presence of his glory with exceeding joy (KJV).

The main problem Jude addresses in this postcard-sized epistle is false teaching. He urges his readers to recognize the errors of those who "change the grace of our God into a license for immorality" (v. 4). He uses strong language to put down those heretics, but then he changes tone to comfort the weak. "Be merciful to those who doubt" (v. 22), he says, closing with the supportive benediction of verse 24. No matter how confusing the theological climate might be, God can keep you from falling.

A bit later she heard a speaker close a sermon with, "O Lord, we know Thou art able to keep us from falling," a benediction taken from the Epistle of Jude. Then at mealtime, when Carmichael's companions complained about their mutton chops being improperly cooked, Carmichael wondered, "What does it matter about mutton chops? O Lord, we know Thou art able to keep us from falling." Amy Carmichael, who kept track of insignificant dates in her life, wrote down, "September 23, 1886, the mutton-chop, keep-us-from-falling day."

Bible verses connected with her father's death, an encounter with an old woman, and a meal with poorly cooked mutton chops were used by God to shape Carmichael's life. Each verse, in its own way, reminded the teenager that eternal things were the only things that truly mattered.

In 1892 Carmichael applied to the China Inland Mission for overseas service but was turned down by the mission's doctor. Yet she was certain that God wanted her in mission work, so she applied and was accepted by another mission for service in Japan. However, after a whirlwind fourteen months in Japan, Carmichael became ill with what one doctor called "brain exhaustion" and another called "Japanese head." She returned home to recover. The following year she headed back to Asia, this time to India, where she worked without a furlough for the next fifty-six years until her death in 1951.

Strong-minded and enterprising, Carmichael eventually severed ties with her missionary society and began the Dohnavur Fellowship, which rescued children from prostitution. She had been horrified by the practices of Hinduism, which encouraged the temple slavery of children and the selling of boys and girls to Brahmin temple priests.

The Dohnavur Fellowship grew to accommodate hundreds of children who had been rescued from temple prostitution. The children who came to Dohnavur were cared for, educated, and trained for lives of productive service. Partly through Carmichael's efforts, the practice of dedicating little girls to the temples became illegal. The work at Dohnavur continues today. Its properties now cover about four hundred acres, including a hospital, sixteen nurseries, and several compounds, and many of the former temple prostitutes have become outstanding Christian workers.

In 1931 Amy Carmichael suffered a serious fall and was crippled for the rest of her life. Using her experiences with suffering, she wrote book after book, many of which have become Christian classics. Among them are *Rose from Brier, Gold Cord,* and *If.*

It is interesting that after God spoke to Amy Carmichael through a verse about how he keeps people from falling, it was a physical fall that resulted in her classic writings that helped change the world.

The Apostle of the Haphazard

OSWALD CHAMBERS (1873-1917)

Perhaps the biggest problem Oswald Chambers had was that he was gifted in so many different areas. As a boy he was an accomplished musician, and as a teenager he went to an art school in London. In his twenties he went to the University of Edinburgh, wrote poetry, and studied art along with archaeology. "My life work," he wrote, "is to strike for the redemption of the aesthetic Kingdom of the soul of man—music and art and poetry, or rather, the proving of Christ's redemption of it."

Then one day he heard God telling him, "I want you in my service—but I can do without you." Not accustomed to hearing voices, Chambers took the message seriously. When he returned to his lodgings, he saw a report from a ministerial training college in western Scotland, and he enrolled there immediately.

> ### Luke 11:13
>
> *If ye then, being evil, know how to give good gifts unto your children: how much more shall your heavenly Father give the Holy Spirit to them that ask him?* (KJV).
>
> ---
>
> Philosophers call this an argument from the lesser to the greater. We give good gifts to our kids. God is greater than we are. Therefore we can count on God to be even greater at giving good gifts. A few verses earlier we find the Lord's Prayer, along with the exhortation "Ask and it will be given you." As Oswald Chambers learned, we can rely on our loving Father to give us good things.

The turning point in Chambers's life came in 1906 after several very difficult years. "The Bible was the dullest, most uninteresting book in existence," he wrote, "and the sense of depravity, the vileness and bad-mouthedness of my nature, was terrific. . . . I was getting desperate. . . . I knew that if what I had was all the Christianity there was, the thing was a fraud. Then Luke 11:13 got hold of me." This verse says that although people can "give good gifts . . . how much more shall your heavenly Father give" (KJV).

Chambers simply claimed the promise "in dogged committal on Luke 11:13." He said, "I had no vision of heaven or of angels. I had nothing. I was as dry and empty as ever, no power or realization of God, no witness of the Holy Spirit." But when he spoke at a meeting and forty people came forward for prayer, he knew something was different.

He left school that year and became a missionary/teacher in Japan, the United States, and England. In 1910 he married Gertrude Hobbs, a stenographer who transcribed his sermons and later put his messages into book form, including the best-selling *My Utmost for His Highest*. He founded a Bible college in England and became a military chaplain with British troops serving in Egypt. He died in 1917 at the age of forty-three, from peritonitis after an appendicitis attack. At the time of his death he had no books published.

Chambers was always full of surprises, which made him a delightful speaker and writer. He told one man: "My strong advice to you is to soak, soak, soak in philosophy and psychology, until you know more of these subjects than ever you need consciously to think. . . . The man who reads only the Bible does not, as a rule, know it or human life."

"God never has museums," he said at another time, urging listeners to be unique specimens of what God wants to do in them and through them. "Let God be as original with other people as He is with you." He also said, "Never allow that the haphazard is anything less than God's appointed order, and be ready to discover the divine design anywhere."

Seven years after he died, Chambers's wife took her shorthand notes of his sermons and talks and began transcribing them. Not only did she produce *My Utmost for His Highest,* perhaps the best-selling daily devotional of all time, but more than thirty other Oswald Chambers books as well.

The General Who Prayed
DOUGLAS MACARTHUR (1880-1964)

General Douglas MacArthur had a colorful and sometimes controversial military career during the first seven decades of the twentieth century. He served as Theodore Roosevelt's aide in 1906; he was a much-decorated hero of World War I; he became West Point superintendent in the 1920s; he was appointed field marshal of the Philippine army in the 1930s; and then he retired from the U. S. Army.

Recalled to duty in 1941, MacArthur commanded all the U.S. Army forces in the Far East and then became commander of all the Allied forces in the Southwest Pacific. In 1945 he accepted the Japanese surrender on the battleship *Missouri*. As supreme commander of the Allied occupation forces in Japan, he brought a new liberal constitution to the conquered country. In 1950 when North Korea invaded South Korea, he became commander of the United Nations forces there at the age of seventy, but after strongly disapproving of President Truman's handling of the Korean War, MacArthur was relieved of his command. Returning to America, he was honored with ticker-tape parades and was asked to address a joint session of Congress. And in 1964, shortly before he died, he begged President Lyndon Johnson to stay out of Vietnam.

Though he was one of the most decorated military heroes, what he treasured most was his role as a father. In fact, his greatest hero was his own father, General Arthur MacArthur, who died suddenly at a reunion

Luke 11:2

And he said unto them, When ye pray, say, Our Father which art in heaven, Hallowed be thy name. Thy kingdom come. Thy will be done, as in heaven, so in earth (KJV).

The disciples had asked Jesus to teach them how to pray, and Jesus gave them this model. Elsewhere he warns against "vain repetitions" (Matt. 6:7 KJV), so it's doubtful that he intended for his followers to recite this prayer without thinking. Yet it does give us a great pattern to follow, and these words can easily express the praises and longings of our hearts. And many people who aren't sure what to say to God—perhaps people like Douglas MacArthur—can use this prayer to guide their hearts.

of Civil War veterans. As his father was making a speech at this reunion, he collapsed, and the ninety veterans of his regiment gathered around him, repeating the Lord's Prayer. Douglas MacArthur never forgot the trauma of his father's death. "My whole world changed that night. Never have I been able to heal the wound in my heart." And never would he forget the Lord's Prayer.

Although MacArthur was not a churchgoer, he was an avid Bible reader. Every morning the MacArthur family would gather for prayers at eight, read from the Anglican Book of Common Prayer and from the Bible, and pray the Lord's Prayer.

In 1942, during the darkest days of World War II, MacArthur got a letter from the National Father's Day Committee of Alvin, Texas, naming him Father of the Year. MacArthur responded: "Nothing has touched me more deeply. . . . By profession I am a soldier . . . but I am prouder, infinitely prouder, to be a father. . . . It is my hope that my son when I am gone will remember me, not from the battle, but in the home, repeating with him our simple daily prayer, 'Our Father who art in heaven.'"

Three years later when he was able to lead troops back into the Philippines and retake Manila, he officially restored the capital to the loyal Filipino officials who had survived the fighting. He announced, "Your country is again at liberty to pursue its destiny to an honored position in the family of free nations." Then, overcome with emotion, he buried his face in his hands and concluded brokenly, "In . . . gratitude to almighty God for bringing this decisive victory to our arms, I ask that all present rise and join me in reciting the Lord's Prayer."

General MacArthur was a military leader who delighted in building peace on earth, but more than that, he was a man who delighted in being a father who prayed to his heavenly Father.

Opening the Windows
POPE JOHN XXIII (1881-1963)

The Roman Catholic cardinals had gathered in the Vatican's Sistine Chapel to choose a successor to Pope Pius XII, who had died earlier that month. In early voting, four or five candidates seemed to be favorites. In the ninth and tenth ballots a dark horse emerged: Cardinal Angelo Roncalli, patriarch of Venice. On the eleventh ballot he was chosen.

Why was he chosen? At seventy-seven years old, Roncalli didn't have any enemies and was known to be a good man. The other cardinals thought Roncalli would quietly go about his business, but little did they know what would happen in the next five years.

When Roncalli was asked, "By what name do you wish to be called?" he surprised the cardinals by responding, "I will be called John." No pope had taken the name John since the fourteenth century.

> ## 1 John 4:7
>
> *Beloved, let us love one another: for love is of God* (KJV).
>
> ---
>
> Love is the key word in John's epistles. This is not surprising, since he was known as "the disciple whom Jesus loved" (John 21:7). Of course, he and his brother James were also called "Sons of Thunder," possibly because of their violent tempers. But somewhere along the trail with Jesus, John learned how to love. He is the only gospel writer to record Jesus' Last Supper discourse, when Jesus gave his commandment to love one another (John 13:34). John seemed to understand more than anyone that this was what Jesus was all about.

He explained, "The name John is dear to me because it is the name of my father. . . . But we particularly love the name John, because it was borne by two men who were closest to Christ the Lord. . . . John the Baptist and John the disciple." Then he quoted from John's first epistle, "My children, love one another. Love one another, because this is the greatest commandment of the Lord" (1 John 4:7).

He had another surprise for people when he expressed the desire to update the church and bring it into the twentieth century to renew the life and worship of every Catholic. Less than three months after he was elected, he shocked everyone by announcing an ecumenical council, the first in nearly a century. When asked what its purpose would be, he responded, "To let some fresh air in here."

In his encyclical *Mater et Magistra* he set forth his concerns for the poor in industrialized nations and in emerging nations. He said that all people must share in the wealth produced by modern technology, and this was a revolutionary statement for a Roman Catholic pope.

The Vatican Council convened in 1962, with nearly three thousand Roman Catholic leaders and observers from seventeen other Christian denominations present. St. Peter's Square was mobbed by thousands of cheering Romans, and the pope quieted them and said, "Go home, and make love grow from here to everywhere."

No infallible pronouncements were made at that council, which became known as Vatican II. But a new climate was established. The Catholic mass was permitted in the language of the local country. Differences were not to be feared. Ecumenical dialogue could begin. "Holy liberty" was established. Previous councils had often been convened to condemn a heresy or to begin an inquisition, but now Pope John said that the church "prefers to make use of the medicine of mercy rather than that of severity." He was indeed opening the windows of the church to let some fresh air in.

In his final letter to his Roncalli kinfolk, he wrote, "This is what matters most: to make sure of eternal life, trusting in the goodness of the Lord. . . . Go on loving one another, all you Roncallis."

And that is what the apostle John said too.

The Hiding Place

CORRIE TEN BOOM (1892-1983)

The first forty-five years of Corrie ten Boom's life were quite ordinary. The daughter of a Dutch watchmaker in the city of Haarlem, she had operated clubs for girls and for handicapped youths for about twenty years. She also became the first woman in the Netherlands to qualify as a watchmaker.

Then Nazi troops invaded the Netherlands, intending to carry out Hitler's plan to conquer Europe and exterminate all the Jews on the continent. The ten Boom family decided to resist. Corrie's eighty-four-year-old father was told that if he persisted in hiding Jews in his home, he would face imprisonment. He responded, "If that should happen, then it would be for me an honor to give my life for God's ancient people, the Jews."

The ten Booms began hiding Jews in their house when German soldiers ransacked the shop of a Jewish merchant across the street; the ten Booms took the merchant in. Soon other Jews fled to their home, and the ten Booms built a secret room, a hiding place behind a false wall. Whenever Nazi soldiers came to the door, the Jewish residents were quickly shuttled into the hiding place.

Eventually the ten Booms were betrayed, and thirty-five of their friends and family were led to the police station. They sat together on a gymnasium mat, not knowing what the future held. Father ten Boom asked Corrie's brother, Willem, to read Psalm 91, which begins, "He that dwelleth in the secret place of the most High shall abide under the

Psalm 91:1

He that dwelleth in the secret place of the most High shall abide under the shadow of the Almighty (KJV).

We don't know that David wrote this psalm, but he could have. Running through the caverns of the Judean desert, staying a step ahead of the murderous King Saul, David would have known the value of shelter and secret places. Later this psalm depicts God as a giant bird, a mother hen of sorts, spreading her protective feathers over her brood. Does God protect us from all misfortune? Of course not. Corrie ten Boom lost her father and sister to the Nazis. But there is a spiritual security we find in him, and a strength to deal with our trials.

shadow of the Almighty. . . . He shall cover thee with his feathers, and under his wings shalt thou trust" (vv. 1, 4 KJV). For many months Jews had come to live in the secret place of the ten Boom home; now the ten Booms were committing themselves to the "secret place of the most High" (v. 1 KJV).

That was the last time Corrie saw her father—he died ten days after his arrest. Corrie and her sister, Betsey, were taken from one concentration camp to another. Corrie later recalled, "During my months of solitary confinement, I often felt lonely and afraid. In such moments I recalled that last night with my elderly father, sharing Psalm 91 and praying." Eventually Corrie and her sister were taken to Ravensbruck, which was known as the concentration camp of no return. Betsey died there, but before she died she told Corrie, "After the war we must go around the world telling people . . . how wonderful God is, and how his love will fill our lives, if only we will give up our hatred and bitterness."

A week after Betsey's death, Corrie was set free because of an administrative blunder. After the war ended she established a rehabilitation home for victims of concentration camps and a home for refugees on the site of a former concentration camp.

She was in her sixties when she began her international ministry, speaking in more than sixty countries, sleeping in more than a thousand beds. Her book about her family's work during World War II, *The Hiding Place,* became an international best-seller as well as a Christian classic, with sales in the millions. Worldwide Pictures made the book into a film that has been translated into many languages.

But for Corrie the important book was not *The Hiding Place* but the Bible. She carried it in concentration camps and around the world. Why? Because it "is almost bursting with Good News. And there has been plenty for everyone."

One truth she often repeated was "For the child of God, no pit could be so deep that Jesus was not deeper still." In the concentration camps as well as in the other deep pits of life, Corrie ten Boom lived the truth of Psalm 91:1.

Hitler's Nightmare

MARTIN NIEMOLLER (1892-1984)

Martin Niemoller was a thorn in Adolf Hitler's side—the Nazi dictator didn't know what to do with him. Niemoller was imprisoned for his outspoken opposition to Nazism, but because of his international reputation, the Nazis hesitated putting him to death. As Niemoller's life hung in the balance, he clung to Romans 14:8 more tightly than ever: "Whether we live therefore, or die, we are the Lord's" (KJV).

When Hitler was named chancellor of Germany, Niemoller was a forty-one-year-old pastor in Berlin. He had served as captain of a German U-boat in World War I and considered himself a German patriot. In fact, he initially supported Hitler. A month after Hitler became chancellor, the Reichstag, Germany's historic parliament building, went up in flames. Hitler blamed the Communists, claimed a national emergency, and suspended all constitutional rights. He said he was saving the country, and most Germans believed him. In six months Hitler took over the labor unions, removed all Jews from civil service, outlawed opposition parties, and imprisoned his foes. Very few complained.

Only the church was a potential problem. Hitler negotiated with Rome to remove the Catholic Church as a possible foe and then worked to unite all twenty-eight Protestant denominations under one head, whom he would name. When a new church leader was announced, every church in Germany was to be decorated with Nazi flags, and a

> ### Romans 14:7–8
>
> *For none of us liveth to himself, and no man dieth to himself. For whether we live, we live unto the Lord; and whether we die, we die unto the Lord: whether we live therefore, or die, we are the Lord's* (KJV).
>
> ---
>
> These verses occur within Paul's discussion about the "weaker brother" (Rom. 14:1–8). In some matters good Christians will disagree with one another. Some will be vegetarians; others won't. Some will observe certain holidays; others won't. Each person is responsible to the Lord for these decisions, so we shouldn't pass judgment on one another or create stumbling blocks. Since we live and die for the Lord, we should operate according to his priorities. We need to show love to others and leave the judging to God.

proclamation was to be read in each church, giving thanks to the Nazi party for reorganizing religion.

In response, Niemoller, Dietrich Bonhoeffer, and a few others formed the Young Reformation Movement. They wanted to make sure that Nazism wouldn't twist the church to serve its own purposes. When the Nazis banned all Jews and those married to Jews from holding church office, Niemoller launched the Pastors Emergency League and signed up more than two thousand pastors. On Reformation Sunday that year, with Gestapo officers present, Niemoller preached about Jesus Christ, a Jew, the rabbi of Nazareth.

The following day Niemoller was suspended from his pastoral duties. Three months later Niemoller and other pastors of the Pastors Emergency League were summoned to appear before Hitler. Some of the pastors backed away from a confrontation with the Führer, but not Niemoller.

In 1937 the Nazis arrested Niemoller and sent him to Moabit Prison. There he was visited by a chaplain who asked, "And brother, what brings you here? Why are you in prison?"

Niemoller responded quickly, "And brother, why are you not in prison?"

Eight months later a judge released him, but as soon as Hitler heard of his release, Niemoller was rearrested and sent into the Sachsenhausen concentration camp, with thirty thousand other prisoners. He was moved to Dachau in 1941 and preached from his jail cell to anyone who would listen. To stop his preaching, the guards placed him in solitary confinement. Planks were nailed across the bottom window of his cell so people could not see his face. But his cell was near the prison yard where prisoners did their daily exercises, and as they came by he would encourage them with verses of Scripture. He remained in Dachau until 1945 when he was rescued by American soldiers.

Later Niemoller wrote his famous confession: "In Germany they came first for the Communists, and I didn't speak up because I wasn't a Communist. Then they came for the Jews, and I didn't speak up because I wasn't a Jew. Then they came for the trade unionists, and I didn't speak up because I wasn't a trade unionist. Then they came for the Catholics, and I didn't speak up because I was a Protestant. Then they came for me, and by that time no one was left to speak up."

But this pastor did eventually speak up against Nazism and he did so courageously because he recognized the importance of Romans 14:7.

Speaking Our Language
W. CAMERON TOWNSEND (1896-1982)

In 1917 twenty-one-year-old Cam Townsend was trying to sell Spanish Bibles in Guatemala, but he soon realized that 60 percent of the people didn't speak Spanish, much less read it. When a Guatemalan Indian asked him, "Why hasn't God learned our language?" Townsend knew he had to do something about it. So he decided to learn the tribal language Cakchiquel and translate the Bible into it, even though he had no linguistic training. For the next ten years he and his wife worked on the translation. They also started an elementary school, a Bible school for preachers, an orphanage, and an agricultural cooperative.

Townsend then began thinking of the five hundred or more language groups in Latin America that didn't have the Bible

> ## Exodus 23:20
>
> *Behold, I send an Angel before thee, to keep thee in the way, and to bring thee into the place which I have prepared* (KJV).
>
> ---
>
> This verse was spoken to the Israelites at Sinai, just a short while after they received the Ten Commandments. This angel would lead them, guide their behavior, and help them in battle. An angel already had led them across the Red Sea and screened them from the pursuing Egyptians. Perhaps the angel took the form of the pillar of cloud and fire that led them through the wilderness.

translated into their tongue. He had a vision of doing even more things: "There must be an intensive literacy campaign. The masses must be taught to read. Other tribes must receive the Scriptures in their own native tongues. God will send young men and women with a burning desire to plant His Word in every language. I tell you, the tribes of South America will have the Bible. And North America, Africa, and Asia also."

A fellow missionary told him there were fifty tribes in Mexico without the gospel. Townsend liked the idea of starting in Mexico, but he didn't want to get tied down to one tribe. His vision was larger—he wanted to start a summer training school where missionaries and future missionaries could learn how to translate Scripture into the different languages.

However, when Townsend asked the Mexican government for permission to bring in missionary translators, he was turned down. Finally he and his partner were allowed in on the condition that his partner would not preach and Townsend would not translate. That evening in a motel in Monterrey, Mexico, the missionaries turned to Scripture for encouragement. Then they came upon Exodus 23:20: "Behold, I send an Angel before thee, to keep thee in the way, and to bring thee into the place which I have prepared" (KJV).

"Praise the Lord," Townsend responded. "We felt like shouting after that verse," he said later. "It seemed as though God Himself was speaking to us from heaven."

The next day their situation looked even more bleak, but Townsend, assured by the verse in Exodus, was confident. "The Lord has brought us this far and He will carry us on."

After visiting several government officials, he was allowed to study the rural education system but not the Indian languages. Townsend researched the system and wrote articles about it, which impressed Mexican officials. In 1934 he announced his "Summer Training Camp for Prospective Bible Translators," which was soon renamed "Camp Wycliffe" after John Wycliffe, the translator of the first English Bible. When Townsend reapplied to the Mexican government to let his workers in as "linguistic investigators," the president of the country approved because they were providing a practical service for the Indians.

One by one other countries like Suriname, Togo, and Papua New Guinea opened up to the translators. Eventually Wycliffe Bible Translators (as their organization came to be called) became the largest independent Protestant mission agency in the world, with more than two thousand workers overseas in about thirty countries.

In addition to his translation work, Townsend pioneered in various missionary methods: partnering with foreign governments, assisting mainline denominations, working with Roman Catholics, and sending single women missionaries to remote tribes. Some of these innovations were criticized, but Townsend had his vision of what needed to be done to get the Bible into every language in the world, and he didn't let criticism deter him. But one wonders if he would have quit before he ever got started if he hadn't been convinced that an angel of the Lord was going before him.

When Townsend retired at the age of seventy-five, he was asked if he had anything to say. Of course he did. "Out there are two thousand tribes who still don't have the Bible! I believe God is going to help us reach them all. Don't you?"

By the Numbers

DONALD A. MCGAVRAN (1897-1990)

Missionary Donald McGavran was troubled. He had been a missionary in India for a dozen years, his parents had been missionaries, and his grandparents had been missionaries. He had translated the New Testament into the Chattisgarhee language. He had been a rural evangelist, a hospital administrator, a church planter, and an educator. But as he read the Book of Acts and then looked at mission work in India, he felt that something wasn't working the way it was supposed to work.

In the Book of Acts, three thousand were saved at Pentecost and later five thousand were saved; in Acts 5:14, it mentions "multitudes both of men and women" (KJV) who were converted; in the next chapter it says "the number of disciples multiplied . . . greatly" (6:7 KJV). But in India it was not working like that at all. Despite a lot of effort, prayer, and Spirit-filled missionaries, McGavran's mission still had only twenty to thirty small churches, hardly any of them growing.

> ### Acts 5:14
>
> *And believers were the more added to the Lord, multitudes both of men and women* (KJV).
>
> ---
>
> In the days and months following the outpouring of the Spirit at Pentecost, the church exploded. Acts 2, Acts 3, Acts 4, Acts 5—it seems like we're always reading about the apostles preaching or working miracles, and crowds responding. The first few entries—Acts 2:41 and Acts 4:4—mention specific numbers, but then Acts refers only to multitudes. It also seems apparent that many of these early converts were pilgrims visiting Jerusalem from other cities around the Mediterranean. They eventually went home and started churches in their own areas.

Impressed by the verses in Acts 5 and elsewhere, McGavran left his administrative position and began to research what makes churches grow. He looked at 145 mission stations in India that represented a variety of denominations and independent boards, and nine of these had doubled in attendance in the previous three years. He investigated these mission churches, asking, "Why, in seemingly identical situations, with missionaries equally faithful, do some churches grow and some do not?"

After seventeen years of research, McGavran published his findings in a book called *The Bridges of God*. The book set in motion a revolution in missionary thinking and a new way of looking at church growth in countries like the United States and Canada, where the Christian church was already well planted. The Church Growth movement had begun.

McGavran was convinced that church growth was dependent on Spirit-directed evangelism. He used the social sciences to understand the problems; he analyzed different cultures scientifically. But he realized that eternal results would be accomplished only by the Holy Spirit. Most mission philosophies believed that a person only needed to be faithful and let God work, but McGavran asked leaders to analyze everything. He talked of entire villages being swept into the kingdom and the need to convert entire groups, not just individuals.

In 1961 he established the Institute of Church Growth in Portland, Oregon, to train missionaries on furlough. Four years later he moved the institute to Fuller Theological Seminary in Pasadena, California.

Church-growth thinking as it applied to foreign missions was revolutionary enough, but when it was applied to North America, it raised even more eyebrows. Terms like "seeker churches" and "seeker-sensitive congregations" began to surface. Marketing techniques were being used. Surveys were being taken. Worship services were being changed dramatically. New congregations like Willow Creek in Illinois and Saddleback in California followed McGavran's advice and found that multitudes were responding, just as in the Book of Acts.

Of course, there was criticism for this approach. Too much emphasis on numbers? McGavran pointed to the three thousand people mentioned in the early chapters of Acts. Too much emphasis on secular marketing tools? Why not, he would ask, if it gets the gospel out? Not enough social concern? McGavran would say that can come later.

When McGavran first started asking questions about why churches in India were not growing like the early church in Jerusalem, he was simply concerned about making a dent in India for Jesus Christ. You might disagree with McGavran's methods or theories, but you have to acknowledge him as a world-changer. It is said that Paul and Silas turned the world upside down, and the same thing might be said of Donald McGavran.

The Happy Atheist
Changes His Mind

C. S. LEWIS (1898-1963)

Few twentieth-century authors have had the impact on Christians that C. S. Lewis has had. Hundreds may have come to Christ through *Mere Christianity*. Perhaps thousands have gained a new perspective on the Christian life through *The Screwtape Letters*. And probably millions of children have fallen in love with Aslan, the Christlike lion of *The Chronicles of Narnia*. Romantics love the story of his late-in-life marriage to Joy Davidman (dramatized in the movie *Shadowlands*). Social critics cite his prophetic observations in *God in the Dock* and *The Abolition of Man*. Even science fiction nuts have his imaginative space trilogy to read.

Yet this brilliant Oxford don was an atheist for the first thirty years of his life.

Born in Belfast, Clive Staples Lewis was

Exodus 3:14

And God said unto Moses, I AM THAT I AM (KJV).

When Moses received his call to confront Pharaoh with the message "Let my people go," he worried that people wouldn't believe God had sent him because he didn't know God's name. Then God gave him this calling card: "I AM WHO I AM." In fact, the name Yahweh, used in the Old Testament for "the Lord," is similar to the Hebrew verb of being. But there's more involved here. Modern theologians have called God the "ground of being." He is the One who is and the One who gives existence to others.

---

educated in English schools and served briefly in World War I until he was wounded. Then he entered academic life, teaching at Oxford and later at Cambridge for the rest of his life.

He always had a great imagination, but he had a keen intellect as well. "The two hemispheres of my mind were in the sharpest contrast," he writes in *Surprised by Joy*. "Nearly all that I loved I believed to be imaginary; nearly all that I believed to be real I thought grim and meaningless."

At Oxford he spent time with a number of other intellectual Christians, such as the writer J. R. R. Tolkien. Lewis was also very familiar with the works of Scottish tale-teller George MacDonald and British pundit

G. K. Chesterton—both clever proponents of Christianity. But personal faith was a step Lewis didn't want to take. That would require a transformation in his life, and he was quite happy being an atheist.

But Lewis reasoned that there might be some sort of universal Spirit and the more he thought about it, the more he was drawn to the idea. "The real terror," he wrote, "was that if you seriously believed in even such a 'God' or 'Spirit' as I admitted, a wholly new situation developed. As the dry bones shook and came together . . . so now a philosophical theorem, cerebrally entertained, began to stir . . . and stood upright and became a living presence."[1]

This "living presence" didn't want to argue; he just said, "I am that I am." This wasn't a case of a man searching for God—this was God searching for the man.

In 1929 Lewis gave in, accepting that God is God. But it was still a few years before he became a Christian. As a classics scholar, Lewis knew many ancient myths about gods interacting with humans, and he was especially interested in stories about dying gods. Tolkien and others tried to convince him that these myths might be shadows of a truth— that God in Christ really did die for us. These friends urged Lewis to read Romans. And then, as it happened, on a trip to the zoo C. S. Lewis came to believe that Jesus was the Son of God.

It didn't take long for him to begin his career as a Christian writer. In 1933 he published *The Pilgrim's Regress,* putting his quest for faith in fictional terms. His space trilogy began with *Out of the Silent Planet* in 1938. *The Problem of Pain* was released in 1940. And he continued producing thoughtful and imaginative works until his death in 1963.

The sense of "I am that I am" carries through most of Lewis's work. That is, he consistently presents God on God's terms. A writer of Lewis's intellect could make up all sorts of new descriptions of God, but he kept coming back to God's self-description. "God is to be obeyed because of what He is in Himself," he wrote. Lewis always said that he wasn't a theologian, but his works give us great theology—perhaps because he let God speak for himself.

Author Elisabeth Elliot was once asked how a Christian could deepen his theology and think more clearly. Read the Bible, she said, and read C. S. Lewis.

---

1. C. S. Lewis, *Surprised by Joy* (New York and London: Harcourt Brace Jovanovich, 1955), 227.

Costly Grace

DIETRICH BONHOEFFER (1906-1945)

Dietrich Bonhoeffer lived what he believed, and he believed that following Jesus was a serious thing. "When Christ calls a man, he bids him come and die," Bonhoeffer once wrote. This phrase has special meaning because that was exactly what Christ called Bonhoeffer to do.

Growing up in Berlin, Germany, Bonhoeffer was surrounded by educated people. His father was a psychiatrist, and other relatives had been ministers, academics, and theologians, so no one was surprised when young Dietrich did well in theological studies.

Some of his early academic writings began to explore a theme that would fascinate him throughout his life. To what extent should Christians inform, affect, and even judge the society in which they live? This would become a crucial question as Germany came under the control of the Nazis.

> ## Matthew 16:24
>
> *Then Jesus said to his disciples, "If anyone would come after me, he must deny himself and take up his cross and follow me."*
>
> In a quiet moment with his disciples, Jesus asked who they thought he was. Peter responded that Jesus was the Messiah, and he received high praise for that response. But then Jesus began talking about going to Jerusalem to die, and Peter felt compelled to talk the Master out of such a foolhardy plan. But Jesus responded, "Get behind me, Satan!" (v. 23). In this verse Jesus went on to challenge his disciples to follow him fully—even to death. As it happened, Peter denied Christ to avoid being crucified with him but then was crucified for Christ some thirty-five years later.

In 1930 Bonhoeffer went to study at Union Theological Seminary in New York City. There he helped teach a Sunday school class at an African-American church in Harlem. This might have been the most valuable of all his classes, because he saw firsthand the struggle of an oppressed people. These lessons would be important as Bonhoeffer returned to his homeland.

Back in Germany he taught systematic theology at Berlin University from 1931 to 1933, but then the Nazis took power with Hitler at the helm. Some pastors went along with Hitler's efforts to control the churches; Bonhoeffer could not. He took a teaching position in London to escape the madness, but how could he run away from such a challenge to the church? Didn't true discipleship demand that he stand up for Jesus, whatever the cost?

Returning to Germany in 1935, Bonhoeffer got involved with the resistance movement. He was forbidden to speak in public or to enter Berlin, but he set up an illegal seminary to train new ministers who would not obey Hitler's demands. In 1937 he published *The Cost of Discipleship*.

This book is a Bible study about the Sermon on the Mount and other passages in Matthew, and Bonhoeffer draws out every challenge that Jesus issued. "Cheap grace is the deadly enemy of the church," he begins, and he adds, "We are fighting today for costly grace." He didn't deny that grace is a free gift from God, but he wondered how we, the recipients of grace, can take up our cross and follow the One who gave his life for us.

With the winds of war blowing, friends hustled Bonhoeffer out of Germany in 1939, but once again he felt he had to return. "I shall have no right to participate in the reconstruction of Christian life in Germany after the war if I do not share in the trials of this time with my people," he said. After returning to Germany he got even more involved with the resistance. Though a pacifist, he participated in a plot to kill Hitler. When the plot was discovered, Bonhoeffer was arrested. Held in a concentration camp, he wrote many letters to friends and well-wishers, some of which were later published as *Letters and Papers from Prison*.

In the early months of 1945 Allied troops were closing in on the Germans. By personal order of Heinrich Himmler, Bonhoeffer was hanged on April 9, just a few days before the Allies arrived to free the camp.

Who knows what preaching and writing this man might have done if he had survived the war? But the fact is that Christ called him to "come and die." Bonhoeffer left a legacy of words and thoughts, and these are all the more powerful because he took up his cross and followed Jesus.

Serving the Thirsty One

MOTHER TERESA (1910-1996)

Agnes Bojaxhiu was a most unlikely candidate to be an internationally known celebrity. Born to Albanian parents in Yugoslavia, she followed a call to become a Catholic missionary nun when she was eighteen. After a year in Ireland learning English, Teresa (the name she took when she became a nun) was sent in 1929 to Calcutta, India, where she taught geography and catechism at a Catholic high school. Most of the sisters there thought of her as rather ordinary, hardly someone who would make a mark on the world.

In 1946 she was stricken with tuberculosis and was sent away to recuperate. While on a train from Calcutta to Darjeeling (in the foothills of the Himalayas), she received what she described as her "call within a call."

> ### John 19:28
>
> *I thirst* (KJV).
>
> ___
>
> Jesus said seven things from the cross, according to the gospel writers. The cry of need in this verse underscores Jesus' humanity. Some early heretics suggested that Jesus was a spiritual being who only appeared to have a body. John smashes this teaching again and again in his writings, so it's fitting that he records the words "I thirst."

"It was on that train," she said, "that I heard the call to give up all and follow Him into the slums—to serve Him in the poorest of the poor. I knew it was His will and that I had to follow Him. The message was quite clear. I was to leave the convent and work with the poor while living among them. It was an order. I knew where I belonged, but I did not know how to get there."

The call, she said, was to follow Jesus in ministry to those who, like him, "had not whereon to lay their heads," to those who were naked, despised, and forsaken as he had been, and to those who were crying "I thirst" (John 19:28 KJV) as he had.

Yet she had to get approval. She had taken lifetime vows as a Loreto Sister, so when her request was brought to the archbishop, he was upset. A solitary nun on the streets of Calcutta? Ridiculous. She was told to wait a year, and she was sent to a convent three hours away where she

189

managed the kitchen. After a year she was allowed to go and minister to the poorest of the poor in Calcutta's streets. In 1950 Teresa founded the Missionaries of Charity.

Biographer Eileen Egan writes of her first visit with Mother Teresa: "As we walked, children naked or near naked began to follow us. . . . One naked child lay on a piece of cloth, his eyes half open. . . . Women in discolored saris stood listlessly holding brass and tin pots. Mother Teresa explained that the only water for drinking and for washing came from the washrooms. . . . Large beetles scurried among the massed bodies. . . . Yawning before me was a steaming pit of misery. The mingled fumes of arriving steam engines, of diseased and sweating bodies, or cooking pots over the dung-burning stoves, of half-decayed goods guarded for future meals settled almost palpably over the teeming scene. I felt that the odor would cling to me until I left Calcutta. Mother Teresa seemed not to notice the stench."[1]

"Our work," said Mother Teresa, "calls for us to see Jesus in everyone. He has told us that He is the hungry one. He is the naked one. He is the thirsty one. He is the one without a home. He is the one who is suffering. These are our treasures," she said as she looked out on the masses. "They are Jesus. Each one is Jesus in His distressing disguise."

Beginning with Calcutta's poor, Mother Teresa then began Missionaries of Charity in Latin America, Africa, the Middle East, Australia, Asia, Europe, and even in the inner cities of North America. The aim of the order is "to quench the infinite thirst of Jesus Christ on the cross for love of souls by the profession of the evangelical counsels and wholehearted free service to the poorest of the poor." Each chapel is humble, but all of them blazon the words "I thirst" over their altar.

Mother Teresa was awarded the first John XIII Peace Prize in 1971, the first Templeton Prize in 1973, and the Nobel Peace Prize in 1979.

1. Eileen Egan, *Such a Vision of the Street* (Garden City, N.Y.: Doubleday, 1985), 46.

Moses with a Dream

MARTIN LUTHER KING JR. (1929-1968)

African-Americans have always identified with the Israelites in Egypt. Both groups were once slaves and both looked to God for deliverance.

In colonial times slaves found hope in the core of the gospel message. Jesus was a suffering Savior for suffering people. They knew he could set them free in a spiritual sense, and they hoped that someday there would be a Moses to lead them out of physical slavery.

In the mid–nineteenth century the abolition movement effectively used biblical imagery, especially the story of the exodus. Harriet Tubman liked to be called Moses and used verses from the Book of Exodus as code words in the Underground Railroad. But the Emancipation Proclamation and the Civil War only started a process of liberation. By the early 1960s African-Americans were still in bondage, at least economically and socially. Strict laws, especially in the South, kept blacks as second-class citizens.

But although African-Americans were held back socially and economically, their religious commitment had grown strong. Once freed from slavery, they could freely assemble to worship. Black churches became the center of community life, so it only made sense that the next Moses for these people would be a minister.

This man's name was Martin Luther King Jr. A pastor's child from Atlanta, King went to Morehouse College at age fifteen and then went to Crozer Theological Seminary, later getting a doctorate at Boston University. In 1954 he became pastor of the Dexter Avenue Baptist Church

Exodus 9:1

Then the LORD said to Moses, "Go to Pharaoh and say to him, 'This is what the LORD, the God of the Hebrews, says: "Let my people go, so that they may worship me."'"

This verse is the message that Moses repeatedly gave Pharaoh on God's behalf. God was sending plagues of frogs, flies, and hail upon the land, but Pharaoh refused to yield. Finally the angel of death struck down the Egyptian firstborns, and Pharaoh relented, at least temporarily. This story is relived each year in the Jewish Passover celebration.

in Montgomery, Alabama, where he served for five years. During his time at that church a woman named Rosa Parks refused to give up her bus seat to a white man and was arrested. In response, King organized a successful boycott of the city bus system. This action brought King to national attention—especially when the U.S. Supreme Court ruled that bus segregation was unconstitutional.

In 1960 King moved to Atlanta to copastor his father's church and to continue the fight for civil rights. This fight was decidedly nonviolent. Jesus had taught about loving enemies, and the Israelite slaves in Egypt let God do their fighting for them. While other leaders were advocating a forceful revolution, King held to his peaceful approach. "Peace," he once said, "is not merely a distant goal that we seek, but a means by which we arrive at that goal."

In August of 1963 King was one of several leaders of a march on Washington. A quarter of a million people took to the streets, and in front of the Lincoln Memorial, King delivered his famous "I Have a Dream" speech. Perhaps this was the moment when King took on the mantle of Moses for the movement. Speaking of a world where people would be judged not by the color of their skin but by the content of their character, he was essentially describing the Promised Land.

King received the Nobel Peace Prize in 1964, and the Voting Rights Act was passed in 1965, but the following years saw mounting opposition. He refused to confine civil rights issues to the South and called for change in northern states as well.

On April 3, 1968, a weary Martin Luther King truly sounded like a modern-day Moses: "I don't know what will happen now. We've got some difficult days ahead. But it really doesn't matter with me now, because I've been to the mountaintop . . . And I've seen the Promised Land. I may not get there with you. But I want you to know tonight that we as a people will get to the Promised Land."

The next day he was assassinated.

Shelter in a Fog

FRANCIS SCHAEFFER (1912-1984)

Francis Schaeffer has been called an evangelical guru and a guide to students struggling with existential and philosophical problems. Amazing as it was that students were able to find him tucked away on a remote Swiss mountaintop, it is even more amazing that Schaeffer became a guru at all.

After serving pastorates in Pennsylvania and Missouri between 1938 and 1947, he was asked to conduct a fact-finding survey of Europe's spiritual conditions. Upon his return, he and his wife Edith were asked to go to Europe permanently. They were unsure of this, but they went anyway. Edith Schaeffer later wrote, "I am impressed by the constantly repeated opportunity in life to trust the Lord in a fog." They expected to stay in Switzerland for three months before heading elsewhere, but God had other plans for them.

Their work there was discouraging. Most European churches seemed dead and lifeless, and secularism had swept the continent. The problems seemed overwhelming.

Nor did they find solace during their missionary furlough in 1953. Their small denomination was on the verge of splitting, and if they stayed in America, they would be embroiled in a denominational battle. They didn't have money for the trip back to Europe, but Schaeffer made reservations anyway. Just before they were supposed to leave, they received enough money for their passage back to Europe.

Isaiah 2:2–3

And it shall come to pass in the last days, that the mountain of the LORD's house shall be established in the top of the mountains, and shall be exalted above the hills; and all nations shall flow unto it. And many people shall go (KJV).

Isaiah has a picturesque vision of the Temple Mount in Jerusalem. The Israelites always had a sense that they traveled up to meet with the Lord in his temple. This might be because the temple was built on one of several hills in Jerusalem, and so they literally had to climb to get there. But this vision shows the temple as the mountain of the whole world with people from every nation on earth streaming up to it.

While on board the ocean liner, the idea for L'Abri began to take shape. *L'Abri* is the French word for shelter, and they thought that perhaps their chalet might provide a spiritual shelter for skiers and other young people. But after arriving in Switzerland, they heard that a letter had been sent to pastors of European churches, asking them not to invite the Schaeffers back. In addition to that, avalanches had almost wiped out their home, the Swiss government did not want the Schaeffers to stay in the country, and their children were having health problems.

It was then that Edith Schaeffer, in her daily Bible reading, saw Isaiah 2:2–3: "The mountain of the LORD's house shall be established in the top of the mountains . . . and all nations shall flow into it" (KJV). Edith wrote later, "I put 'L'Abri, January 1955,' in the margin of my Bible . . . and I imagined a stream of people coming . . . from many nationalities and nations, to inquire about the existence of God. . . . I was comforted after all the upheavals, and hugged that comfort to me like a hot-water bottle, keeping out 'cold fears.'"

That promise in Isaiah convinced them to move ahead with L'Abri. A few months later a nearby village said the Schaeffers could move to a chalet in Huemoz. L'Abri was officially begun.

A stream of people began coming to L'Abri. Some visitors would stay for a night or a weekend, and others would become longtime students. Hippies came with drug problems; dropouts came seeking to make sense out of life. After a meal Francis Schaeffer would invite the students into the living room, where they could ask questions and receive answers about anything they could think of. Before long, tapes of Schaeffer's messages were being sent around the world.

By 1965 Schaeffer was speaking at Harvard, MIT, Cambridge, and other universities. His lectures became his first book, *The God Who Is There,* and other books followed, as well as radio messages and film series. Schaeffer helped many to understand the world in a Christian way. This response to Schaeffer from a young minister is typical: "My Christian faith used to be just a jumble of puzzle pieces. . . . For the first time I can see the beautiful picture of Christian truth."

Billy Frank Drives the Pickup

BILLY GRAHAM (1918-)

Sixteen-year-old Billy Frank was sitting as far back as he could in a large tabernacle in Charlotte, North Carolina. The tabernacle had been erected for revival meetings led by the fiery Southern evangelist Mordecai Ham. A neighbor had invited Billy Frank to come along but the boy was reluctant. When the neighbor said that Billy Frank could drive his truck to the revival, the sixteen-year-old accepted the offer.

At the service, Billy Frank Graham, now known as evangelist Billy Graham, began to have thoughts that he had never known before. Later Graham recalled, "The evangelist had an almost embarrassing way of describing your sins and shortcomings and demanding, on pain of divine judgment, that you mend your ways." Billy Frank found that he couldn't stay away from the meeting the next night or the night after that. He talked to a cousin about his unusual feelings, and the cousin urged him to keep attending.

> ### Romans 5:8
>
> *But God commendeth his love toward us, in that, while we were yet sinners, Christ died for us* (KJV).
>
> ---
>
> In the first few chapters of Romans, the apostle Paul masterfully makes the case that all people are sinners. Whether we've been raised on God's law or not, we have violated God's perfect standards and we deserve to be God's enemy. But that's not the end of the story. Though we are sinners, God offers redemption. He loves his enemies enough to send his Son, who died for the ungodly.

The next night Billy Frank sat near the front, and it seemed that Mordecai Ham was talking directly to him. The revivalist was preaching on Romans 5:8, and every time he quoted this verse about God loving sinners, young Graham thought that Ham was looking directly at him. The invitation was given to approach the altar, and the choir was singing, but Billy stayed in his seat. When the choir began singing the gospel hymn "Almost Persuaded," the teenager got up and walked forward. "It wasn't the invitation hymn," Graham said later. "It was Christ."

That night he felt wonderful, but before he went to sleep, he thought to himself, "I wonder if this will last."

Four years later at Bible school, Billy Graham was wondering what to do with his life. The things he enjoyed most were playing golf and baseball, but people kept telling him that he should be a preacher. At first he shrugged it off—he felt that he was too poorly educated. Maybe he could be a country preacher with a small church in the backwoods somewhere, but that was the extent of it. Then one night in March 1938 he sat down on the eighteenth green of a golf course and gave in to God. He knelt on the edge of the green and prayed, "O God, if you want me to preach, I will do it."

Seven years later he became Youth for Christ's first full-time evangelist; in nine years he was named president of Northwestern College in Minneapolis; in eleven years he achieved national fame in a spectacular seven-week Los Angeles crusade; a year after that the Billy Graham Evangelistic Association was launched, followed by his *Hour of Decision* radio program.

Graham was so successful that he became the confidante of U.S. presidents. *Time* magazine's David Aikman wrote: "No other human being this century, living or dead, has had such intimate conversations with so many of the age's powerful and famous, from Winston Churchill to Mikhail Gorbachev, from Generalissimo Chiang Kai-Shek to Queen Elizabeth of England, from Pope John Paul II to North Korea's fiery Communist leader Kim Il-Sung."[1]

In his ministry he has preached in most countries of the world. In face-to-face preaching he has addressed about one hundred million, and by radio, TV, and films, hundreds of millions more. Some two million individuals are known to have responded to his gospel invitation.

And it all began when a neighbor let him drive his truck, and an evangelist pointed a finger and said, "Even though we are sinners, Christ died for us."

1. David Aikman, *Great Souls* (Nashville: Word, 1998), 3.

Bright Days Ahead

BILL BRIGHT (1921-)

"Frankly, I was a happy pagan," Bill Bright recalls, speaking of his early twenties. He had left Coweto, Oklahoma, which is hard to find on even the best maps, and had gone to California, where he hoped to enter military service. When he was turned down, he went into business instead. "I set my goals as a humanist, materialist, self-sufficient person," he recalled. Business was good. His companies, Bright's California Confections and Bright's Brandied Foods, were booming.

Then he met some young professionals who went to Hollywood Presbyterian Church. He started attending, always sitting in the back row, but one spring evening in 1945 he got involved in a meeting of the young adult group. Dr. Henrietta Mears was speaking on the conversion of the apostle Paul. The two questions that Paul asked were "Who art thou, Lord?" and "Lord, what wilt thou have me to do?" These two questions, she said, were the most important questions anybody could ask God.

Acts 22:8, 10

And I answered, "Who art thou, Lord?" . . . And I said, "What shall I do, Lord?" (KJV).

One day when the apostle Paul visited the temple in Jerusalem, he caused a riot because people mistakenly assumed he had brought a Gentile into the area reserved for Jews. Paul had to be rescued by Roman soldiers, but then he was given permission to speak to the crowd, and he told them his conversion story. On the road to Damascus he was knocked off his horse by a bright light from heaven. When he asked, "Who art thou?" he learned that it was Jesus of Nazareth. When Paul asked what to do, he was told to go to Damascus. Ultimately he was given a mission to reach the Gentiles with the good news of Christ.

That night when Bright returned to his apartment, he got down on his knees and asked God those two important questions. "In a sense, that was my prayer for salvation," he recalls, and soon he began to grow in his new commitment and love for the Lord.

In 1951 he and his wife Vonette drew up a "Contract with God," in which they agreed to do whatever God wanted them to do and go wherever he wanted them to go, no matter what the cost. Bright was now seriously asking the second question that the apostle Paul had asked. A week later while studying for a Hebrew exam at seminary, Bright was called by God into evangelistic work, specifically to a ministry for college and university students.

Though he had shared his faith at other meetings, Bright had never asked students to receive Christ as their Savior. One night before speaking at a sorority house at UCLA, he prayed, "O Lord, please let there be at least one who will respond, to confirm the vision You gave me." That night more than half of the sixty women in attendance responded to the invitation. More meetings followed, and in the next few months more than 250 UCLA students had committed their lives to Christ.

And that was the start of Campus Crusade for Christ. In 1952 staff members were dispatched to serve on four campuses. By 1958 Campus Crusade went international, reaching out to South Korea and then to Pakistan and the Middle East. Next came Bright's Lay Institutes for Evangelism (LIFE), which later evolved into the Here's Life ministry. Then came Athletes in Action, as Campus Crusade athletic teams toured the country.

Bright had long envisioned a motion picture on the life of Christ, and in 1974 everything started coming together to make it happen. Following the text of the Gospel of Luke, *Jesus* was filmed at 200 different sites in Israel and used a cast of more than 5,000 people. The film was released in 1979, and by the end of the century an estimated 4.5 billion people had seen it and heard it in 575 languages. These figures by far exceed the totals for any other motion picture in history.

By the end of the century, Campus Crusade had more than 20,000 full-time staff members and more than 650,000 trained volunteer workers. And Bill Bright keeps asking, "Lord, what will you have me to do?" as the Lord keeps expanding his vision. Now he is praying for a staff of 100,000 by 2020. "The best," he says, "is yet before us."

Opening the Gates
JIM ELLIOT (1927-1956)

On January 8, 1956, five young missionaries were martyred as they attempted to teach the Auca Indian tribe the gospel of Jesus Christ. One of the five was Jim Elliot.

Radio reports blazoned the news to the western world. Then *Life* magazine sent a photographer to Ecuador and featured the story worldwide. During the next year, Jim Elliot's widow, Elisabeth, wrote *Through Gates of Splendor*. Not only did it become a best-seller, but it opened New York publishing doors to other missionary biographies.

In the twentieth century, many missionaries died martyrs' deaths, but none of those martyrdoms shook the world as did the deaths of the five in Ecuador. All five were outstanding in different ways, but it was Jim Elliot who became the best known. No doubt this was partly because Elisabeth wrote Jim's story in another best-seller, *Shadow of the Almighty*. But it was also because Jim Elliot himself wrote his thoughts honestly, wrestling at times with God as well as man.

> ## Isaiah 42:16
> *I will bring the blind by a way that they knew not; I will lead them in paths that they have not known* (KJV).
>
> Isaiah 42 begins by talking about God's servant, who will "bring justice to the nations" (v. 1). God is announcing a new way of life. Idol worship is out; glory to God is in. Captives will be freed. Blind people will see. Verse 16 shows God (or God's servant) carefully leading those who trust him over difficult terrain. Of course, the New Testament explicitly names Jesus as this servant who brings a new kind of life to his faithful followers.

During his senior year at college, he wrote, "I am quite at ease about saying that tribal work in the South American jungle is the general direction of my missionary purpose." But other opportunities for Christian service were in front of him, and Elliot found himself drawn to the millions in India who had never been evangelized. Elliot was torn between India and Ecuador. What about the tribes in Ecuador that had never heard the gospel? These were not large tribes, but hadn't Jesus said that the gospel needed to be preached to everyone?

In April of 1950, nearly a year after his college graduation, he was still weighing the matter. "Found some difficulty in discerning the Lord's will," he wrote. Then God gave him Isaiah 42:16: "I will bring the blind by a way that they knew not" (KJV). Elliot commented, "I fulfill the qualification for once, Lord; most surely I am blind." From then on, he could see God's direction more clearly. Within a few days he was accepted at Wycliffe's Summer Institute of Linguistics, and within a few days he had the assurance that he should serve in Ecuador.

Three and a half years later, Elliot and other missionaries were discussing the best way to bring the gospel to the Auca Indians. One member of the group, Nate Saint, wrote, "We had just decided that it was the Lord's time to try to contact the savage Auca tribe." They knew that earlier efforts had ended in failure, so they planned carefully. To win the friendship of the Aucas they would drop gifts for them from an airplane and later approach them on the ground. They learned Auca phrases, and Elliot carried some of these phrases on cards in his pocket.

He discussed with his wife the possibility of not returning. "If God wants it that way, darling, I am ready to die for the salvation of the Aucas."

Once in the area, their last radio contact was simply: "Will contact you next at four-thirty." But no contact was made. Soon news flashed around the world: FIVE MEN MISSING IN AUCA TERRITORY. Search parties were sent in, and one by one the bodies of the slain missionaries were found.

The deaths had amazing impact, and many new missionaries were inspired by the dedication of these men. The Auca tribe eventually opened up to the gospel, thanks to some of the widows of the martyred missionaries.

"Consume my life, my God, for it is Thine. I seek not a long life, but a full one, like You, Lord Jesus," Elliot had written in 1948.

"He is no fool who gives what he cannot keep to gain what he cannot lose," he wrote in 1949.

And in 1950 he added, "I must not think it strange if God takes in youth those whom I would have kept on earth till they were older. God is peopling Eternity, and I must not restrict Him to old men and women."

A Higher View

APOLLO 8 (1968)

The years 1967 and 1968 had not been good years for America. As 1967 began, three American astronauts lost their lives when a fire swept through their command module, on what was to have been the first manned mission to the moon. The unpopular war in Vietnam was being waged with more and more casualties. There was war in the Middle East, and China exploded its first hydrogen bomb. Russia invaded Czechoslovakia, and North Korea seized a U.S. Navy ship with eighty-three on board. Racial violence was breaking out in many of America's major cities. Amid the turmoil in 1968, President Lyndon Johnson announced that he would not accept renomination to the nation's highest office. Then civil rights leader Martin Luther King Jr. was assassinated in Memphis. Two months later Robert F. Kennedy, who had just won the California primary election, was shot and killed.

> ### Genesis 1:1
>
> *In the beginning God created the heaven and the earth* (KJV).
>
> The first verse of Scripture is foundational to Jewish and Christian thought. In Romans Paul says that even those without Scripture can sense the basic identity of God by observing what he has created. Genesis 1:2 shows the Spirit of God (or his breath) moving across this empty expanse to bring things into being. Sure, there are all sorts of arguments about how and when God created, but the main point is that he did make us. We owe our life to his Breath.

No, those weren't good years. It seemed that humanity was drained of all hope.

After the disaster that took the lives of the three astronauts in 1967, many questioned the U.S. space program. Critics said it cost too much money, that it reeked of showmanship not science, that it jeopardized American lives, and that it was a childish stunt to try to get to the moon before the Russians.

But the Apollo space program continued. The first flights had been unmanned; later flights had carried astronauts. Some flights had achieved their mission; some had not. Apollo 8 was the next big challenge. On that voyage the astronauts were going to orbit the moon. The astronauts chosen for the mission were Frank Borman, James Lovell Jr., and William Anders. Borman was a devout Episcopalian, a lay reader in his church. Lovell had recently become a Christian.

Thousands lined the Florida beaches to watch the liftoff. Government officials, foreign dignitaries, business executives, engineers, newsmen, and tourists were all watching. Monitoring stations had been established around the world.

Shortly before 8 A.M. on December 21, Apollo 8 lifted off out of the billowing flames. The critical launch had been successful. The astronauts beamed back to earth pictures of the moon they were headed to and pictures of the earth they had just left.

On the day before Christmas there was excitement at mission control in Houston. The flight controllers were watching to see how a crucial rocket engine would fire. As Apollo orbited the moon, that engine would have to refire and send the spacecraft back to earth. The astronauts took ten orbits around the moon, as Lovell carefully described to Houston what he saw.

Then at 9:30 P.M. on Christmas Eve, as the whole world watched, Borman announced, "Apollo 8 has a message for you." The camera provided a close-up of the moon as Anders read, "In the beginning God created the heaven and the earth. And the earth was without form, and void; and darkness was upon the face of the deep" (Gen. 1:1–2 KJV). Then Lovell picked up the reading: "And God called the light Day, and the darkness he called Night" (Gen. 1:5 KJV). Borman concluded with: "And God called the dry land Earth; and the gathering together of the waters called he Seas: and God saw that it was good" (Gen. 1:10 KJV).

After that, Borman simply said, "Good-bye, good night. Merry Christmas. God bless all of you, all of you on the good earth."

The Country Preacher
Takes the Big City

DAVID WILKERSON (1935-)

It all started when David Wilkerson, the young pastor of a rural church in the mountain town of Philipsburg, Pennsylvania, was reading a story in *Life* magazine about a murder trial in New York City. Seven gang members were charged with brutally attacking and killing a fifteen-year-old polio victim.

Suddenly the thought came to Wilkerson that he had to go to New York and help those gang members. It was a crazy notion and he knew it; he was certainly not equipped for inner-city work. But he couldn't get the idea out of his mind.

He asked his congregation for money to make a trip to New York City with his youth director. Seventy-five dollars was donated, enough to get to Manhattan and back. As the two rode along, Wilkerson confided, "I wish I could be sure that this isn't some crazy notion of mine, and that it really is God leading me." Wilkerson asked the youth director to reach into the backseat, get a Bible, open it at random, and read the first passage he put his finger on. The passage of Scripture that the youth director put his finger on was Psalm 126:5–6: "They that sow in tears shall reap in joy" (v. 5 KJV). It was the encouragement that Wilkerson needed for what lay ahead.

The first trip seemed to be an embarrassing failure. Wilkerson was kicked out of the courtroom, and photographs of his ejection were fea-

Psalm 126:5–6

They that sow in tears shall reap in joy. He that goeth forth and weepeth, bearing precious seed, shall doubtless come again with rejoicing, bringing his sheaves with him (KJV).

This is a psalm about captives returning to their homeland, possibly referring to the Babylonian captives. There is a dreamlike quality here, with both great joy and the memory of great sorrow. In the farming culture of Palestine, it would be natural to use the image of seed-sowing to describe the painful experiences that yield joyous results.

tured in New York newspapers. He began to have doubts whether those verses were really meant for him.

Despite the failure, he felt he had to go back a second time. This time, to his surprise, when he was parking his car, he was recognized by some gang members from his picture in the paper and was regarded as one of them. After all, the police apparently weren't on Wilkerson's side any more than they were on the side of the gangs.

For the next four months, Wilkerson made weekly visits to the city, and each time God seemed to increase his courage. One time, a gang member named Nicky told him, "You come near me, Preacher, and I'll kill you."

"You could do that," Wilkerson replied. "You could cut me in a thousand pieces and lay them out in the street and every piece would love you."

Within two years Wilkerson and his wife had moved to New York and started a television program for youth. Plans were laid for the first Teen Challenge Center, where gang members and drug addicts could talk with counselors. When the Center opened, Wilkerson was surprised to see what had been carved over the fireplace in the room they would use as the chapel. It was a bas-relief of a sheaf of wheat, tied and harvested, a perpetual reminder to him of those verses in Psalm 126.

The Cross and the Switchblade, a book that tells the Wilkerson story, became an international best-seller with sales in the millions. Meanwhile, Wilkerson was starting Teen Challenge Centers in other metropolitan areas. Today there are 120 such centers in the United States and 250 worldwide. After a few years away from New York, Wilkerson returned to start the Times Square Church in the heart of Manhattan.

Randomly picking verses of Scripture isn't usually the best way to get divine guidance, but Psalm 126:5–6 certainly gave David Wilkerson the encouragement he needed to begin a ministry to gang members in New York City.

The Peaceful Revolution

DESMOND TUTU (1931-)

Recipient of the Nobel Peace Prize, Anglican archbishop of Capetown, South Africa, and staunch opponent of apartheid, Desmond Tutu was a key player in one of the most miraculous revolutions of the twentieth century—the peaceful overthrow of the apartheid government in South Africa.

The son of a Methodist schoolteacher, Tutu was educated at a Swedish mission boarding school near Johannesburg, and he taught school before entering the Anglican ministry when he was twenty-six. He rose quickly in the clerical ranks, going to London to study. There he enjoyed a freedom and gained a self-respect that he could not find in his own country. "The most horrible aspect of apartheid," he wrote, "is it can make a child of God doubt that they are a child of God, when you ask yourself in the middle of the night, 'God, am I your stepchild?'"

> ### Romans 8:35, 37
>
> *Who shall separate us from the love of Christ? Shall trouble or hardship or persecution or famine or nakedness or danger or sword? . . . No, in all these things we are more than conquerors through him who loved us.*
>
> ---
>
> We get the idea from the Book of Romans that it was tough to be a Christian in Rome. History tells us there were disputes in Rome between Jews and Jewish Christians, and that the Romans were cracking down on both groups. In hard times, it's natural for devout people to wonder what they did wrong. Paul assures the Roman believers that they are not being condemned for their sin (8:1) and that nothing can separate them from the love of Christ (8:37–39).

He returned to South Africa in the late 1960s, a time of seething unrest. Apartheid laws had become increasingly strict and dehumanizing; blacks responded by secretly forming armed resistance units. Tutu, now a lecturer in South African universities, sympathized with the black students and influenced them to protest in nonviolent ways. Once, when students were being arrested for peacefully protesting campus injustice, Tutu walked to the police and said, "If you are arresting the students you can count me, as their chaplain, with them."

Sadly, this oppression was going on in a land that was supposedly Christian. Tutu put it like this: "We had the land and they had the Bible. Then they said, 'Let us pray,' and we closed our eyes. When we opened them again, they had the land and we had the Bible. Maybe we had the better of the deal."

Tutu had always loved Scripture. A text that motivated him in his ministry was "If God is for us, who can be against us?" (Rom. 8:31). He firmly believed that God was on the side of the oppressed Africans. In the Bible, Tutu said, "God did not just talk—he acted. . . . He took the side of the slaves, the oppressed, the victims. He is still the same even today." Tutu saw that Jesus came to preach deliverance, but he urged his listeners not to cast off oppression only to put on the garments of bitterness and division.

Tutu talked about "the tingling joy of being accepted by God." Not only was he confident of God's love, but he knew that nothing could separate him from that love (Rom. 8:35–39), and this gave him boldness. "The worst thing that they can do is to kill me," he said during one crisis, "and death is not the worst thing for the Christian."

In 1980 Tutu said prophetically, "We need Nelson Mandela, because he is almost certainly going to be that first black prime minister," even though Mandela was imprisoned with a life sentence at the time. But Mandela was eventually released from prison, and he held a press conference in the official residence of Desmond Tutu, now the archbishop. Three years later Mandela, in his inaugural speech after a free election, said, "We enter into a covenant that we shall build the society in which all South Africans, both black and white, will be able to walk tall."

Desmond Tutu couldn't have said it any better. His friend Nelson Mandela had chosen to forgive his enemies, and as a result, it was an amazingly peaceful transfer of power and a stunningly effective healing of old wounds. The oppressed people of South Africa had won a great victory, but Archbishop Tutu was not surprised. After all, "We are more than conquerors through him who loved us" (Rom. 8:37).

Term of Endearment

JIMMY CARTER (1924-) AND CHARLES COLSON (1931-)

Throughout the centuries, Christians have used the term "born again" to describe their salvation. This term was a particular favorite of George Whitefield, the energetic preacher who echoed these words of Jesus: "Ye must be born again." He was calling people out of a formal faith and into a personal commitment.

That's exactly the way the term "born again" has been used in the twentieth century. Fundamentalists in the twenties and evangelicals in the fifties used it as a kind of code word. Many people considered themselves Christians merely because they went to church, so "I am a Christian" didn't mean much. But "I am a *born-again* Christian" would indicate a personal experience with Christ.

The phrase burst into public awareness again in 1976 as two very different world-changers hit the headlines. Jimmy Carter, the peanut-farmer-turned-governor from Georgia, was running for president. Just a few short years after the Watergate scandal, Carter's simple honesty was a breath of fresh air. A devout Southern Baptist, he clearly stated that he was a born-again Christian.

The other newsworthy born-again figure that year was Charles Colson, a veteran of the Watergate scandal. He had gone to prison and written a book, just like others from the Nixon White House, but his book was different. Dwelling very little on the background of Watergate, it talked instead about his religious conversion. He entitled it *Born Again*.

> ### John 3:3
>
> *I tell you the truth, no one can see the kingdom of God unless he is born again.*
>
> ---
>
> This was Jesus' opening remark to the Pharisee Nicodemus, and it stunned him. Some scholars suggest that the text could read "born from above," but that makes it harder to explain Nicodemus's response. John uses the term "born of God" in several other places, and Peter uses "born again" (1 Peter 1:23), but Paul doesn't. Paul prefers legal terminology like atonement, redemption, and reconciliation, but he's talking about the same thing. "Born again" remains the most graphic description of conversion, and that might explain its popularity.

Colson wrote at the book's climactic point: "Was I to accept without reservations Jesus Christ as Lord of my life? It was like a gate before me. There was no way to walk around it. . . . While I sat alone staring at the sea I love, words I had not been certain I could understand or say fell naturally from my lips: 'Lord Jesus, I believe You. I accept You. Please come into my life. I commit it to You.'"

Critics assumed that Carter was just shilling for votes and that Colson was just seeking public sympathy, but the following years proved the integrity of these men. Carter had a difficult presidency, making many political enemies, but his faith kept shining through. After leaving office, he got involved with Habitat for Humanity, building houses for poor people. Colson's experience behind bars helped him establish Prison Fellowship, the world's leading prison ministry. He also wrote several thoughtful books for Christians who interact with the world.

The late seventies saw the words of Jesus from John 3 become an ad slogan, a hot product name, a cliché on the lips of every celebrity. People were claiming to be born again through fad diets, crystals, and sexual experiences. The metaphor was stretched way out of shape.

In the eighties a few popular TV evangelists were publicly disgraced, and as a result the public began to associate the term "born again" with everything they didn't like about Christianity—hypocrisy, insensitivity, arrogance, judgment, and greed.

Now when someone asks, "Are you born again?" you need to be careful. You might have to explain exactly what Jesus meant by the term. But the truth is that a multitude of folks over the last two millennia have seen their lives begin anew because of a personal relationship with Jesus. Some of them, like Jimmy Carter and Chuck Colson, have been headliners. Others have changed the world in quieter ways. Perhaps someday we can reclaim the simple beauty of Jesus' metaphor.

The Mysterious Pattern

JONI EARECKSON TADA (1949–)

Seventeen-year-old Joni Eareckson had just graduated from high school and was looking forward to college. She had no desire to change the world; she didn't even know what to do with her life. She was just another teenage girl, interested in boys, sports, and having fun. But she was a committed Christian too, and she knew God wasn't pleased with the direction of her life. So she prayed, "Lord, please do something in my life to turn it around."

A few days later, after diving into the Chesapeake Bay, she was pulled out of the water a quadriplegic.

In a state institution, Joni prayed for a miracle. "What young girl lying numb and motionless with tubes running in and out of her wouldn't?" she later said. A friend read a passage from John 5 about a man who had been unable to walk for thirty-eight years and whom Jesus healed. "I can't wait that long," Joni pleaded. "Heal me now, Lord."

Friends shared other passages of Scripture with Joni, but the one that really affected her was Romans 8:28: "And we know that in all things God works for the good of those who love him."

She had been familiar with this passage before, but now she heard it when she was fighting despair and depression at the prospect of living a life with permanent paralysis. As Romans 8:28 was explained to her, she came to realize that her accident was no accident at all. She calls this realization "a major turning point," and Romans 8:28 became her "scriptural anchor." It was life-changing to understand the sovereignty of a God who loved her and had a plan for her.

> ### Romans 8:28
>
> *And we know that in all things God works for the good of those who love him.*
>
> ---
>
> The apostle is talking about present sufferings and future glory. All of creation groans as it waits for its full redemption, and we humans experience the same frustration. But in the meantime we can trust that God has a purpose, that he is working for our good, and that he will never stop loving us.

"He has a plan and purpose behind your pain," she wrote in *Glorious Intruder*. "Even the evil over which you have no control—evil men or evil schemes or injustice or iniquity—works mysteriously together in a pattern for your good."

So Joni was no longer a victim. In 1975 Barbara Walters interviewed Joni on the *Today* show, and Joni demonstrated how she could draw while holding a pen between her teeth. In 1977 her autobiography *Joni* became a best-seller. In 1980 Worldwide Pictures released a film about her life, and soon she was making guest appearances at Billy Graham Crusades.

But for Joni there was still more. Convinced that she must be a "doer of the Word and not a hearer only," she began an organization called Joni and Friends, which helps disabled people achieve their dreams. The organization is now in twenty European countries and in Latin America and Asia. In addition, she established Wheels for the World, which maintains wheelchair restoration sites in several countries and distributes wheelchairs in developing countries.

In 1982 she married Ken Tada, and together they reach out to the world's six hundred million people with disabilities. She has written more than twenty books and continues to paint with a brush between her teeth. Her Christmas cards and paintings have earned her a wide audience of art fans.

Other verses in Romans 8 have been influential in her life too. Verse 17 says, "We share in his sufferings in order that we may also share in his glory." Verse 18 says, "Our present sufferings are not worth comparing with the glory that will be revealed in us." And verse 37 says, "We are more than conquerors through him who loved us." But Romans 8:28 remains her anchor. That verse changed Joni, and she is changing the world.

The Person in the Mirror

If you've been counting, you know we've presented ninety-nine Bible verses that have changed the world. In most cases these verses changed *people* who went on to do world-changing things. There are plenty of other influential Christians through the centuries who have been changed by Scripture, so we could easily come up with a hundredth entry.

But we have found the hundredth person somewhere else . . . in your mirror. You've been reading stories of people who encountered God's Word and let it shape them. They went out and did something that made a difference. And so two questions come back to you as you finish this book: (1) How is the Bible changing you? (2) How will you change the world?

We both grew up learning 2 Timothy 2:15: "Study to show thyself approved unto God, a workman that needeth not to be ashamed, rightly dividing the word of truth" (KJV). This image has stayed with us through the years. Careful students take a scalpel to Scripture, understanding who was writing what to whom and why.

In Hebrews 4:12 the image is reversed. "For the word of God is living and active. Sharper than any double-edged sword, it penetrates even to dividing soul and spirit, joints and marrow; it judges the thoughts and attitudes of the heart." So the word of truth is "rightly dividing" us as well. The common theme of the ninety-nine world-changers is that they let the Bible cut into their lives. At some point they stopped doing surgery on Scripture and let it operate on them.

We encourage you to take 2 Timothy 2:15 to heart. Study, work hard to understand Scripture, but then let that sword do its work on you. "Do not merely listen to the word, and so deceive yourselves," says James. "Do what it says" (James 1:22). He follows with the illustration that if you listen without doing, you're like the person who sees his reflection in a mirror "and, after looking at himself, goes away and immediately forgets what he looks like" (v. 24). The idea is that he sees something wrong—say his hair is mussed, or there's spinach between his teeth—but he doesn't do anything to fix it! The whole point of looking in a mirror is to see what's wrong and correct it. The same thing applies to studying Scripture. When you see your reflection in Scripture and don't do anything to change, you're just deceiving yourself.

So what have you read from Scripture recently? What verses have been influential to you? What Bible verse is knifing into your soul? And what difference is it making?

Now consider the next question: How will you change your own part of the world? Your community. Your church. Your family. What difference are you making for people as a result of the way God's Word is operating on you?

You might be saying, "Not me. I can't change the world. I can't even change my socks." You might be ashamed of a certain sin in your life, or you might feel that God hasn't given you any talents. When you feel this way, glance back through the history lessons of this book. God used a persecutor like Paul, a playboy like Augustine, a slave trader like John Newton. He used a hothead like Martin Luther and a sad sack like John Wesley. He used the sickly Amy Carmichael and the quadriplegic Joni Eareckson.

The ultimate conclusion is that it's not about you! It's about the awesome power of the Word within you. You don't have to write a masterpiece or start a reformation, but just let God use you to make a difference in people's lives.

And then we can write about you in the sequel.

Subject Index

Scripture Index

10:42   117
12:11–12   109
16:24   187
17:4   135
18:21–22   25
24:14   21
28:19–20   129

Mark
3:25   125
8:36   49
11:22   147

Luke
6:31   167
7:37   107
11:2   173
11:13   171
15:20–21   59

John
3:3   207
3:7   85
3:16   151
6:12   163
7:37   87
8:32   65
12:24   137
15:15   127
17:3   47
19:28   189

Acts
2:4   153
5:14   183
8:30–31   79
22:8, 10   197

Romans
1:17   41
1:20   29
5:8   195
5:18   61
8:1–2   83

8:28   209
8:31   45
8:35, 37   205
13:13–14   19
14:7–8   179

1 Corinthians
1:27   155
1:30   69
3:11   43

Galatians
6:9   95

Ephesians
5:16   97

Philippians
4:4   131

Colossians
3:17   157

1 Timothy
1:17   81

2 Timothy
1:12   91
2:2   15

1 John
3:2   133
4:7   175
4:19   39
5:4   73

Jude
24   169

Revelation
5:9   75
11:15   77
19:6   77
19:16   77

William J. Petersen served as editorial director of *Christian Life Magazine* and *Christian Bookseller Magazine* before becoming editor of *Eternity* magazine. A past president of the Evangelical Press Association, he was the first recipient of the Joseph T. Bayly Award for "outstanding service to Christian periodical publishing." He was awarded a doctorate by Eastern College for his contributions to religious journalism.

He was editorial director of the *Revell Bible Dictionary* and has written Bible study curriculum and Bible study aids for various curriculum and Bible publishers. He has written more than twenty books on various subjects, including biography, Bible study, cults, hymnology, and travel. With his son Randy Petersen he has written three previous books: *The One Year Book of Hymns, The One Year Book of Psalms,* and *100 Christian Books That Changed the Century.*

Bill and his wife, Ardythe, are the parents of three grown children and live in Pennsylvania, where he continues to serve as senior acquisitions editor for Fleming H. Revell.

Randy Petersen has served as editor of the *Bible Newsletter* and on the staff of *Christian History Magazine.* He was content editor of the *Revell Bible Dictionary* and has written a considerable amount of Bible study curriculum for youth and adults. He is the author of more than thirty books and was co-author of *The 100 Most Important Events in Church History* and *100 Christian Books That Changed the Century.* His other books range from *How to Fear God without Being Afraid of Him* and *Angry with God* to *The Family Book of Bible Fun* and *The Complete Book of Bible Puzzles.* Other books have dealt with sports, psychology, devotionals, and fiction. Active in his Methodist church in New Jersey, Randy also acts, directs, and teaches in local theaters and schools.

Explore the twentieth century's most influential works!

Discover writings—from *Up from Slavery* to *Mere Christianity*—that literally molded the mind-set of evangelical believers.

After exposure to the summaries of these pivotal works, you too will begin scouring your favorite sources for classics that not only changed the twentieth century, but which also are destined to change your life.

—JERRY JENKINS,
CO-AUTHOR OF
THE LEFT BEHIND SERIES

This is a wonderful, highly readable compendium of the most important works of the twentieth century. Christians need to read this to appreciate the best of our modern heritage.

—CHARLES COLSON,
PRISON FELLOWSHIP
MINISTRIES

"*Classics that are destined to change your life.*" —JERRY JENKINS

100 Christian Books That Changed the Century

WILLIAM J. PETERSEN and RANDY PETERSEN

0-8007-5735-1 $12.99 p